# Guaranteed Notes

*Memoirs of the*
*Three Erdman Brothers and*
*The United States Marine Band*
*"The President's Own"*

D1565743

Fredric Erdman • Timothy Erdman

James Erdman

ISBN: 1470045109
ISBN 13: 9781470045104

Library of Congress Control Number: 2012902461
CreateSpace Independent Publishing Platform
North Charleston, South Carolina

# Table of Contents

*Dedicated to our father, Frederick James Erdman.*

# Foreword

"'Administrations come and go, but the band plays on forever,' said an account of the Marine Band concerts on the White House grounds in 1891. During the final decades of the nineteenth century America was caught up in a tremendous band craze. Not only were military bands all the rage, but so were industrial bands, Salvation Army bands, circus bands, and school bands. Outdoor band concerts after the Civil War became more than just an institution, they were an active social force. Hardly an event could be observed without a band. ...The Marine Band during the second half of the nineteenth century was much more than 'The President's Own.' It was the people's as well. And it linked the presidential family with the nation like no other social or cultural phenomenon of the period."

—Elise K. Kirk, *Music at the White House: A History of the American Spirit*, Urbana: University of Illinois Press, 1986.

***A taping session of The Marine Band for the NBC show, "America Speaks."***
***(Photo courtesy Department of Defense)***

"Growing from fifes and drums to 100 of the world's most expertly played instruments, the colorful Marine Band marches melodiously through the Nation's history."

—*National Geographic*, 1959

*Freddie Erdman:*

Imagine a widget containing ten thousand moving parts. Imagine further that the manufacturer of this widget has promised—*guaranteed*—that not one of those ten thousand moving parts would miss or fail. Ever. Would you buy it? Now translate those ten thousand widget parts into ten thousand musical notes.

Colonel Albert F. Schoepper (SHOW-purr), director of the U.S. Marine Band from 1955 to 1972, asked—or more appropriately, *demanded*—his musicians promise—*guarantee*—that they would not miss *any* of those ten thousand notes in any given performance. Hence, the title *Guaranteed Notes: The Demand for Perfection.*

No musician in his or her right mind, no matter how talented and experienced, would or could make that promise or offer that kind of guarantee. After all, a musician isn't a widget. A musician is a human being. You are about to meet a group of musicians who came as close to making that guarantee as any probably ever will—the United States Marine Band under Colonel Albert F. Schoepper.

This book tells many stories, but one of the best is found in Chapter Thirteen and epitomizes the book's title, "Guaranteed Notes." The incident happened in Boston, Massachusetts, during the middle of one of our nine-week cross-country tours. Two misplayed notes, one by the solo cornetist, the other by me, resulted in a strong chastisement issued by our leader, Colonel Albert F. Schoepper, who then went on to decree: "You must guarantee me ALL the notes." That dressing illustrates the demands of performing in The United States Marine Band under Schoepper. His "guaranteed notes" dictum was the tail that wagged the dog. His reputation as a musical despot who ruled the band through raw fear and intimidation could paralyze any player at any given time. Woe to the player who took it personally!

His band was Sousa's band, a 135-piece ensemble with its own box seat to history, steeped in tradition and a living symbol of American patriotism. Its primary mission: to perform music for the nation's President, a job dating back to John Adams, who signed into law in 1798 the Congressional act that established the Marine Band, christened by Thomas Jefferson—a musician himself—"The President's Own."

Realizing that not everyone can become part of the pulse of our country at a level of national importance, it has been my privilege, as a thirty-year veteran of "The President's Own," to experience this connection to American history on a national stage through the many functions and events for which we performed.

Like the recurring four seasons of nature, the yearly cycle of duties repeated its own rhythm: spring and summer concerts in the nation's capital, followed by the arduous sixty-three- to sixty-seven-day concert tour each fall to different parts of the country. Our mettle was sorely tested during each tour by the relentless grind of daily bus travel from city to city and town to town. We were our own traveling slice of Americana visiting other slices of Americana.

Our work in the Capitol area often required outdoor performances in sweltering heat and humidity, where breathing felt like being covered in a hot, wet washrag. During the cold-weather months, outdoor funerals in Arlington National Cemetery meant wind-blown cold, fierce enough to freeze lips to mouthpieces!

My years with the Marine Band have also been well-seasoned with the camaraderie, humor, and cherished friendships of my fellow Marine Band members. You are invited to walk back with my brothers and me through the years of an extraordinary journey to share a unique slice of life and, above all, the powerful inspiration of superbly performed music.

*"In this imperfect world, perfection is seldom obtained. But the striving for it results in excellence."* —*Vince Lombardi*

**Tim Erdman:** I think it was Michael Erdman who years ago encouraged his three older brothers to get the four of us together about once every August or September for a reunion of sorts. So we did, gathering for a few hours once a year at the Hunt Valley Hampton Inn in Hunt Valley, Maryland. We did what siblings typically do—catch up on each other's lives and reminisce about old times. And each time we got together (including both funerals for our parents) we'd ultimately go back to our days as members of the United States Marine Band, in large part at Mike's goading, who always seemed fascinated by our stories. His interest, of course, compelled each of us to add another tale each time the previous one had been completed, a resurgence of memory that always tried the patience of our waiter, who had been ready to clear off our table and move us out hours ago.

At one of those reunions, Freddie showed up with two spiral bound "books" containing diary-like entries, in chronological order, of memories from his days spent as the premier cornet soloist of the "The President's Own." As a professional writer, I appreciated his body of work, thinking that finally, someone took the time to sit down and do what many had been suggesting to us over the years: write a book about those halcyon days in the world's most distinguished symphonic band. I offered to look over what he had written and perhaps perform a light edit to his manuscript. Freddie was happy to take me up on my offer.

The subject of this endeavor came up sometime later in a conversation I had with Cathy Murphy, our editor, and who at the time was in charge of editing a couple of industry magazines that I was also writing for on a monthly basis. Cathy saw a bigger story when she learned that not one, not two, but three brothers had served in the United States Marine Band, all at the same time. She was herself a fan of the band, and when I amused her with the recounting of a couple of my own memories, she said, "Tim, I think what Freddie has done is wonderful. But the fact that all three of you served in that band at the same time makes me think that there's a bigger story to be told!" I thought about what she had said, then got back to Freddie. I suggested that his memoirs might be more universally received if (a) Jim's experiences along with my own were added, and (b) that all our stories could be better framed and told in a broader context of the band itself, including references to other band members who themselves had stories to tell during the same era of our service, which spanned from 1955 to 1985. Freddie agreed wholeheartedly.

Experiences, when they are told through the prism of one's own eyes, are subject to one's own internal bias. For me, this book is an attempt to not only relate our own personal experiences, but to paint a picture, as accurately and justifiably as reasonably possible, of what everyday life was like in those days spanning six presidential administrations, from Eisenhower to Reagan. It has been my pleasure and deeply felt responsibility to construct the narrative backdrop for the telling of *Guaranteed Notes: The Demand for Perfection.* ❖

# Prologue

## On History's Stage: The United States Marine Band

### Birth in Turbulent Times

An Act of Congress created the Marine Band in the very difficult year of 1798. President John Adams signed the act into federal law on July 11 in Philadelphia, Pennsylvania, then the capital of an infant and struggling United States of America. Adams himself was being criticized as the "Second Coming of Napoleon." At his insistence and in that same year, Congress also passed the highly controversial Alien and Sedition Acts. Americans managed their lives under a threat of war with France. Spies and traitors "were everywhere," as the prevailing paranoia went, the legacy of a revolutionary hysteria that spread like cancer from overseas to these very shores of freedom. Just five years before in Paris, Louis XVI, the monarch and friend of Benjamin Franklin who had so prominently helped America defeat the British, had been decapitated by the guillotine, his head rolling along the bloody way of the French Revolution.

Adding to America's woes were the acts of rampant piracy taking place in sea-lanes used by commercial American vessels. Adams desperately needed a Navy and the marines to back it up. Seeking to help protect its commerce from privateers on the high seas, the 1798 law re-established what had been, since the end of the Revolution, a defunct United States Marine Corps. Along with revitalizing the Marine Corps, the law's wording included a mandate for "[a] drum major, fife major, and 32 drums and fifes." Those words breathed life into the United States Marine Band.

Thirty-two drummers and fifers: a fledgling unit, to say the least. In any military setting that could be enhanced with music, however, fifes and drums found their place, providing the rhythm and song of America's patriots, instilling morale and inspiring men and women to go forward, in harm's way or otherwise. At first, good musicians were hard to come by. In 1799, along with a significant enlarging of the Marine Corps, eighteen more musicians were added to the "Marine Band." Some served on men-of-war fighting vessels; others, on missions of recruitment. The remaining stayed in Philadelphia to play music for government leaders. At the time, no one knew it as "The President's Own," a title that was to come later under Adams' successor, Thomas Jefferson.

If its beginnings were humble, so was the musical repertoire. Under Jefferson, the Marine Band's music "library" was a polite misnomer for a tiny collection that included a handful of titles such as "Yankee Doodle," "Hail Columbia," "Auld Lang Syne," and "Jefferson's March." Who could have foreseen two centuries later, when the Marine Band would grow to become the world's preeminent military concert band? And indeed it did, staking its claim to being the oldest continuously active professional musical organization in America, consisting of over 150 of the world's finest musicians, and today possessing over 100,000 musical scores, making its music library the world's largest.

## From Fifes and Drums to "Rock Band"

Almost everyone knows that the Marine Band played for Jefferson's inaugural in March 1801 and for every presidential inaugural since. But it became much more than the ceremonial band for a president raising his right hand while taking the oath of office. The Marine Band went on to perform weekly concerts on the White House grounds, and during the 1840s, it began a tradition of regular concerts for the public on the East Plaza of the United States Capitol.

Throughout the life of a nation that went from a handful of quibbling colony-states to union to superpower, the Marine Band has occupied its own special seat, front and center to the ever-expanding stage of America's history. It serenaded Dolly Madison; first performed "Hail to the Chief" for President John Quincy Adams; rode with Abraham Lincoln to Gettysburg; reached into America's homes with the longest sustained network radio broadcast ever (known as The Dream Hour); and played a historic wartime concert for Franklin Roosevelt and Winston Churchill.

The band led the funeral procession of murdered president John F. Kennedy; played in New York City amidst the splash of light and fireworks during the rededication of the Statue of Liberty; became the only military band to tour the Soviet Union before its downfall; and was the first musical institution inducted into the American Classical Music Hall of Fame. Its leaders included John Philip Sousa, legendary "March King," American patriot and music icon extraordinaire. The Marine Band was already well known by the time Sousa took it over as director in 1880, but under his strict baton, it achieved "rock band" status. With Sousa, no one dared question his downbeat or musicianship. Convinced that his revered band should be heard outside the Washington, D.C. limits, Sousa organized and launched the Marine Band's very first tour in 1891.

Seventy-five years later, another taskmaster became leader—Albert F. Schoepper. Except perhaps for Sousa, no other ruled with more iron-fisted authority. Under Schoepper, every rehearsal and performance was played under a cloud of intimidation that could best be described as "fear of God" . . . or "fear of Schoepper," whichever was worse and more effective. But the music was as close to God as any conductor of the Marine Band could bring it. And Schoepper brought it.

## A Proud Family Tradition . . . of Families

The Marine Band's history is a family history. In the early 1800s, Gaetano Carusi, a native of Catania, Sicily served in the band with his two sons: Samuel and Ignazio. Antonio Sousa was a trombonist in the band; his son, John Philip, enlisted as an apprentice musician before becoming its most famous leader. Another notable name in the band's history is that of Santelmann. "No family has had longer or more influence on the Marine Band than the Santelmann family," says the Marine Band's distinguished web site (www.marineband.usmc.mil). The father, William H., joined the band in 1887 under Sousa and became its leader in 1898, 100 years after the Marine Band was created. His son, William, auditioned for his father for a spot in the band—and didn't make it the first time around! In a subsequent audition, however, he was accepted and later was named the band's twenty-first director in 1940.

Another father-son combination was the Sevenhuysens. Theodore joined "The President's Own" in 1893 as a bassoonist and violinist. Following in the senior Theodore's footsteps, Theodore Jr. joined the band in 1921 as a trumpet player. The Harphams (Dale and Dee, trombone), Saverinos (Angelo, tuba, who also was awarded the Bronze Star during World War II; and Louis, tuba, contrabass clarinet, string bass, and composer), Greenhoes, (David, trumpet; Gary, trombone), Patrylaks (Daniel, trumpet; Thomas, clarinet), Mergens (Michael, trumpet and Paul, tuba), and Crowes (Donald, French horn, and James T. [Tom], trombone) were sets of brothers that served in the Marine Band, either concurrently or at different times throughout the band's two-hundred year history.

The Barclays were another father-son act. Robert joined the band in 1950 as a clarinetist and violinist; son John followed suit 38 years later, first becoming a member of the clarinet section, then moving over to E-flat clarinet in 1990. Dennis Burian joined the band in 1969 as a clarinetist and was appointed one of its assistant leaders. His son, trumpeter Douglas Burian, joined in 1997 and played for a time under his father's baton.

Christopher Franke, violinist, is a third-generation member of the Marine Band. His father was principal euphonium Philip Franke; and his mother, Susan, joined the band in 1981 as a violist. Susan's father was David Johnson, the band's principal trumpet for many years and a contemporary of the three Erdman brothers.

While they had a combined fifty-nine years of service to the Marine Band, Fredric, James, and Timothy Erdman served together for only six years and during that time were featured as The Erdman Trio. They all served under Schoepper's unfailing, exacting baton. They played together, argued with one another, stood by one another, and ultimately, made history as the first and, to date, only brother trio in a major service band. Like their fellow musicians in the Marine Band, the Erdman brothers lived by the dictum that was defined by the likes of a man perhaps more demanding, more intimidating, and more musical, than any other before or since his time, the dictum of "guaranteed notes." ❖

## Chapter 1

# A Tribute from Colonel
# Albert F. Schoepper

In 1994, moved by the celebration of a scholarship presentation to Lebanon Valley College in our father's name, Jim Erdman had invited Colonel Albert F. Schoepper, USMC Retired, to attend and speak during the evening festivities. The former conductor of "The President's Own" United States Marine Band, graciously accepted. Schoepper's appearance required his making a 150-mile trip from his home in Arlington, Virginia to Lebanon, Pennsylvania. His speech, a tribute to our father and his friend, Fred Erdman, summed up an interesting piece of Marine Band history.

*Schoepper:*

"*Speaking at this point in the program, I feel much the same as the ninth batter up in the old Yankee lineups of Ruth and Gehrig or Maris and Mantle. All the home runs have been hit and a lot of runs batted in. And by now, all Fred Erdman's well-deserved accolades already have been paid to him. However, I shall try to add a few more, along with some chronological facts in the Erdman family's musical saga.*

*"I am here because forty years ago this past spring, a young cornetist from Lebanon, still a high school junior and musically trained by his father, drove to Washington to audition before the Director and Assistant Director of the United States Marine Band. He gave a flawlessly brilliant performance of "The Carnival of Venice" which I, as Assistant Director and in my twenty-first year with the Band, rated unequaled by any other brass player during those years. He was the young Fred Erdman, first of the Erdman prodigies.*

*"Fred was accepted on the spot by the Band's Director, Lieutenant Colonel Santelmann, and told to return after high school graduation. But Santelmann retired the following spring, and I became Director for the next seventeen years.*

*"One of my first moves was contacting Fred to notify him that now I was expecting him. However, I found him somewhat ambivalent about joining us at that time, because he was thinking of entering a music school such as Curtis or Juilliard.*

**Program of the 1994 Scholarship Concert
honoring the father, Fred Erdman**

2

"So, I told him that four more years on that path would lead him only to obscurity in the trumpet section of a symphony orchestra, playing fanfares and afterbeats. My sales pitch worked, and after only two weeks in the band, Fred was dazzling thousands at the Capitol and Watergate summer concerts. So, score one for Fred, for his father, and for the Marine Band.

"One year later, another Erdman fledgling appeared. He was younger brother Jim, and seeking an audition on the trombone. Naturally, with his surname and musical background, I was receptive to his request. Like Fred, he had been taught by his father and like Fred, he had it all . . . tone, technique, and at seventeen, a world of self-confidence, plus, even a dash of chutzpah thrown in! So, score another win . . . this time for Jim, his father, and the Marine Band.

"Jim started immediately on his greatly successful solo career and in the band, I placed him on the solo trombone stand as assistant to the famed Bob Isele, who had performed there for 20 years. Four years later, upon Isele's retirement, Jim became head of the trombone section and also the youngest E-9 in the Marine Corps, E-9 being the highest attainable enlisted rank.

"A few years passed and then I was told—I wonder by whom—of yet another brother, and this time it was Tim. Tim was a cornetist, and like his older brothers, a pupil of his father. Tim, too, would like to audition for the Marine Band. By then I was ready to say, 'If he's another Erdman, trained by the family teacher, why bother with the audition? Just bring him down and we'll suit him up, because he's bound to be ready.' Naturally, Tim did audition and again the notes flew around my office as he polished off the "Finale" of the Mendelssohn Violin Concerto.

"So, Tim was in, and so was formed the Erdman triumvirate, a fraternal trio, a group unique in the history of the Marine Band and one that drew vast audiences and great acclaim whenever the brothers appeared. They came to the Band as superbly equipped young technicians, and as they matured, they made the most of their talents, justifying every promotion they received and so obviously deserved.

"Above all, I am indeed grateful to their father, Fred, for the splendid musical schooling provided them, and to both Catherine and Fred for planting in their sons the highest standards of discipline and character so prevalent in the boys' personal and professional lives. Our honoree, Fred Erdman, richly deserves the accolades he is receiving tonight as teacher, conductor, and forceful musical leader. I extend my congratulations to him and all his family, along with my deep appreciation for being here." ❖

*The Erdman Trio, July 1970.*
*(Photo courtesy Department of Defense)*

# Chapter 2

# Of Scarlet, Braid, and Brass

The Marine Band we Erdman brothers knew was a melting pot of personalities, a collection of "who's who," some quite young, some nearing retirement, but all highly accomplished professionals, banded together in scarlet, braid, and brass—red-coated musicians who manufactured only the best in concert band sound under one man, Colonel Albert F. Schoepper, and his incomparably unyielding baton.

All rehearsed, joked, laughed, and cried in that famous hall, the one that occupied the southwest corner of the Marine Barracks, Eighth & I Streets, Southeast, Washington, D.C., where the "March King" himself, John Philip Sousa, rehearsed his band from 1880 until 1892. Above all, when the chips were down, as an ensemble, the band embodied Marine Corps values. While that may sound trite, especially in an era of national doubt and the pain of Vietnam, the band didn't forget the Marines it represented and the ideals of honor, courage, and commitment that defined the Corps' own core values.

Some bandsmen were combat veterans themselves and had distinguished themselves in World War II. Tubist Angelo Saverino was awarded the Bronze Star Medal. Percussionist Boyd Conway was a tail gunner on B-29s and flew missions over Japan just before the end of the war. Harpist Claude Pedicord flew bomber crew missions over Germany and received the Distinguished Flying Cross Medal. And Jack Kline, who eventually became the band's director, served in the U.S. Army in Germany and France; his awards included the European-African-Middle Eastern Area Medal with five stars, the Legion of Merit Medal, and the French Fourraguere.

More bandsmen were WWII veterans, including Edmund DeMar, the band's drum major who as a combat Marine served in the Pacific theater ; George Durham, Louis Hegedus, James Hubbard, Stephen Rammer (who served in a band on the ship USS Franklin), Frank Reda, Ben Sanger, Robert Shapiro, Lee Sheary, and Bob Stuart (Patton's band),

Then there was talent. From playing musicians to arrangers and tubists to triangle player, the United States Marine Band was a mother lode of musicianship. Experience in symphony orchestras and other world-class ensembles was a two-way street: some were coming, some were going. Many members had played in major-league symphony orchestras before coming into the band, and many others would eventually leave the band to play in world-class civilian ensembles. Many were career bandsmen who stayed in for the full term of twenty years or more, then said goodbye to the best concert-performing organization they ever knew for a fifty percent pension, often at the age of 41. Jim Erdman, the band's principal trombonist and the youngest ever in the United States Marine Corps to be promoted to master gunnery sergeant, opted out at the age of thirty-seven. Despite leaving after twenty years of service, he had set another record: one for longevity, by appearing as the band's featured soloist in front of matinee and evening tour audiences for ten straight concert tours, each sixty-three days long and no days off. During this period, he also accomplished the amazing feat of performing in nineteen tours in a row.

## Tour

The tours the band made each autumn took it to thousands of cities and countrysides. It was the Marine Band's way of reaching out to America's heartland (and sometimes its hinterlands) and its music lovers. Each year for nine grueling weeks, the band would travel through a particular region of the United States, playing two concerts a day. The tours were like religion to some of the career guys, who loved the idea of seeing America from a bus window. They loved the prospect of playing in a different town every day; it was exciting and had a certain air of unpredictability. Anticipation was palpable among the "tour veterans" as summer wound down, and especially as September approached and the sixty-three-day grind was just around the corner.

If that was the upside, there was also the downside: sixty-three days, two concerts a day, no days off—a daily, intense, no-letup grind, with an itinerary that frequently included towns where the hotels were located on the outskirts, just too far to walk and see or experience anything noteworthy during the off-hours.

Concerts were held in the best and worst of concert halls, including gymnasiums, arenas and amphitheaters. The music, especially during afternoon matinee concerts, was frequently directed at the kids (tomorrow's leaders, they'd say) who, one would *think*, would be grateful and inspired by the band's magnificent sound, patriotic flair, and forty-eight-man ensemble of dress blues. There were times when the performers didn't sense any such gratitude, especially when fending off flying spitballs between notes.

Then there was the inevitable ennui, a sort of "tour trance" that one experienced while embarking and disembarking from the same bus ten times a day and over 600 times throughout a two-and-a-half-month period. Around the second or third week, few knew or cared what day it was or where they were, except when someone would look at a map and discover that Monday's concert site was 400 miles from Tuesday's location but only twenty-five miles away from Wednesday's. Tour veterans called it "zig-zagging" and it happened quite often, much to the dismay of those who liked to sleep in. Freddie was one of those. On his first tour, he was late for the morning's bus departure five times.

## From Tangos to Tear Gas

The band's permanent residence or "station" is the Marine Barracks in Washington, D.C. Known as the "oldest post of the Corps" and a haven of history, the barracks' cornerstone was laid in 1801. That was home, the official residence of The United States Marine Band.

The band wasn't called "The President's Own" for nothing. Several times each week, the White House became its point of destination, its place of employment, its home away from home. This was especially true for the Marine Band Orchestra and small Marine Band combos that were responsible for providing the music for dining, dancing, and other White House social events. On some occasions, the band or orchestra would play on the outside lawn. Inside, a quartet of fanfare trumpets could be heard as the President and First Lady, each resplendently attired, descended the White House's grand staircase. Later that evening, the couple—along with their guests—would dance the night away to the music of the Marine Band's White House combo.

While playing for the nation's chief executive was the more glamorous part of the job, band members sometimes found themselves marching in the wake of controversy. Such an episode occurred while the band played in formation on the White House's South Lawn for the Shah of Iran's state visit in the late 1970s. Though weakened by cancer, the Shah was a controversial figure, and his presence on the South Lawn triggered a near-riot as pro-Shah demonstrators met up with anti-Shah protestors. To keep the confrontation from getting out of hand, police unleashed tear gas to disburse the mob. A menacing cloud formed and knew no boundaries. The gas engulfed Marine Band members, ready to play appropriate music for the President as he was paying his personal tribute to a toppled and dying leader.

So there we were, eyes tearing and nasal linings feeling as if they were being ripped apart. Still, we managed to stand at attention on the pristine-cut-and-colored green grass, stifling coughs and pretending to ignore the blaring sirens, haunting megaphones and screams of protest less than 100 yards away.

Somehow amidst the strains of martial music and the cacophony of chaos, order prevailed and everyone survived, their burning membranes and "charred" vocal chords destined to heal for another day.

## "High" Notes

Just about everyone in the band performed every type of job that came along, whether it was a funeral at Arlington Cemetery, a state reception at the White House, or a concert. Sunday evening concerts were held on the Potomac River below the Lincoln Memorial, on a floating concert barge known as "The Watergate." Tens of thousands attended those wonderful performances; unfortunately, the shell was positioned squarely in the flight path of planes from nearby Washington National Airport. Many an overture's climactic measures were drowned out by a plane's engine noise; thousands of listeners never heard countless wonderfully played strains of music. In June of 1972, the barge was destroyed by Hurricane Agnes. By 1973, the band was performing its Sunday evening concerts at the Jefferson Memorial.

Those attending the summer concerts experienced the musical precision and accuracy of one of the world's greatest service bands. However, a Marine Band concert was not always about perfection. One of the concerts at the Jefferson Memorial in fact was notable for falling short, due to a very high summit.

The French horn player playing the principal horn part that evening was a young player who had entered the band about three years earlier. On this particular concert, he had an important solo, the famous horn call to Wagner's opera, *Siegfried*. A fine player, he was directed by the assistant conductor at that time, John R. Bourgeois, to ascend the steps to the very top of the Memorial, then play the call. "Ascend" meant climbing what must have seemed like over 100 steps. This would be like asking a musician to go to the gym and do a stepper routine for five minutes and then execute a virtuoso passage without missing a note.

As ordered, he climbed all those steps and proceeded to play. Of all the notes he played (or attempted to play), many were missed or just didn't "speak" at all, much to the chagrin of both horn player and conductor. The next time the piece was performed, the conductor decided to have a "canned" recording by the band's first woman member played instead. Despite the improved quality and gender aside, John Philip Sousa, who at one time expressed disdain for music recordings, would have turned over in his grave.

## Heroes' Farewell

Marches were always part of the musical bill of fare, even for such sobering occasions as the ubiquitous military funerals at the nation's most famous national cemetery. The band paraded countless times through Arlington for at least a mile, sometimes more, shiny instruments projecting out to the skies and heavens above, playing the strains of *Our Fallen Heroes* by Joseph H. Peckham, Beethoven's *Funeral March*, and, of course, *The Marines' Hymn*, played as a dirge as the procession approached the gravesite. Solemn marches like these provided the musical portion of military honors for what seemed like an endless stream of dead men and women Marines returned home from war. During the early 1970s, it was always about Vietnam, or at least it seemed that way to us.

As the decade came to a close, the "parade" to the gravesite grew to several miles in length along the macadam path that wound around and through the sea of uniformly white grave markers (or gray, depending on whether the day was sunny or overcast). The service always began with the arrival of the casket, which was then borne with solemn military bearing by Honor Guard pallbearers who carried it with a reverent if deliberately and painstakingly slow gait, to inside the multi-denominational Fort Myer chapel.

Back in the parking lot and during the chapel service, we'd sometimes find ourselves standing at parade rest alongside the Honor Guard, mounted soldiers of the Caisson Platoon of the Third U.S. Infantry Regiment (the famous Old Guard), holding the reins of their stout and dignified equine companions, steeds admirable in their stance and relatively still hooves. Every so often, however, despite the decorum, dignity, and ingenious contrivances to avoid unseemly accidents, nature could not be denied. We would receive a malodorous "gift" from a nearby horse, obviously as uncomfortable as we were.

And we'd never as much as flinch one sinew of irritated muscle.

*Freddie:*

*Finally, the troops and the band were called to attention as the chapel ceremony ended. The band played a hymn as the pallbearers carried the casket from the chapel to place it on the horse-drawn caisson. The funerals in the cold stand out most in my memory.*

*After a brief moment, the Drum Major called out, "Band—Forward . . . 'arch!" We stepped off on the march to the gravesite with the somber beat of the drums. We played two or three funeral marches throughout the procession.*

*The clip-clop, clip-clop of horses' hooves echoed hauntingly from the road into icy air, evoking memories of the vast numbers who have died in battle. The horses' timbers were so shivered in this penetrating cold that their steamy evacuations could barely be restrained as the funeral procession moved along and arrived at the burial site.*

*As we stood at attention, we played one last hymn, after which the chaplain offered final words of comfort and thanks. The American flag that had draped the casket was ceremoniously folded and presented to the seated survivor.*

*"Taps" was then sounded. After the last note faded away, the service concluded.*

## Quadrennial Festival

Like a cyclical comet, the nation's "main event" comes around once every four years and catapults the Marine Band into the national spotlight. Considering all its trappings and staging, the Hollywood-style production known as the "presidential inauguration" is the nation's most grandiose ceremony. It affirms democracy and pays homage to it and its chief caretaker, amid a gaggle of press, television cameras, Hollywood moguls and celebrities, Wall Street barons, and members of Congress—an array of VIPs that somehow lends the highest degree of honor and drama to the occasion.

Every presidential inauguration includes two oaths. One is taken by the vice president, which is followed immediately by the Marine Band playing twelve measures of "Hail Columbia." The other, of course, is the Presidential oath, followed by thirty-two measures of notes that rank at the top in all of music officialdom: "Hail to the Chief," the musical signature of the President of the United States of America. And played by "The President's Own," The United States Marine Band. Scripted accordingly, no presidential inauguration would ever be complete without "The President's Own," and brothers Freddie and Jim played their share—a total of twelve presidential inaugurations between them (fourteen, counting mine).

*The Marine Band plays for Dwight David Eisenhower's inauguration.*
*(Photo courtesy Department of Defense)*

For a Marine Band member, Inauguration Day was the longest day of the year. You'd report at the crack of dawn and be dressed by 7:30 a.m. in full dress, overcoat, white hat and whatever else you could fit into underneath for warmth's sake. Then you'd board the bus for the short jaunt to the Capitol and its staging area. At approximately 9:00 a.m. you'd get off the bus and walk up and onto the inaugural platform. For a little while you could crane your neck to to watch the arriving celebrities and dignitaries. At a certain designated time, you'd find your way to your seat in concert formation for rehearsal, then spot-rehearse a few places in the music, just to make sure everyone was on the same page.

Then you'd play the pre-inaugural concert and hear some polite applause at the end of each number. But you really didn't care, because while the inaugural audience was applauding, you were praying for the sun to stay out and direct its rays on you.    After the ceremony, you'd board the bus, eat a quick box lunch, get back off the bus and form up to march in the Inauguration Parade. At around 3:00 p.m., when the band's portion of the parade was finished, you'd board the bus once again for the return trip to 8th & I, smearing your chapped and quivering lips with salve, Vaseline, or some substance derived from the innards of cows. But the day wasn't over. Later that evening, there were the inaugural balls to be performed. For a Marine Bandsman, it could be the longest day of the year, and the proudest one to be a part of.

Presidential inaugurations were always at the high end of the band's visibility spectrum. But the job just wasn't about playing for the nation's Chief Executive.  In addition to the funerals, parades, inaugurations and concerts, there were the "patriotic openers," which helped to set the tone in the beginning of a ceremony (for example, an FBI graduation) and often comprised much of the band's weekly schedule.

Such was the kind of job Freddie Erdman found himself in as he walked onto the oldest post of the United States Marine Corps on a warm day in June.

## The Erdman Trio Begins

"Wednesday, June 14, 1955, Flag Day," Freddie remembers. "Eisenhower is in the middle of his first term in office. Eight days earlier, I had celebrated my nineteenth birthday, the same day as the eleventh anniversary of the Normandy Invasion. I weighed 145 pounds and stood six feet, one inch tall."

On that same day, after completing his physical in Harrisburg, Pennsylvania, his Dad drove Freddie down to Philadelphia to have him officially enlisted and sworn in at the Marine Corps recruiting center, which simultaneously made him an E-5 "buck sergeant" in the U.S. Marine Corps, for duty with the United States Marine Band only.

(The Marine Band is the only major service band that does not require its musicians to attend and experience boot camp.)

The new Marine and his father proceeded to Washington, D.C. That evening, after dinner with a friend who had encouraged Freddie to join the band, the three went to attend a portion of the Marine Band concert at the East Capitol plaza. The band put on a striking appearance, its members decked out in dress blues with white trousers. It was the first time in his young and impressionable life that Freddie actually saw a string bass and harp used in a concert band.

Two years earlier, when he was seventeen, Freddie had auditioned for Lieutenant Colonel William F. Santelmann and Captain Albert F. Schoepper. This was a reversal in thinking: he originally aspired to attend the Curtis Institute in Philadelphia. "George Wood had some influence on my decision," Freddie remembers. "Mr. Wood worked for the Agriculture Department in Washington, D.C. and was also the groundskeeper for the Marine Barracks at Eighth and I. He met his wife Irene in Lebanon, Pennsylvania, my hometown. On one of his commutes to Lebanon, he and Irene decided to take a trip to Hershey Park, where my Dad's American Legion Band happened to be playing.

**William F. Santelmann.**
**(Photo courtesy**
**Department of Defense)**

"When they heard me play, they approached Daddy and suggested I audition for the Marine Band." After several visits to the Erdman home and telling his Dad in Freddie's presence everything they knew about the Marine Band, the Woods succeeded. Freddie decided to audition for the Marine Band instead of Curtis.

Under Santelmann and his predecessors, anyone auditioning for the Marine Band had to be able to play two instruments at a professional level. Freddie's instruments were cornet, trumpet, and piano. Although he "endured" five years

13

of piano training, his abilities on that instrument did not quite reach the professional level. Freddie played the Del Staigers *Carnival of Venice*, arranged by Mayhew Lake, a flashy cornet solo that he had first performed publicly at the age of 13 with the Palmyra American Legion Band, in front of a crowd of three thousand at the old Hershey Park Band Shell. "Both the colonel and captain complimented me on my technique," he said, "but told me to go back and complete my high school education. Then I was to come back and play for them again." Nearing his graduation in 1955, he auditioned a second time, playing the same cornet solo for Santelmann (Schoepper was absent), who then challenged him with three sight-reading selections: Paul Creston's *Legend*, *My Heart at Thy Sweet Voice* from the Camille Saint-Saën's opera *Samson and Delilah*, and excerpts from Jules Massenet's opera *Le Cid*.

He passed the audition.

"Report for duty with the Marine Band immediately upon graduation from high school," said Lieutenant Colonel Santelmann. ❖

***Freddie's 1955 high school
graduation photo.***

# Chapter 3

# Road to Washington

On Thursday, June 15, 1955, at 8:30 a.m., Freddie Erdman reported to the Marine Barracks at Eighth & I Streets S.E. in Washington, D.C. for briefings and to check in with the administration noncommissioned officer (NCO), Sergeant Manifold at Operations. During the orientation he learned that General Shepherd was the Commandant, and that the Marine Band had two leaders: Captain Albert Schoepper and his assistant leader, Warrant Officer Dale Harpham. The band's staff, starting on the first floor in "the office," included one drum major, Edwin DeMar, a Marine Corps veteran of World War II in the Pacific theater. Sergeant Manifold was the "admin" man, and Sgt. Virginia Pickel, the band publicist. On the second floor (or "deck," as it was commonly called) was the library, run by the chief librarian, Sgt. Eugene Kuhns, and one assistant. Recording engineer Ross Ritchie supervised the recording lab. On the third deck (or "topside") was the instrument repair shop, manned by Sgt. John Tilley, a brass repairman; Sgt. Stewart Hanna, reeds; and Sgt. Paul Sieben, strings. As Freddie was to learn, the entire show that was the United States Marine Band was run by all of twelve people.

At about 10:15 a.m., his errands down the arcade of the ceremonial post and briefing completed, he was free to enter the band hall, sit down, watch, and listen to "The President's Own" in rehearsal.

**Drum Major Edwin DeMar. (Photo courtesy Department of Defense)**

*Freddie:*

*While choosing a seat in the middle of the hall, and while the band was playing, I saw they were dressed in khaki uniforms. I also noticed that the cornet section sat at the director's immediate right, with the first cornets abouut three feet from his right hand. (This could be intimidating to the best players, but especially to anyone lacking self-confidence in playing the solo chair or first book.) I was immediately awed by its sound and the stature and conducting of its new leader, Captain Schoepper. He wielded a very strong, authoritative baton. I was so thrilled at seeing and watching the band in action—it had me smiling continuously. This is great! The band was rehearsing a transcription of Liszt's Second Polonaise. "Oh my God!" I remember saying to myself. I didn't have words to describe the power and impact that I was feeling from this band. After that splendid rendition, I heard Schoepper call out somebody's name. A man from the cornet section rose up and stood in front of the band to rehearse a solo. It's Charles Erwin. Ah! He's playing "Spanish Caprice," a cornet solo written by Leonard B. Smith. I like this solo and he's doing a good job with it. I also like his stance and the way his embouchure looks. Very impressive!*

Charles "Chuck" Erwin was one of the band's pre-eminent principal players. He joined the band in the late 1940s and soloed frequently. Hailing from Evansville, Indiana, with his jet black hair and dashing good looks, lean athletic build and military bearing, Erwin "sang" through his cornet with a powerful, operatic sound that frequently dominated the band.

*John Philip Sousa Band Hall, 1955.*
*(Photo courtesy Department of Defense)*

*Charles Erwin.*
*(Photo courtesy Department*
*of Defense)*

**Robert Isele.**
*(Photo courtesy Department of Defense)*

*After the rehearsal ended, I exited the hall to go home. I hadn't yet met any of the musicians, but I knew I'd be getting that chance the following day, my first time of sitting in the section at rehearsal. I did recognize Bob Isele, legendary trombone artist, and Harold "Bud" Malsh, clarinetist of equal stature. I had heard of these guys even while growing up in Lebanon. As I made my way home, I remember thinking that I must get at least three hours practice in today, the usual. I was also thinking of the professionalism I just witnessed and heard this morning. What an experience!*

## Bandmates

Bob Isele, a native of Harrisburg, Pennsylvania was a magician on the trombone. In high school, he won three national solo competitions in a row, from 1933 through 1935. He spent twenty-four years in the Marine Band, and another sixteen with the National Symphony Orchestra in Washington. Harold "Bud"

Malsh was the band's principal clarinetist. Also a native of Harrisburg, Malsh developed a reputation for never missing a note. An accomplished tennis amateur, he had the grace of an antelope on the court and could frequently be seen dueling with yet another Harrisburg native, Marine Band clarinetist Don Carodisky. "Ski" was a quiet-mannered man who became known as "Schoepper's valet" on tours, ensuring that all of the leader's belongings were always safely carried to and from the bus.

The following day at 8:45 a.m., Drum Major DeMar took roll call. He notified Freddie to sit in the cornet section, playing the fourth stand, third part, last chair. As he took his seat in the section, Freddie could see about sixty musicians, a number typical for concerts performed by the Marine Band. (The number was reduced to forty-eight when the band went on tour.) Joe Rasmussen, playing third cornet, was the first man to introduce himself. "He made me feel welcome," remembers Freddie.

*Harold "Bud" Malsh.*
*(Photo courtesy Department of*
*Defense)*

*Freddie:*

*What feelings of grandeur I have, playing with this awesome band! I find myself very much respecting Captain Schoepper as a commander and conductor. At 10:15 a.m. he gives us a fifteen-minute break, during which time everyone in the cornet section introduces himself to me, along with other musicians throughout the band. They all seem like a great bunch of guys. There are no women in the band at this time.*

## Solo So Soon?

Nine days later after rehearsal ended, everybody packed up and left—except Freddie. After being told, "The Captain would like to see you," Freddie dutifully entered Schoepper's office.

"Erdman."

"Yes, sir?"

"How about rehearsing *The Carnival of Venice* next Tuesday?"

The tone of Schoepper's voice was a bit intimidating to Freddie. "All right, sir."

"Good. That's all."

"Yes, sir."

Freddie was surprised to be called upon to rehearse a solo so soon. He had been in the band all of nine days!

That evening, he got his first taste of the post's regular weekly ritual called the "Sunset Parade." Along with the Drum and Bugle Corps, the band was led out by the drum major from the band hall to the parade deck where they awaited, at parade rest, the sounding of the bell which starts the parade. The highlight of this event was, of course (and still is to this day) a stunning performance of rifling choreography by the Silent Drill Platoon.

*Freddie:*

*Mid-June, 1955*

*Drum Major DeMar takes roll call. After announcements about various jobs and duties, DeMar leaves the podium. Most of us then continue to warm up or practice a part in the concert folio.*

*At precisely nine o'clock, Schoepper enters the back doorway, strides through the band, and ascends the podium. He epitomizes "dignity." The band falls silent. In a brisk manner, he calls out the composer's name of the piece he wants to rehearse, then sometimes, but not always, mentions the title of the piece. This is unusual—most conductors call out the title first. As a result, most of us are nervously scrambling through the folio, looking for the piece he wants to rehearse.*

*Schoepper takes the band through several pieces. As I am sitting on the last cornet chair, I begin to strongly sense how my lips—"chops"—are feeling.*

*When will he call my name?*

*Damn! This must be what a death row inmate feels like.*

*"Erdman. Staigers. 'Carnival of Venice.'"*

*I am just short of shock. His sharp tone of voice, commanding manner is so arresting, abrupt, intimidating. I leave my seat as everybody pulls out his part to the "Carnival of Venice," and make my way to the front of the band, positioning myself to Schoepper's left. I find myself standing in front of Bud Malsh. I am still in civilian clothes—Louie the Tailor, whose shop is located directly across the street from the Marine Barracks, hasn't yet completed the fittings of my summer Service C khakis and the full dress uniform of scarlet tunic and white trousers.*

*Schoepper doesn't look at me as I stand in the "ready" position. He raises his baton then brings it down forcefully, as if pulling a big switch that turns on the stage lights of a Broadway theater. I hear the band sound the first of three fortissimo B-flat major chords. On the third chord, I strike the first note of the slurring cadenza and slowly roll into the series of major triads. I now feel myself accelerating gradually into a rapid speed and acceleration to the end of the series. Every note is coming out. I can feel my confidence growing.*

*After successfully executing my way though the following three variations and the band releasing the final chord with me, I hear resounding applause and the shuffling of feet from the musicians. Even Schoepper is applauding. "Very good!" he exclaims with a smile.*

Sunday, July 17, 1955, on a hot evening in the nation's capitol, nineteen-year-old Freddie Erdman would debut as a soloist with the Marine Band at the Watergate concert barge. Daddy and I—his seven-year-old half-brother—drove down from Lebanon, Pennsylvania, our hometown, to hear Freddie play. Mom didn't make the trip. She remained at home to care for our three week-old baby brother, Mike.

As the afternoon wore on, the weather threatened. Eventually it managed to rain. "Looks good to me!" thought Freddie. Rain would more than likely cancel the concert, which meant that Freddie wouldn't have to perform the solo, a relief to his growing anxiety. As the three were having dinner at a nearby restaurant, however, the skies cleared. It was time to face the music after all!

The Sunday night concert was on. Freddie would have to suit up in his uniform upon our return from dinner. The nerves were coming back. He had played earlier that day, and everything was working. But he couldn't rid himself of the apprehension.

*Freddie:*

*7:15 p.m. Time to take off for the Watergate. Even though the concert started at 8:30 p.m., I was already worried about getting there in enough time to warm up. We drove down Pennsylvania Avenue and headed west for about five miles, then onto Independence Avenue, still heading west. We ended up at the bottom the steps of the hallowed Lincoln Memorial. I was in full dress uniform. The supply people could not find a scarlet red tunic that would fit me properly, so I had to wear one that was much too big for me. A white belt encircled the outside of the tunic. I must have looked like a wheat sack tied in the middle!*

*We parked the car on Independence Avenue and as we got out, I felt intimidated by the environment. Walking along the stately boulevard and seeing more people, I also spotted two or three Marine Band members making their way to the concert site.*

*As we kept walking, the barge suddenly came into full view. I said goodbye to Daddy and Tim and, increasing my pace nervously, headed toward it. I saw a fifteen-foot-long gangplank, extending from the stone-walled shoreline of the Potomac River to the barge. I walked the plank to cross over onto the stage, sensing movement. The barge rested quietly on its moorings with a barely detectable sway. I wondered if I was going to sway back and forth during my solo. I then made my way to the backstage area, greeted a few of my bandmates, pulled out the horn and began to warm up. It was about ten minutes to eight. Plenty of time.*

*8:25 p.m. I notice the band is not tuning up. This band never tunes up! It never has to!*

*8:27 p.m. Time to go onstage. I am ready but anxious.*

*8:30 p.m. We start off with a fanfare and as we are still playing, Sgt. Redkay, our concert moderato (as well as pianist for concerts and the White House), greets the audience and introduces "Captain Albert F. Schoepper," who struts out, bows to the audience, and takes his position on the podium. At the thunderous strike of the tympani, we arise from our seats and play the national anthem. At its conclusion, we resume our seats while Sgt. Redkay announces the opening overture. As we are playing along, I feel good that I am playing in the low register; it will keep my chops loose. Another piece follows. Damn! I hate this waiting around! Please, Dear God, give me an earthquake, a tornado, anything! Just get me out of this!*

*Another piece follows, and I can see from the order of our parts that I will be next. After the conclusion of the last piece, Sgt. Redkay introduces me. The audience greets me with polite applause as I make my way to the front of the band. I assume my stance. Captain Schoepper looks over at me. I look over at him. He then addresses the band with his baton and comes down with the beat. I attack on the third chord, and we are off to the rolling thirds that proceed very smoothly. Good! We've got it made! My performance lives up to what I wanted. In the professional world, a live performance is like a parachute jump. Ya gotta get it right the first time.*

*After I play my last note, the applause from the audience resounds across the Potomac. Schoepper smiles, shakes my hand, and says, "Congratulations."*

*I notice that the seating on the Memorial steps and the grassy plot below is filled to capacity. Someone recently told me that the seating capacity was ten thousand. The overall venue is beautiful and unique with the Lincoln Memorial looking down from a distance at the Watergate barge on the Potomac River.*

*Now I'm glad I played. What a feeling of relief and excitement!*

## Full Dress Uniform

Louie the Tailor eventually finished outfitting Freddie. He received his own perfectly tailored uniforms—no more "wheat sack tied in the middle" look. The scarlet tunic and white trousers of the full dress uniform bear an historic pedigree. When the United States Marine Corps (and with it the Marine Band) was established in 1798, the band's uniform followed the European pattern of reversing the color scheme worn by the regular troops. The Marine uniform was a dark blue coat with red trim. The musicians' coats were red with blue trim. Since musicians were used by commanding officers to send signals to the troops in battle, they needed to stand out on the battlefield: the reversed colors made the musicians easier to spot. The band has kept this reversed color scheme since 1798. In 1904, the Marine Corps adopted a "special full dress uniform" for the most formal of formal occasions. In 1912, the Marine Corps dropped this uniform, but the band continued to wear it and still does today.

An article in a 1959 *National Geographic* issue says that crowds of eight thousand and more actually attended these concerts at the Watergate barge. That summer saw our Mom and Dad make several trips to see and hear their nineteen-year-old son and cornet virtuoso. In those days, such trips were anything but an afterthought. Interstate 83 hadn't been constructed yet. The Interstate Highway System had yet to be authorized by the Federal-Aid Highway Act of 1956—which meant we had to go from Lebanon through York, Pennsylvania; then continue motoring down through and over the Conowingo Dam in Maryland, just south of the Pennsylvania border. On those long trips inside the confines of our Dad's two-tone Pontiac, we anticipated the nexus known as Washington, D.C. that could drive our mother into verbal spasms.

"Fre-eeedddd! Take it easy!" She was an inveterate "back seat" driver and was constantly on Dad's case.

Bad weather certainly didn't do much to allay Mom's fears of the road. Going across the dam and passing the huge hydroelectric plant at Conowingo, I can remember the severity of thunderstorms and lightning. I was always afraid that one of those gigantic electrical towers would be struck by lightning and fall down on top of us, crushing us into motorist oblivion. It seemed so bad at times, I had visions of Scarlett O'Hara and Rhett Butler madly driving their horse-drawn carriage through Atlanta's firestorms.

For our parents, it would become a trip made more frequently over the years, a remarried father and dedicated mother rewarded with not one, not two, but eventually *three* sons in the United States Marine Band, "The President's Own," all at the same time. During a tour concert in Annville, Pennsylvania in 1975, Dad would be invited onstage to guest-conduct the band. It seemed only fitting. ❖

# Chapter 4

# Roots

*Our Father. . .*

*. . . suggests the opening of a familiar prayer, and in his particular instance it might very well fit. He excelled on the cornet and trumpet—those were his instruments, although he wasn't a bad sub on my instrument from time to time. Dad would occasionally switch to the trombone when Lebanon's historic Perseverance Band, formed during the Civil War, needed an extra 'bone player. Let's face it, the brass instrument known as the cornet or trumpet certainly is not in danger of becoming extinct! We definitely need more trombonists to compete with that thing!*

*Playing the snare drum as early as fourth grade and moving on to the cornet in fifth grade, I had broken the drumhead. Since cost to replace it was not "in the cards" at that time, I moved onto an old, used baritone and experimented with that during the beginning of sixth grade, tiring of it halfway through. Then there was the time when Dad was washing a trombone in the tub, slushing the slide back and forth. Enjoying the scene of washing and sloshing, I blurted out, "Let me try it!" "Fine," he replied patiently, "but then this is what you stick with."*

*And that was that. I learned the slide positions fluently in less than two weeks, and that was the genesis of my career. Little did I know!*

*For as much as my father loved me and, yes, I did study for a brief time with him when I played the cornet, he was not quite as thorough with me as he was with Freddie or Timmy. My lessons, as I recall, were extremely frustrating to Dad, because this very young "Jimmie" was very easily distracted and very silly. Dad would become very exasperated and disappointed, knowing full well that I simply had other things on my mind. At that point, the lessons would come to an abrupt halt.*

*He never showed anger. But it was obvious he recognized that his son Jimmie was not the "serious" player that Freddie was. (Timmy, of course, was still in diapers!)*

*I think it's important to note that I was not a "soloist" during my high school years as was Freddie; therefore, Dad was not cognizant that I had that capability. One of my most loving memories is of Dad's emotional reaction after one of my first solo performances with the Marine Band at the Watergate Concert barge, where an audience of nearly ten thousand had gathered the night he came down to hear me play in front of the band. "I had no idea you played like that," he exclaimed. "You really are a phenomenal player!" That statement, easily understood as coming from a very proud parent, may well have been a bit exaggerated. But it meant more to me than he ever realized.*

*(Years later, brother Michael, the only non-player in the family, studied the trombone for a brief time with Dad. However, his interests pointed in a different direction, and we became particularly proud of his career as a senior health physicist at the Penn State Milton S. Hershey Medical Center in Hershey, Pennsylvania.)*

*Dad deserves more than a sentimental accolade for his part in this story. One must understand that, when his divorce occurred in the 1940s, it was highly unusual for a father to receive custody of his children, especially when they were ages six (Freddie) and four (me). It was his steadfast intention to do all he could for us. As I consider the rather extensive knowledge I have of my biological mother, that successful custody was primarily the cause of our success!*

## "Men of the Earth"

"Dad" was born Frederick James Erdman in 1914 in Lebanon, Pennsylvania.

His father—the Erdman brothers' grandfather and a stern taskmaster—was James Erdman. The boys called him "Pop." Jim Erdman was a gentle man, a hard-working type. His gentlemanly and quiet demeanor belied a tough-as-nails steel inspector in a stress-filled job overseeing the machines that produced railroad spikes. With forearms like Popeye, he also fashioned a living making wrought-iron railings for local homeowners. In the latter half of his eighty-five years, he kept one hand on his King James Version Bible and the other in "the shop," a twenty-foot by forty-foot concrete structure behind our house on Third Avenue in Lebanon. Here, as a self-employed contractor, he turned inch-square steel rods into wonderfully-twisting banister railings. His was an art form rarely seen in homes any longer, perhaps only in the most upscale residences.

Before that, he eked out a living during the Great Depression, selling fruits and vegetables. His daughter Ruth, our dad's sister, helped out by baking cookies that she'd sell to the neighbors.

Despite austere times, the Erdmans managed to make ends meet. German blood ran thick. Our name "Erdman" in German means "earthman," and no one was more down to earth than Grandpa. He and his brothers and sisters were known for having a strong work ethic. Most lived long lives. Bill ran a mincemeat business in the 1940s and 1950s, and no friend of the family could ever turn away a piece of mince pie made from Erdman's Mince Meat. As a lively, frolicsome centenarian, Bill was known to scoot up and down the halls of Cornwall Manor Nursing Home on his motorized wheelchair, spreading jokes and good cheer right up until the day he died at the age of 104. His brother Charles Erdman helped in the mincemeat business and lived to be 103.

## Mazie

Jim's wife Mazie Amanda (Bowman) Erdman lived to be 99. An accomplished pianist and organist, Grandma suffered from arthritis and osteoporosis in her last 50 years and rarely walked without the aid of a walker or on the strong and constant arm of Grandpa, her faithful companion and husband. Jim even rigged a buzzer from the kitchen to the shop where he would be forging, hammering, and twisting out another wrought-iron railing. Whenever Mazie needed Jim, she'd ring the buzzer. Grandpa would put down whatever iron piece he was cutting, shaping, bending, drilling, or welding. He'd grab a rag and wipe off his grease or oil-marked arms and hands, then walk out the shop door and down a series of steps to the house and into the kitchen where Mazie would be sitting, waiting. He had the patience of Job, to go along with a deep and abiding love of his family that complemented his unfailing discipline as a self-employed worker.

Both made time for leisure, which often included card games like canasta and pinochle. They loved their cards. Opposite friends in their living room, Mazie took pride in the strategically played hand. She didn't like to lose. "Oh pshaw!" she'd exclaim upon realizing a losing hand. When she lost after competing with arthritis for many years, and her hands became unmercifully gnarled,

Jim bought her an electric automatic card shuffler. He also purchased an electric wax bucket that melted wax for immersing Mazie's hands. Used this way, paraffin was supposed to relieve pain and restore temporary function for the arthritically-wracked hand. Despite these measures, the deterioration worsened, and Jim would eventually have to load the mechanized shuffler himself. The card-playing eventually stopped, when Mazie could no longer hold back the tears from the pain of holding cards.

## Work, Discipline, and Faith

Jim Erdman and his brothers and sisters were known for their stoic ways and practiced the rigid Germanic lifestyle of hard work and prudent spending. While Jim would smoke an occasional cigar, the Erdmans in general refrained from the vices of everyday life, practiced temperance, and rarely wore their emotions on their rolled-up sleeves. Except for Mazie. She had a temper and didn't hold back when it came to voicing her opinion. Grandma wore her emotions on her sleeve. On the other hand, with an Erdman male, what you saw wasn't necessarily what you got, for you never knew exactly what he was thinking. Grandpa and his brothers were just the kind of people who rarely threw caution to the wind in anything they did or said.

*Freddie:*

*Many hours were spent practicing back in Grandpa's shop. Even when Grandpa was around, he seemed not to mind at all. Sometimes he'd have me twist half-inch-square iron bars in his four-foot-high workbench vice, using a three-foot long handle that gripped the bar. I'd go full circle with my arms, bending iron, twisting it, a very arduous process. It was one that Pop performed with relative ease. Although I didn't volunteer for this chore, my reward was that it developed my arms and shoulders. Then I'd go back to practicing. I think he tuned me out!*

*My grandmother was a true taskmaster. She started me on piano. I learned rhythms pretty fast. It was either that . . . or Grandma's ruler on the wrist!*

The family was a churchgoing one but kept an eye on world events as well. Their son Fred, our Dad was a God-fearing man who could recite Biblical verses with one breath and tell salty jokes with the next. He prided himself equally on proper English usage and exacting penmanship. Ocasionally dispensing a fifty-cent word just to impress, he enjoyed conversations that could be as cerebral as life after death, as biblical as a parable, or as earthy as talking until 2:00 a.m. with the local high school football coach, Mike Intrieri, over cigarettes and coffee.

## The ladies in Dad's life

As the only son to Jim and Mazie, Fred grew up in a church-going household of mostly women. With his younger sister Ruth, Fred was nurtured mostly by his mother, grandmother, and any number of aunts who happened to be residing with them at the time. In an autobiography for a college English professor (the essay earned a B-minus) he wrote:

"…with the exception of my father, I was the only male resident of our home, pitted against the wiles and favors of three generations of the fair sex. In short, I was spoiled."

As a child, Dad's aunts were his mentors; and girls, his playmates. His elementary school peers came to regard him as a sissy, and he paid the price by having to high-tail it like Forrest Gump from home to school and back, with a couple of bullies always a few steps behind in hot pursuit. But far from doing him any serious social harm, Fred's matron-oriented upbringing endowed him with an ability to listen and empathize.

He would come to attach a special importance to listening. As a result, people found him easily approachable and frequently sought out his advice. From the late 1950s to the early 1960s, Fred served on the Lebanon school board and was elected president. He got more votes than all the other candidates combined and never spent a cent campaigning. Those who knew him regarded Fred Erdman as a gentleman. This exemplary reputation stayed with him until his death on Christmas evening in 1998.

## Beginning a Dynasty

Seventy years prior and on his fourteenth birthday, Fred Erdman walked into Loser's Music Store in downtown Lebanon with Billy Etter. A kind and generous friend of the family, Billy purchased for Fred his first trumpet, a Buescher model. It had cost Billy $50, a serious sum back in those days.

The investment certainly did return dividends. Fred began taking lessons and in just a couple years could outplay his teacher. Schooled in the fundamentals of embouchure development and technique, he soon attained first chair in his high school band. In short order he went from student to teacher, amassing a weekly teaching load of over sixty students shortly after graduation. As his clientele expanded, so did his reputation as a musician.

During the 1930s and well into the 1940s, he played to local audiences as the area's premier cornet soloist. Soon out of high school, he joined the vaudeville circuit, performing on weekends throughout the eastern region of the state. He even subbed on trumpet at "The "Roxy," one of the more prominent vaudeville houses in New York City. One of his favorite stories—and one the family always liked hearing—involved a rainy "gig" night that ended in an event nothing short of the mystical. He was in his twenties by this time, driving to and from gigs with a couple of musician-friends who wailed alongside him in a band called The Criterion Cadets.

Late one rainy night, the Cadets were on their way home from a gig, and Fred was at the wheel of the car, trying to negotiate through nasty, relentless thunderstorms on the back roads behind Hershey and Annville, less than fifteen miles from Lebanon. The car had no windshield wipers, compounding the difficulty of negotiating through the severe driving conditions. Rain began pelting down so hard that visibility was next to impossible. No one was sure where they were or if they were even headed in the right direction. Someone finally spoke up. "Fred," he suggested, "Why don't you stop the car, get out and see where we are? Maybe you'll see a road sign somewhere."

What happened next might convince the most fervent atheist of the existence of angels. Fred took a high-beam flashlight, got out of the car, walked in front of the headlights, and pointed the flashlight down to the ground and straight ahead. There, in front of the vehicle by less than two car lengths, was the edge of a cliff overlooking one of the area's numerous limestone quarries.

*At 18, our dad was playing vaude-ville. This photo depicts him in his Criterion Cadets Orchestra uniform.*

## Our Teacher

Dad was Freddie's first trumpet teacher—also Jimmie's and mine—sternly teaching us everything he knew. Some would later say that Freddie forgot more than Dad ever knew. This included all the musical terms, most of them in Italian. Terms like *allegro* and *vivace*.

And then there was *tacet*, a particular term Dad learned the hard way.

During one vaudeville rehearsal, the conductor told Dad and the rest of the group that they were to mark a certain section *tacet*. In a heavy Italian accent, the leader pronounced "tacet" as "tocket." Dad didn't know that the word meant "don't play" and instead guessed it meant something else like "expressive." So he marked the music *tacet* as ordered. When that point in the music occurred, he played the passage *espressivo*. The conductor stopped the rehearsal and rapped his baton repeatedly on the podium. "*Tocket*, I said," he insisted in broken but vehement English, looking straight at Dad. "*Tocket!*"

Dad nodded, a blank stare on his face, then played the passage again, this time more *espressivo* than before. The conductor once more stopped the rehearsal and, rapping his baton sharply on the stand, shouted at Dad, "*Tocket*, Erdman, *TOCKET!*" His own patience wearing thin, Dad thought, "Okay, if he's going to yell at me, I just won't play it, period." The next time the orchestra came to the passage, Fred sat with his trumpet on his lap, training his eyes on the conductor.

The conductor looked up at Fred and smiled.

## Local Celebrity

Fred would become a conductor himself one day, leading the Palmyra American Legion Band in the 1940s and 1950s at the old Hershey Park band shell. On summer Sundays the band performed regularly on the bandshell, which frequently brought in major ensembles like the United States Navy Band. Fred's band consisted of talented artists and helped launch many a professional performance career.

When he wasn't waving the baton, he taught private trumpet lessons. In fact, Fred became one of the area's most successful trumpet teachers, as evidenced by his students' successes in music and other professions. Among the hundreds of students he taught over the years, Stan Mark was a standout; he could blast down the walls of the Erdman home on Saturday mornings at his nine-o'clock lesson time. Stan eventually became Maynard Ferguson's lead trumpet player for nine years. David Boltz came over for lessons on Saturday mornings as well, and in the eighth grade was already ripping through the Arban's "Characteristic Studies" with pinpoint accuracy. David became a career assistant principal cornetist in the United States Air Force Band.

James May joined the Marine Band for four years, then became an Army chaplain, ultimately becoming Colonel May in charge of the Fort Myer Army Chapel on the grounds of Arlington Cemetery. Allen "Skip" Fenner also joined the Marine Band, then left after four years to become one of the top salesmen for a leading recording-tape manufacturer. By the time Fenner successfully auditioned for the Marine Band, the band's austere leader, Albert Schoepper, was convinced of our dad's expertise in grooming first-rate trumpet players.

*Dad was known for his student trumpet trios, featured throughout the region of Lebanon, PA. This circa 1954 photograph shows, from left to right, James Checket, Freddie Erdman and Art Sherman. The three performed Leroy Anderson's "Buglers Holiday" on the Ted Mack Amateur Hour held in New York City and narrowly missed winning the nationally televised competition. Checket went on to become a professional trumpeter, educator and musical composer.*

It was hardly any wonder that being with him sometimes made his family feel as though they were tagging along in the presence of a local celebrity. Many times when going out to dine in some downtown Lebanon restaurant, someone would walk up to greet Fred Erdman. If the Erdmans went to a picnic where a local community band was playing, Fred would inevitably be called up to the stage to guest-conduct the band. "I see Fred Erdman is with us tonight . . ." began the announcer.

When he conducted, his baton spoke with distinctive authority. One local Lebanon musician formed the Lebanon Community Concert Band in 1991 and asked Fred to be its first director. He agreed, and more than sixty musicians showed up for that first rehearsal, all of them either his former trumpet students or veterans of his Palmyra American Legion Band.

## Berdine

Fred's first wife was Berdine, Freddie and Jimmie's biological mother. She was a striking beauty with long, flowing jet-black hair. She considered herself a free spirit, evidenced by six other marriages that followed in successive years. One of her husbands was a close confidante to Howard Hughes, the famous aviator and reclusive billionaire. A passionate devotee of the arts, she could express herself admirably in several art forms, including dance and piano—she was an accomplished cocktail pianist. She could recite a line of verse that she herself occasionally wrote. She especially loved to play drums; a pair of drumsticks could set her off in serious motion. As she attained professional competence, Berdine dreamed of drumming in a nightclub band, all the while feeling the weight of marriage and motherhood.

Freddie remembers that, in fits of frustration, she would hold him, as a toddler, under cold showers. Other than that, he had no memories of her. As an adult, he realized that his parents were musically gifted but had diverging priorities. Despite his musical prowess, Dad wanted job security and a secure household in which to raise their family. Living in Lebanon as a performing musician meant anything but job security.

On the other hand, Berdine desperately wanted to perform.

As a result, Freddie grew up in a conflicted household, the product of two musical talents, but with disparate career goals and seemingly incompatible life-goals. The economic aftershocks of the Great Depression by this time had gripped the nation, and Fred and Berdine Erdman were not immune to them. The family wasn't poor, but it wasn't swimming in the lap of luxury, either.

What little we know about Berdine is mostly contained in Fred's college autobiographical essay.

Dad:

"We settled down in our cozy apartment. I was working with my dad, learning to know the ins and outs of the job at which he excelled ('Pop' ran the railroad spike machine), and more importantly, learning to know and admire him in a way I could only obtain in the man-to-man, day-after-day relationship we had, for I was one of the fifteen or twenty men under his supervision, and dad played no favorites. Some of my spare time was applied to trumpet instruction, in which I was on the issuing terminal.

"The remainder of the time was spent on marital instruction, in which I was on the receiving end. Berdine and I had the natural and exciting happiness that is the experience of all newly married couples. We also had those dubiously frolicsome experiences . . . Our sea of matrimonial bliss was alternately peaceful, then stormy, then peaceful again, then stormy again. The winds of [my] irate but subtle mother-in-law were ever-threatening to mar the more placid expanses of time the three of us were privileged to enjoy.

"*. . . As my income increased due to wage increases and a growing student clientele, we moved to roomier and more favorably located apartments. My wife was of invaluable aid to me in my musical endeavors, as she was an accomplished pianist and her piano accompanying left little to be desired. However, when our baby was eighteen months old, Berdine's mother came for a month's visit to our home, and at the end of the month Berdine and the baby went back with her to her home sixty miles away (near Allentown, Pennsylvania). Berdine's intent was to leave for good and obtain a divorce. On the twenty-first day of her absence I received a telegram from her asking me to meet her at Reading (a town twenty-five miles east of Lebanon and fifty miles west of Philadelphia). She wanted to come back, and it was revealed to me that when I met her, she had to literally escape from her mother under whose vigilant guard her every movement for those twenty-one days was watched.*

"*So we started again. This time I had every reason to hope that the troubled waters would be forever calmed. A year and three months later we were blessed with our second boy, Jamie, and these two children, I thought, would surely cement our marriage.*"

(At that time, Dad apparently was calling Jimmie "Jamie.")

In 1941, the plant at which Fred and his father were employed had liquidated—an opportune time, Fred decided, to try his hand at teaching music for a living. "For nine months I did this with surprising success," he wrote.

Dad:

"*Then came Pearl Harbor, and the combined chauvinistic spirits of my wife and myself demanded that I get a job to do my part . . . I secured a position as a time-study man in a key defense industry, and after a period of intense training, became a time-study engineer in my own right. In addition to my job, I was still teaching fifty pupils per week. A great responsibility was placed on my wife, for there wasn't a whole lot of time I could devote to my family, and still carry on these two activities. During all these years since my wife's return she and I constantly improved our musical standing, and through that, our social standing in our community.*"

Fred's students were performing everywhere, playing solos, duos, and larger ensembles at various special events throughout the city and region, a fact that pleased Berdine.

*Dad:*

"... in her flair for the spectacular, which she displayed continuously, she was partially satisfied with the contacts these engagements presented. I was also the first chair cornetist and soloist in the prominent band in our city, and this too delighted her; otherwise, I should have relinquished that position many times.

"Thus we moved along until October of 1942, when a steel firm in Jersey City, having knowledge of my experience on the spike machines and my ability to handle them . . . proffered to me the position as assistant superintendent of their factory in Hagueville. When they realized that I was also a time study engineer they spared no words in telling me how badly they needed me . . . I decided in March of 1943 to accept this position."

The young family packed its bags and moved to Jersey City, and Berdine and Fred were at peace.

*Dad:*

"Her mother came to live with us 'for a while.' We lived there sixteen weeks; she was with us nine-sixteenths of the time.

"New York was Berdine's Babylon and my Waterloo. In short, she became career-minded and decided that if I refused to take advantage of my talents she would reap whatever benefits she could gain from hers. She had many times encouraged me to accept opportunities with 'name' bands and to go on the road, travel, meet people, and gain new experiences. My convictions told me my place was with my wife and my children; hence, I never accepted or considered accepting any of these offers.

"She decided to leave then, in September of 1943, and her desire was to place the children in a home, a desire which would be fulfilled, in the modern vernacular, over my dead body. There was but one way out, and that course I pressed with all my being. I brought the two boys, aged seven and four, to my parents in my hometown [of] Lebanon. Although my mother Mazie was in no condition to assume this responsibility, her love for the children, coupled with a like devotion on the part of Dad, made them take and care for Freddie and Jamie as they cared for their own. My wife went her way, a way that is not yet clear to me, for in her own words, she has 'so many irons in the fire.' She was and is a beautiful woman, and perhaps someday she may reach the top of whatever ladder she may be climbing . . .

*"This cataclysmic event had, by its very asininity, unexpectedness, and irrevocableness, completely nullified my mentality for a time. After the first drug-like effects had worn off, I was left with a sensation . . . of numbed remorse. But, with the end of passion came the beginning of wisdom. Things could not be forever like this . . ."*

## Freddie:

*We were in the middle of the war in 1943 when Daddy, Jimmie, and I drove back to Jersey City after having visited Grandma and Pop one Sunday evening. Upon arriving at our apartment, we could not find Berdine. When Daddy saw the note on the bedroom bureau, he said to us, "Come on, boys, we're going back to Lebanon."*

*I think from that moment, he became my hero. He was all I had.*

*It was late at night when Daddy drove us back to Grandma and Pop in Lebanon. I think he was driving a black Ford coupe at that time. We lived there for six years. The first couple of months of those years were quite an emotional trip for all five of us. Daddy still had his job in Jersey City. It was always terribly painful to see him have to leave us Sunday evenings. He had to get back to his job, and it must have been doubly painful for him to leave two crying little boys, pleading and begging him not to leave. I can still see and hear Jimmie wailing at the front door as Daddy made his way out.*

**Jimmie, Freddie, and their dad, Fred Erdman in this 1945 photograph.**

*A month or two later, Daddy got hired at the Lebanon Steel Foundry where he worked with Jimmie's future father-in-law, Frederick D. Koons. For the most part, we were a happy family, at least as far as I was personally concerned. Daddy was my model of what a man should be—physically and in terms of character and personality. He could do no wrong. Knowing how fascinated I was with the sousaphone, he obtained for me an old helicon from the Perseverance Band. I can still remember marching up and down Church Street between the back porch and the high school stadium wall tooting that thing. It must have been quite a spectacle for the neighbors.*

## Problems Solved

In 1943, young Freddie was having problems as a first grade student, and his teacher suggested he repeat first grade, adding that his mind often seemed thousands of miles away. His father did what he could to help Freddie with his academics, spending many late hours, especially with math reading problems. Dad displayed a flair for innovation, as evidenced by an approach he devised to help his son.

> *Freddie:*

*With the idea of getting me interested and focused on these reading assignments, he devised a football scoring system, knowing how much I liked football. This motivated me to get more correct answers. His plan worked!*

*In 1943, Daddy started me on trumpet lessons. He had a unique system of noting his assignments in the lesson book: he used a pen that had four different colors in it. In the student's first assignment, he would write the date in black. If the student had to do it over, Daddy would write that date in red. If the student had to do it over again, he would mark it in green, then blue. I don't remember getting too many greens and blues. I don't know how many Jimmie got.*

*Some time after starting lessons, I was still sucking my thumb. I remember one night when he put me to bed, he said to me that if I kept on sucking my thumb, I'd get buckteeth and wouldn't be able to play the trumpet. From that night on, I never again sucked my thumb.*

*To me, Daddy was a man of the world. I loved him and also feared him if I misbehaved. But he never spanked me.*

*Freddie when he was eight years old.*

## Back from the Brink . . . Twice

In the spring of 1944, Fred left his "job of opportunity." With Freddie and Jimmie in tow, the three moved up to Stowe, Vermont, to "work on a dairy project." Meanwhile, the kids were under the watchful eye of Dad's employer's wife. A few months later, a recurring injury prevented her from caring for them any longer. So, the trio moved back to Lebanon to live once again with Fred's parents. His parental instinct taking over, Fred resolved to make things work out to the betterment of both him and the boys. He wrote, "My children are childishly happy, and they do not consciously miss their mother."

Dad:

*"I know that if I am to pursue this course I have set for myself, I must be doubly diligent, for besides gaining a college education, I must maintain and support my two children, be both father and mother to them, and earn every cent I get during the process of accomplishing these things. But, if I am blest with the continued presence of my parents until I am through these next few years, I shall do it.*

*"What my wife has done I condemn not; certainly I do not condone it. But judging the seemingly obtuse acts of others is not one of my specialties. Maybe she is right. I don't know, but when I lie awake at night sometimes I try to fathom the problem of what my dominant fault was through the years that contributed to the production of this tragedy to our children,*

39

*and in a lesser light, to my wife and myself, for I don't want to make the same mistake again, and I am not so naïve as to believe that I am blameless.*

*"To the Bible and its many comforting phrases and touchstones, I ascribe most of my ability to come back after having stood on the brink of mental disaster. If there is one outstanding bit of the literature of men that held forth like a light unto me during all my heartaches and regrets (for. . .I loved my wife with a love that knew no bounds) it is this from the closing paragraph in Dumas' 'The Count of Monte Cristo': 'There is neither happiness nor misery in the world, there is only the comparison of one state with another, nothing more. He who has felt the deepest grief is best able to experience supreme happiness. We must have felt what it is to die that we may appreciate the enjoyments of life. Never forget, that until the day when God will deign to reveal the future to men, all human wisdom is contained in these words—wait and hope.'"*

## Freddie:

*Many people sought Daddy's opinion and advice, and I was always proud to be with him. People respected him. I always took such delight when we would come outside after Sunday school to hang out and chat with whomever for fifteen minutes or so before we had to go back in for the church service. Inevitably, several men would light up their cigarettes and after Daddy lit his pipe, they would surround him. They sought his thoughts on the football game or whatever sporting event was current at the time.*

*He was a leader of men. We always lived on the other side of the tracks, the industrial north side where the steel plants were. I admired the practical side of him, too. It was always fun every Christmas watching him and Pop erecting the "Christmas yard" model railroad in the dining room at 726 Lehman Street and struggling with the wiring underneath the large eight-by-five-foot platform, in order to get the lights on and the trains running.*

*Some things you just never forget. On a Sunday morning in April 1945, I made my debut as a soloist. In Sunday school, after the superintendant announced, "We will now be favored with a trumpet solo by young Fredric Erdman." I was nine years old. With horn in hand, I made my way up the four-foot high stage, while Daddy ambled over to the piano on floor level. After assuming my position on stage and Daddy assuming his at the piano, he turned, looked at me and said, sotto voce, "Are ya ready, Freddie?"*

*I gave a slight nod and said casually, "Yeah."*

*So, we started. I don't remember the name of the piece I was to play. Maybe it was "The Lost Chord;" I'm not sure. Daddy played me a beautiful eight-bar introduction.*

*On the last bar of the intro, I raised my horn to my face, all set to blow—and there was no mouthpiece! A shock of embarrassment raced through me. As poor Daddy arose from the piano to retrieve my mouthpiece from the trumpet case, a moment of low-key laughter rose from the audience. After he walked up to the stage and handed me the mouthpiece, we began again. We made it all the way to the end of the piece without further incident.*

## Normalcy—and More—Returns

In May 1945, the Allies officially declared victory over the Germans in Europe, while Japan's defeat in the Pacific had yet to be accomplished. Jubilation was everywhere as British and Americans celebrated V-E Day. As a general feeling of "normalcy" returned, Dad's own life began to turn around. He never obtained his college degree. But he got something else much better—someone who could do so much more for him than any sheepskin.

Dad had met the second love of his life and would enjoy another experience of being smitten.

**Our mother, Catherine Schubert Erdman.**

By now he was working in the cooper shop for the Bethlehem Steel Corporation—known to those closest to it as "the BS." He was helping oversee the production of containers that packaged the company's products. Nearby in the gun barrel department, a striking brunette was packing shell casings as part of the BS's war effort. The ranks of women working for the BS had swelled during WWII, and Catherine Barbara Schubert was one of about twenty-five thousand nationwide working for the steel maker. Like so many industrial companies, the BS was marching to the drums of war in its own hard-hat way, and thousands of women like Catherine were in lockstep.

The daughter of Roman Catholic immigrants who came over "on the boat" from what was then Austro-Hungary—the region that is today much of Slovakia—Catherine was a young, vibrant, twenty-seven-year-old, and Catholic to the core. The youngest of Joseph and Mary Schubert's three children, she won the prized and coveted "American Legion" medal in eighth grade for best academic performance, awarded by the school she attended for eight years—St. Gertrude's Parochial School (now St. Cecilia's) at Fourth and Lehman Streets in Lebanon.

She never reached ninth grade. Leaving school soon after her 13th birthday to help her parents make ends meet, Catherine took on a variety of jobs, mostly as a maid and cook for some of Lebanon's wealthier families. The Schuberts spoke English poorly, conversing mostly in a German dialect with an Old World accent, and mingled daily with the local Serbians, Croats, Hungarians, and Slovaks who also lived in the surrounding neighborhoods at the time.

Meanwhile, Catherine developed an expertise for homemaking, learning to cook egg soup, ham schnitzel, and paprikash. These and other imaginative "depression meals" derived their simple, flavorful, and inexpensive combination of ingredients from the dark days of the country's Great Depression. Despite their simplicity, Catherine's culinary delights were said to have rivaled in taste the best cuisine Lebanon had to offer. Mom was a great cook!

Nobody knows if Catherine's cooking had any magnetic influence on Fred. The two fell in love anyway. Fred was divorced by now, a free man in a budding romance; and yet a tough sell to Mr. and Mrs. Schubert, who epitomized the Eastern European Roman Catholic immigrant.

Coming to this country in the early 1900s, Joseph Schubert had settled in Lebanon and found work as a church sexton for St. Gertrude's parish. Sometime later, Mary came over, married Joseph, and helped run many of St. Gertrude's social functions.

The Schuberts were understandably reluctant to have their beautiful and equally hard-working daughter link up with a Protestant divorcé and two feisty young boys in tow. Determined, Fred went to work proving himself, doing odd jobs around the Schubert household and impressing them with his savvy as a handyman, musician, devoted father and model Bethlehem Steel employee. They began to recognize in Dad an attentive, handsome, and ruggedly-built 32-year-old fiancé. What's more, he was dependable. He was also bilingual, conversingwith them and making her immigrant parents laugh in the German dialect they preferred. Dad played his role of courtship with understated relish. It was just a matter of time before the Schuberts embraced him as one of their own.

In Easton, Pennsylvania, on New Years Day 1947, Fred and Catherine were wed by Rev. Paul R. Wert, pastor of St. Paul's Evangelical Church in Lebanon, witnessed only by Fred's sister Ruth and her husband Eugene.

The merger had consequences. Despite pleas to the bishop of the diocese for a hardship waiver, Catherine was excommunicated from the Catholic Church for marrying a divorced man. She also inherited a ready-made family. Freddie and Jimmie had been living under the same roof with their father and were part of the package deal. As a newly married woman, Catherine's lifestyle segued immediately and without fanfare from single, attractive bachelorette to instant mother, one "blessed" with all the joys and trials of parenting two precocious young boys. By agreeing to pick up the pieces of one broken family, she left behind the peaceful coexistence of another.

*The wedding photograph of Fred and Catherine Erdman*

The family set down roots in a little row house on Weidman Street in Lebanon, surrounded by their German-speaking neighbors. I was born a year later, followed in seven years by the family's fourth and final son, our brother Michael.

Catherine had a sharp mind, quick wit, and temper to match, with a fiery tongue aimed at Freddie and Jimmie whenever things seemed chaotic around the growing, young Erdman household. "Mom was long on love," they'd come to say, "and short on fuse."

"When Daddy married Catherine," Freddie said, "he, Jimmie, and I moved out of Grandma and Pop's row home on Lehman Street to go and live in our own house. It was a new life, and I didn't like it. I resented Catherine, my step-mother, and regarded her as an intrusion into my life. We all had difficulty adjusting."

In time though, both Freddie and Jimmie Erdman would adjust to life with their stepmother. In the meantime, Freddie was practicing an average of four hours a day, which was nothing unusual for the young trumpet phenom from Lebanon, Pennsylvania. The most effective way his parents could administer punishment, when deserved for whatever infraction, was to prohibit him from practicing.

## Next step: the Marine Band

Developing a set of "iron chops," Freddie became the star player of many band and orchestra festivals. In his sophomore year of high school in 1953, Freddie was selected to play first part alongside the first-chair player in the All-Eastern Band Festival. The conductor was the famous composer and arranger Erik Leitzen. By the end of the second rehearsal, Leitzen was unhappy with the solo chair cornet-ist's performance. Several of the kids in the band took note and egged Freddie on to approach Leitzen about giving him a chance at the solo passages.

But Freddie refused, so the kids approached Leitzen themselves and informed him about Freddie and his remarkable ability. At the following rehearsal, Leitzen stopped the band after the first cornet solo passage was played, saying that he would like to hear the next gentleman down (pointing to Freddie Erdman) play the passage. Freddie did, and the conductor was all smiles. Without switching chairs, Freddie played all the solo passages for the remainder of the festival.

Freddie's move in 1955 from Lebanon, Pennsylvania, to Washington, D.C. to enter the Marine Band changed his world dramatically. He now held seat in one of the world's finest symphonic bands—an institution that, because of its mission as "The President's Own" band, existed in its own rarefied atmosphere of both history and music.

His parents were proud. So were both sets of grandparents. The name and musical reputation of "Erdman" had crossed from one generation into another, and grew in the process.

In Freddie, the Marine Band had its own right to boast. Not since Herbert L. Clarke—the world-famous solo cornetist in the Sousa Band, and one who has traditionally been considered the finest cornet soloist of the twentieth cen-tury—was there a more electrifying cornet soloist than Freddie Erdman, dubbed sometime later, "the Paganini of the Cornet."

*This tour publicity photo depicts a young staff sergeant Fredric Erdman, who as well as his younger brother James, went on to become two of the Marine Band's legendary soloists.*

In the years to come, three of the four sons sired by Fred Erdman would serve simultaneously in the venerable and prestigious Marine Band—thus creating the Erdman dynasty. In truth, however, that dynasty had begun many years earlier with their father, whose decades of performing and teaching music shaped their destiny. ❖

# Chapter 5

# Longwood. . . Long Road Ahead

Ending on a high "A"note in concert pitch to *The Marines' Hymn*, the Marine Band had just finished its annual series of summer Wednesday concerts on the East Capitol plaza as well as their Sunday evening concerts at the Watergate barge. The change of seasons had arrived. The leaves hinted transformation; a chorus of locusts filled the chilly, late-summer night air; and the government town was itself abuzz with election politics. Beginning in early September and for the next two-and-a-half months, the Marine Band became a road band. It was tour time.

As fall 1955 approached, the band's director, Albert Schoepper, readied the band and himself for the upcoming nine-week concert tour. In early September, he rehearsed the reed sections for two days starting on Monday, taking them through all three folders: matinee, evening, and Sunday afternoon concerts. On Wednesday, he did the same with the percussion section; Thursday, the brass section; Friday, the full band. On Friday, the band's "junior" members were assigned various stage duties. Jack Carey, alto sax, and Freddie were assigned "chimes duty," which meant they were responsible for setting up the chimes before every matinee and disassembling them and packing them up after every evening concert.

Saturday was an "off" day. Sunday was Tour Day One.

The tour band consisted of forty-eight musicians, excluding the leader and the assistant leader. Every musician played the same part on the same stand (or book) every day—there was no switching around. The cornet section carried six players: two on the solo stand, one on second (first part) stand, two on second part and one on third. The trumpet section comprised two players, one on first part and one on second.

*Freddie:*

*This is a Southern tour which will take us as far south as West Palm Beach, Florida; and as far west as Texas. Every musician in the tour band is given a copy of an itinerary. We travel and live in Marine Corps dress blues uniforms: blue blouse with blue belt, blue pants with the red and white piping (stripe), black shoes and socks, and blue cover (hat). We are allowed to remove our blouses only when we are inside the bus or in our hotel room. No air conditioning is available.*

*We are scheduled to play two concerts a day, the same programs every day for sixty-three consecutive days, except Sundays. Sundays could be grueling: the matinees are two hours—as long as the evening concerts. Weekday matinees are less a chore, only one hour long. There are no days off.*

## Tour Etiquette

Two buses were provided by the Atwood Company—one for those who smoked, the other for those who didn't. The non-smokers' bus was the lead vehicle. Everyone except principal musicians was assigned a seat and seatmate. The pecking order was clearly defined: principal musicians (first chair men and soloists) got a double seat all to themselves. This rule applied off the bus as well: the same people also got single rooms.

The tour manager, O.W. Trapp, sat in the very first seat above the wheel well in the lead bus. The same went for the leader in the smokers' bus. One of the musicians, Felix Eau Claire, served as "navigator." *Per diem*, or travel pay, was about $12 a day, out of which the musicians had to pay for hotel room, meals, and haircuts.

On the first Sunday after Labor Day, the two commercially chartered buses, along with a Ryder rental truck carrying uniform trunks, tympanis, chimes, music stands, and instrument cases, would roll out of the driveway at Eighth &

I Streets, past the post sentry box, then head about a hundred miles northeast to an open amphitheatre outside of Philadelphia, in a town along U.S. Route I owning the proud distinction of "mushroom capital of the world," Kennett Square, Pennsylvania.

## Baptism by Fire . . .

The concert amphitheater sat on the grounds of the spectacular Du Pont estate—Longwood Gardens—a panoply of horticultural displays, complete with perfectly manicured grounds and the legendary conservatory organ. Longwood was traditionally the band's first stop, and always one of its finest—save for one simple challenge: the lack of a roof above the stage.

What did Du Pont have against roofs?

An afternoon matinee performance in an open-style amphitheater like Longwood's meant playing a two-hour concert under the constant beating of a hot sun. There was no protection. Bald-headed and fair-skinned musicians like veteran band member and clarinetist Paul French were always "cooked" during a Longwood matinee, and no amount of sunscreen could prevent French's pate from resembling a ripe tomato afterward.

*The Marine Band performing an afternoon concert at*
*Longwood Gardens.*

For a first-time tour soloist, Longwood was the "breakout" concert, the baptism by fire, the stage that "broke him in"—or just broke him. Pull off a relatively flawless performance in relentless heat that seemed fitting for the Mojave Desert, and the soloist felt he could solo anywhere under any conditions.

After the concert was over, band members would go back to the dressing room and remove their sweat-drenched blues, hang them on clothing hangers and pack the swampy-wet assembly inside a black and wooden uniform trunk, squeezing it tightly up against other soaked, sweat-drenched uniforms. There was no way to get around the saturated Longwood matinee uniform. So band members were greeted by a sweaty wool stench upon opening the four-and-one-half feet-high uniform trunks twenty-four hours later—nose-holding time—just before the next matinee performance.

## . . . Followed by a Freeze

The second concert took place later that evening in full dress scarlet tunics and blue trousers, directly behind a row of colorful fountains that simultaneously lit up and rose high into the chilly night amid temperatures that dropped from 60°F at 8:00 p.m. to mid-forties by evening's end. Bandsmen were always surprised at the wide temperature swing between matinee and evening performances.

On that first Sunday after Labor Day in 1955, the first day of tour, Freddie's parents and I met him as the buses arrived and treated him to lunch in Kennett Square.

> *Freddie:*

*We walked over to the Longwood Gardens open-air theater, which seats 2,200 people and is located on the Du Pont Estates, just outside of Philadelphia. The matinee started at two o'clock.*

*I made my way to the backstage area, which was located a level below the stage and where the dressing rooms were. It was time for Jack and me to set up the chimes. It was a beautiful day, but getting hot. I took my horn out of its case to warm up.*

*Schoepper had me scheduled to perform Staigers' "Carnival of Venice" tonight, so I was very anxious.*

*At about 5 o'clock we were served Kennett Square's famous mushrooms with mushroom sauce along with other vegetables and dessert. Our sponsors were wonderful, hospitable folks.*

*At 6:45 p.m., I made my way back to the amphitheater to warm up. At 7:25 p.m., we began to gather in the small area behind the stage. It was very dark. The only light for the entire theater emanated from a row of fountains of various colors situated all along the front of the stage, extending from one end to the other.*

*At 7:29 p.m., we took the stage, seated ourselves, opened our folio and awaited the start of the concert. Because of the fountains, we couldn't see the audience, and they couldn't see us.*

*Suddenly, the fountains dropped all together at once, revealing both audience and the Marine Band, in all its resplendent scarlet and blue. Very dramatic! We opened with a fanfare as the concert moderator greeted the audience. We then stood up to play the national anthem, followed by a march that started the program, then an overture and another selection.*

*Butterflies set in. I would be next.*

## The First Time's Always the Hardest

The march ended. The concert moderator now introduced Freddie, who rose from his chair, walked out to the front of the band as the audience greeted him with applause, and positioned himself to Schoepper's right side. "That applause always helped. It seemed to relax me," said Freddie, who acknowledged everyone with a slight bow. Seeing that he was ready, Schoepper gave the downbeat for the first three B-flat major chords.

*Freddie:*

*Something inside me seemed to say, "All right, just blow the horn." I always do blow just a little more air into the horn than I normally would during my individual practice sessions just to make sure that a sound is going to come out.*

*As before, I attacked my first note of the third chord with security and sailed right through the series of slurred thirds of triads. As I played through the variations, I remember feeling good about how things were going in terms of technique. The performance came off well. My execution was all I had hoped. I made my way back to my seat, the audience still applauding.*

*That's it. No more solos to worry about. Now I can enjoy the rest of the tour.*

*That evening, there was a noticeable chill in the air as the band readied itself for the second half of the concert. It was a rule of nature's thumb: every year the band opened its tour at Longwood, it would be hot in the afternoon, chilly in the evening. Sweat in the afternoon, freeze in the evening.*

*The Marine Band played several more featured selections on the second half of the evening program, and now the concert came to its final number, the last movement of Hector Berlioz's Symphonie Fantastique, "Witches' Sabbath."*

*I remember Schoepper giving the downbeat for the opening's slow, mystical section. Everything's hopping along just fine as the tempo picks up with a flurry of notes. This leads us into the middle of the movement, where the tubas and string bass prevail with a heavy, pronounced descending passage that heightens tension throughout the amphitheater. After a long and drawn-out bass note, things get very quiet, with the lone bass note still sustaining.*

*It is now time for the chimes to sound the three separate notes in rhythm, the famous chimed notes introducing the funereal Dies Irae portion of the piece.*

*Schoepper cues the man behind the chimes.*

*But there are no chimes to be heard! Somebody back there has missed the cue! We're off track! Now what?*

*Schoepper keeps conducting. But nobody is playing, because nobody knows where we are in our parts. For some ten measures, nothing happens. We are moving very close to the precipice. No one's sure of the count or when to play. Are we heading for disaster? Finally, principal trombonist Bob Isele starts playing the chant that occurs after the chimes were to sound. That gets us back on track. Schoepper's pissed, as he has occasion to once again cue the man behind the chimes—a very emphatic cue this time. Would we ever know the wrath the poor percussionist underwent when he was called into the infuriated conductor's dressing room?*

*After the concert ends, we change into our travel dress and pack up our instruments. Jack and I have to disassemble the chimes and pack them up. Then we trek back to the buses, parked on a road behind the theatre. Upon boarding, we see in the wheel well of both buses a bushel basket of Georgia peaches.*

After Longwood Gardens, there were only 62 more days to go and 124 concerts to play. And 630 more times on and off the bus.

A Marine Band tour was the epitome of repetition. ❖

# Chapter 6

# Can't Get There From Here

Freddie Erdman's 1955 tour would be the first of many. Like a wide-eyed boy in a candy shop, he was enjoying so many sights and musical experiences for the first time, at a level of professionalism that few ever have the chance to experience, especially at that age. Hanging over so much of what was new, however, was the ever-lingering shadow of Schoepper.

*Freddie:*

*It was the first week of tour, very hot and humid as we worked our way down south to Florida, especially in dress blues. Our trousers had to be ironed frequently.*

*I found the personalities of these band members so amusing, so much fun: Bob Dehart, the perfect gentleman with a cornet tone that was the most mellow and most beautiful I have ever heard; Bud Malsh, the seemingly carefree solo clarinetist who never missed a note; Doug Stevens, horn, with his quiet, casual demeanor; the very sincere manner of Buddy Burroughs, euphonium; and the very quiet manner and ingeniousness of Louis Saverino and his brother Angelo, both phenomenal tuba players; George Parker, horn, a huge, modest man with the strength of a polar bear; John Gosling, trumpet, whose playing I particularly enjoyed and who displayed a sense of humor so much of the time; Danny Tabler, contrabass, fun to be around.*

**Doug Stevens.**

**Robert DeHart.**

**Bramwell Smith, Cornet and
Post Horn Soloist, 1955.**

Warrant Officer Dale Harpham was fun to be around as well. His imitations of Schoepper and O.W. were hilarious. Bramwell Smith ("Smitty," cornet and post horn soloist on this tour) and Mr. Harpham were roommates and very entertaining to be with when they were together. I frequently dined with them in the hotel dining room.

Captain Schoepper both intimidated us and inadvertently amused us with his abrupt manner of speech and commanding ways. We recognized him as "Der Führer," although some of us also referred to him as "Uncle Al."

*In 1957, three sets of brothers had been serving at the same time in the Marine Band. From left to right, Louis Saverino, Freddie Erdman, Jimmie Erdman, Thomas Patrylak, Daniel Patrylak and Angelo Saverino.*

*Every once in a while, we got out the "Brasso" to polish our belt buckles on the white belt and any other metallic ornaments, such as the brass buttons which lined the front of the blue blouse and full dress red coat, as well as the two brass buttons on the back of the coat. I usually did mine in the bus while traveling.*

*As we approached the third week, tour was already turning into a grind. With the schedule so tight, the only form of entertainment we looked forward to was food and, in some cases, booze. The band, though, was getting tighter and tighter by the day. I felt great pleasure playing in this magnificent ensemble, to hear and feel the organ-like tonal quality and precise intonation. Schoepper's baton technique extracted our uniformity of attack on every note, every chord. It was really something to experience.*

*And yet, he didn't seem to be completely satisfied with any given concert.*

*Hardly a day would go by when he wasn't chewing somebody out for missing a note or needing a haircut, or some other trivial thing. Why was this? I asked myself. Was it because this was his first tour as leader of the Marine Band? He really was getting to a few musicians, including our oboist, who could hardly play the one or two solo passages for which he was responsible. Schoepper, who was turning into a raging tyrant, had totally intimidated the man.*

The band's sense of humor prevailed. To Freddie, young and impressionable, all the guys seemed to enjoy one another's company. He realized with pride that he, Freddie Erdman, was living, breathing, and performing as part of a group of highly talented people, and all quite intelligent. As the leader, Schoepper's intelligence quotient had to be high. He was educated, astute, articulate, and most of all, a master tongue-lasher.

## Trapp's Shortcuts, or Shortcut Traps?

*Freddie*

*The pressure of playing under him every day, twice a day; the relentless grind of the schedule; heat and humidity; and the fact of our having to alight to and from the bus ten times a day, day after day after day, proved quite grueling. Oliver W. Trapp, the Marine Band's booking agent, was called "Shutcher," for "Shut Your Trapp." O.W. was tall in stature, appeared to be in his sixties, and always clenched his teeth when he talked. A chain-smoker, he was the only one who smoked on the nonsmokers' bus.*

*In getting from one town to another, O.W. frequently tried shortcuts, most of which didn't quite work out. During the second week of the tour, while traveling to Salisbury, North Carolina, O.W. tried a shortcut. He told the driver and navigator Felix to "take this dirt road off to the left of the highway." We were about halfway up the dirt road, not really knowing our whereabouts. Then it became apparent: we were in the middle of a wheat field!*

*O.W. spotted a farmer in the middle of the field. He instructed Felix to ask the farmer how to get to Salisbury. The lead bus stopped. Felix called out to the farmer, "How do we get to Salisbury?" The farmer spat out a wad of chewing tobacco and called back, "You can't get there from here!" This was hilarious! Here we were, "The President's Own," lost in the middle of a wheat field!*

*O.W. was frantic. I guess the leader was, too. The threat of being late for the matinee— or worse yet, not showing up at all—was looming large at this point. Somehow, either O.W. or Felix would have to find a way to town.*

*But find our way we did and, arriving late at the hotel and behind schedule, we quickly checked in, got our room keys, dumped our luggage, and immediately headed for the nearest restaurant. We had very little time: it was 12:05 p.m. and the buses were to leave the hotel at 12:30 p.m. for a 1:15 p.m. matinee. After a quick bite, we boarded the bus and arrived* at the concert site at 1:05 p.m., less than ten minutes to warm up before taking the stage. I remember still feeling hungry. But show biz being show biz, I had to play anyway.

It was so hot and humid. I sweated like a pig in July! Somehow, with a great deal of focus, energy, and sheer determination by the stage crew, we made the stage on time and played our way through the show. Then, with the matinee over, it was back on the bus for another half-hour ride back to the hotel. By now the time was 2:30 p.m., which gave us about four hours of leisure time to kill. Following a good dinner, I was still free to relax for an hour or so before having to board the bus again at 7:00 p.m.

After boarding the bus for another half-hour ride to the concert site, we arrived at 7:30, disembarked, and had a half-hour to change into full dress (red tunic) and warm up. We played the concert, then boarded the bus once more for the very last time that day, returning to the hotel. The next morning's departure time was 8:30 a.m.

## Repetition on a Grand Scale

If all of this sounds repetitious, well, it was! A Marine Band tour was repetition on a grand scale. They played the same music day in and day out, got on and off the bus, checked in and checked out of rooms, packed and unpacked and repacked the same suitcase, saw the same faces, heard the same laughter, played the same warm-ups, laughed at the same griping. The same "How many more days?" "It's only day ten!" If one of the more conscientious types made a comment like, "Tour is what you make of it," others would laugh in his face.

But the joke was on them. You didn't make tour. It made you.

*Freddie:*

One day during week three, O.W. spots on his map what he thinks is another opportunity to save time and money—another shortcut. We are rolling along for about seventy-five miles and before we know it, we have left the main highway and are on a two-lane country road. Unsure as to whether his "back road bypass" would work, O.W. becomes crestfallen when he realizes that both buses are suddenly driving through a huge cornfield. Instinctively and without having to be told, Felix calls out to a farmer in a Johnny-on-the-spot display of navigational leadership.

"Can we get to Charleston from here?"

The old farmer squints at Felix, sizes him up, then calls back.

"Brother, you're lost!" The whole bus was laughing.

*We return to the main highway and make it to the next town. We're up against the clock, but again by an act of God make it on time for the matinee. We all hope and pray that this will be the end of the "Trapp Shortcuts."*

*In mid-October, at the University of Mississippi in Oxford, Mississippi, we have a rare "walk" job. Our hotel is only five blocks to the university where we are performing. On this particular day, no buses will be provided.*

## Harpham to the Rescue

*Honoring the astronauts in 1962 at Ohio State University. Left to right, Commander Alan Shepard, Representative William Ayres, Dale Harpham (the Marine Band's assistant director), Lieutenant Colonel John Glenn and Captain Gus Grissom. (Photo courtesy Department of Defense)*

After having dinner with Dale Harpham and Bramwell Smith, Freddie returned to his room and plopped himself down on the bed for a catnap. At some point in his half-conscious state, he heard pounding on his door. "Freddie, open up!!! It's Dale!" It was Harpham, the assistant leader. Freddie forced himself out of bed and opened the door. Harpham rushed into his room. "Where's your blue blouse?" Without asking any questions, Freddie put on his blue blouse.

It was ten minutes to eight, ten minutes before the concert's starting time. "You can't be late or you'll always be seen as being behind the eight ball, and you certainly don't want Schoepper calling you on the carpet," warned Harpham. After grabbing his Marine Corps cover and quickly placing it on his head, Freddie tore out the door, racing as hard as he could to get backstage and to the holding room.

There stood Bramwell Smith holding open Freddie's red tunic for Freddie to jump into.

Chuck Erwin handed him his horn.

It was two minutes to concert time.

*Thank God I made it! It's bad enough that I had been late for the bus three times on this tour.*

Curiously, Schoepper never barked about Freddie's tardiness, not even so much as a whimper. ❖

# Chapter 7

# A Voice of the First Order

After commencing on the first Sunday after Labor Day, the 1955 tour ended nine weeks later, one week before Thanksgiving. Back in Washington, D.C., Schoepper gave the tour band two weeks off, with orders to report back to duty the first week of December. In mid-December, Freddie and the band played for the annual Christmas tree lighting on the Ellipse, just down from the south portico of the White House. It was freezing cold as the band sat and played Christmas music until President Eisenhower came out to light the tree. This was (and still is) a nationally televised event. I remember our mother excitedly turning on the TV to watch "your big brother" play in the band.

Because he did little but play and eat on tour, Freddie's weight shot up, from the nearly 160 pounds he weighed when entering the band, to 180 pounds now. His mind and body had settled into the lifestyle of a Marine Band member.

On New Years Day 1956, at 10:30 a.m., bedecked in the familiar full dress of red coats and blue trousers, the band fell into formation as it prepared to play the traditional "Surprise Serenade" for the new Commandant of the Marine Corps, General Pate. The band stepped out into the arcade, a walkway outlining the perimeter of the barracks and set off by tall Roman arches. Then, to the tap of a solitary drum, the Drum Major marched the band up to the Commandant's House. The day was cold but clear. Red-coated Marines stood in formation, facing the back portico of the house, which in turn faced the parade deck. During the spring and summer months, the "parade deck," a lawn of beautifully manicured grass, approximated the length of a football field. This was the same field on which the Marine Band, Marine Drum & Bugle Corps, and troops all performed in various ceremonies, including the famous Sunset Parades that were held every Friday evening during late spring and all summer.

That day, though, it wore winter's frost as "The President's Own" began its serenade. At the end, everyone remained at attention, while Captain Schoepper delivered a few remarks to the Commandant. The latter responded with his own short speech, then invited everybody into his "Commandant's House" quarters to partake of some punch and hot-buttered rum. Following some schmoozing, Freddie departed at about 11:30 a.m., walked back to the locker room, changed into his civvies, and went home.

(Several years later, the *National Geographic* magazine published an article on the Marine Band. A photo shows our brother Jim shaking hands and speaking cordially to the members of the Commandant's receiving line.)

Rehearsals began a day or two later, with an occasional recording session thrown in. The band also resumed playing patriotic openers, funeral services at Arlington National Cemetery, and official functions at the White House. In February 1956, the winter concert series began, with one concert a week being performed at the Commerce Department in downtown Washington. Downbeat time was 8:00 p.m.

The country was in the midst of a troubling time known as the Suez Crisis in which Marines were deployed to evacuate U.S. nationals from Alexandria, Egypt.

## Changes

To a much lesser extent, times in the band's auditorium were changing as well. Schoepper revised the policy for auditions, so that those auditioning were required to play only one instrument at a professional level instead of two. One of his predecessors was William H. Santelmann, who joined the Marine Band in 1887 after auditioning for Sousa on violin, clarinet, and baritone. His talent on three instruments was reflected in a decision he made after becoming the band's leader eleven years later. Santelmann believed that a string orchestra was better suited than a band for many White House events, so he stipulated that anyone with less than ten years of service learn to play a violin, cello, or other member of the string family. Despite resistance from some Marine Band performers—imagine practicing several hours a day to keep up one's performance level and then having to find more time to learn *another* instrument, and a stringed one at that—the Marine Band Symphony Orchestra, since its founding in 1898, grew in popularity. It became a fixture at the White House over the years as the "Marine Band Chamber Orchestra," the name it carries today. One of the earliest documented appearances by the orchestra was at the Alice Roosevelt wedding in 1906. When Schoepper removed the two-instrument requirement, the band began hiring better musicians for its orchestra, which increased its quality of sound. At about the same time, Schoepper got tough on those who reported late for duty, instituting the infamous "library" penalty.

*Freddie:*

*Spring 1956 brought with it my first Easter Sunrise Service at Arlington National Cemetery Amphitheatre. This was always an early morning gig. We'd leave the barracks by bus at 6:00 a.m.—0600, or what we'd refer to as "o-dark-hundred." Even at such an early hour, there was no excuse for being late. Captain Schoepper had now initiated a policy of punishment for anyone being late or missing a job or rehearsal. Depending on the offense, the offender got "sentenced" to the band's library for one to four weeks. He had to report in at 0800 to the library every weekday, pass out the music folios and perform other library duties until 1600 (4:00 p.m.)*

*Near the end of my first year, I became good friends with Arthur Lehman, the band's principal euphonium player. Arthur lent a mellow and rich tenor sound to the band. He was stocky—built like a bull, and very strong. He worked out with weights and encouraged me to work out with him inside his home garage, where all his weights and barbells were stored. After a one-hour workout, we'd take a half-hour break and he'd make us a milk shake.*

*We had been working out for about a month when, one day, I was doing deep knee bends with at least 200 pounds on my back. Right in the middle of my reps, Arthur proceeded to tell me something. It must have been funny, because I was laughing so hard in the down position that I couldn't get myself back up into a standing position. Thankfully, Arthur relieved me of the weight, both of us laughing until our sides hurt. In time, Arthur would rescue me from other tight spots, too.*

*Arthur Lehman.*

## A Singing Sergeant Joins the Marines

That same year, Bill Jones enlisted into the Marine Band as its baritone vocalist and concert moderator. Jones came from the Air Force Band's "Singing Sergeants" and brought with him an impressive resume. In his youth, he was billed as "the boy with the voice in a million." His voice helped him live a cosmopolitan lifestyle. He was heard in many countries—by some estimates, twenty-six in all—on four continents, before audiences of impressive numbers, some as many as eighty thousand people. "It was for the beautiful baritone of William Jones," said one music critic for the Stuttgart, Germany *Zeitung*, "that the many thousands of listeners remained in their seats to the last tone. Here is a voice of the first order." A concert program from Holland, Michigan described him as "a highly personable gentleman who rubbed elbows with such notables as the Queen of England, the members of the Netherlands Royal Family, the Danish Prince Royal, the Lord Mayor of Chester, The Burgess of Wiesbaden, and many others." His career, it went on to state, included singing before an audience of eighty thousand in Naples, and during dinner at the home of the Libyan magistrate, "where everyone ate from a bowl placed in the center of the floor, without benefit of utensils . . ."

The program continued: "His highly promising career was interrupted by entry in the Armed Forces in 1951, but his civilian musical career was resumed in 1954 when he was engaged as a soloist with the country's leading symphony orchestras, including Washington's National Symphony. So it was that this young man with a baritone voice of remarkable quality was well on his way when . . . Schoepper offered him an opportunity to become the first full-time vocalist and concert moderator in the entire history of America's oldest and foremost symphonic musical organization. In August of 1955 Bill Jones donned the historic uniform of the 157-year-old United States Marine Band, 'The President's Own.'" ❖

*"The boy with a voice in a million..."*
**Bill Jones. (Photo courtesy Department of Defense)**

## Chapter 8

## "I'll Buy That!"

Jim, Freddie's younger brother by two-and-a-half years, auditioned for the Marine Band in May 1956. He played for Harpham first. Then, since Schoepper was engaged at a late-morning White House performance, about an hour later Jimmie played again—this time for the storied leader. The Captain strode in about 12:15 p.m. and ordered, "All right, let's hear something."

Jimmie played Arthur Pryor's *Blue Bells of Scotland* along with another solo. Said Schoepper, "I'll buy that."

As destiny would have it, Schoepper would never hear of Jimmie's problematic sight-reading ability.

When Freddie had entered the Marine Band, the town of Lebanon was abuzz with chatter about one of the local boys making one of the world's finest concert bands. In contrast, Jim's subsequent entrance into the Marine Band was received more like an afterthought. Reaction from the local populace was much more subdued, almost akin to "So what?" Most people, when they remarked on a second Erdman in "The President's Own," wouldn't say, "that young man, James," but more likely, "Freddie Erdman's younger brother."

Jim:

*Sucking hind tit, so to speak, seemed to be my way of life as Fred's younger brother. Not that I wasn't loved and cared for, but you know how it is with the second child. My divorced father and my most-loving grandparents (not to mention my devoted stepmother) raised me the very best they were able. With me, something was different. In our family, I was the unheard-of trombonist.*

*The family focus had been on the cornet and brother Freddie, until I introduced this foreign word: trombone! My father had some knowledge of the instrument and began teaching me. As I approached eighth grade, he felt it was time to move on to a more qualified teacher, namely, R. Leslie Saunders, the local high school band director, and extremely proficient on his "horn," the trombone. Les had played the affluent resorts up and down the East Coast during his younger years, including Grossingers, The Hamptons, and Newport hotspots. He taught and demanded of me advanced practicing routines and slide technique. I credit most of my basic musical knowledge and performance ability to him. Incidentally, he refused to take payment for lessons.*

## Over the Top

R. Leslie Saunders also directed the famed Lebanon High School Band. Saunders was a throwback to another time. He redefined "old school" teacher, throwing batons at wayward students during morning band rehearsals, even rushing back to grab his trombone students by the neck and "shake some sense" into them, wheezing all the while from years of chain-smoking Camels. Even for an era when discipline and corporal punishment were considered *de rigueur* in the public schools, his madman antics were over the top, offset by the level of perfection and musicality he demanded of his band. Like Schoepper, Saunders ruled by fear. As a result, the LHS Band distinguished itself at that time as one of the finest high school bands in the nation.

In keeping with his commitment to music education, R. Leslie Saunders authored a book in 1956 titled "Training the School Dance Band." As a professional trombonist, Saunders was contracted to perform for the "Ice Follies," "Ice Capades" and other top-shelf shows coming to various venues in and around the Pennsylvania region—all this, while putting his high school band on the national map and making it the envy of music educators everywhere.

One of his alumni, Dr. Richard Eiceman, drummer and Class of 1957, recalls a moment when Saunders walked into a conference for the Eastern

United States Orchestra and Band festival in Atlantic City's Convention Hall. The gathering spotlighted the finest high school musicians on the East Coast. "About 2,000 music educators were assembled in the hall, listening to the orchestra rehearse Tchaikovsky's *Fourth Symphony*," recalls Dr. Eiceman. "During one spot when the conductor was talking to the orchestra, Mr. Saunders happened to come through the door, dressed in his black suit and carrying a briefcase. I remember that the room grew very quiet. Then, as if on cue, everyone stood up and spontaneously gave him a rousing ovation. That shows how much respect the man commanded. It was exciting to behold. He must have had tremendous influence. Everyone knew Mr. Saunders."

Like my older brothers, I was fortunate to have played under Mr. Saunders throughout my own years in the Lebanon High School Band. My years spanned from 1962-1966. While the antics of Saunders were wild and legendary, the high school band's performances were outstanding. "Tales of R. Leslie" still serve as fond memories for my friends and me to rekindle some 50 years after the fact. He done us proud!

*Jim:*

*Many of my lessons would last well over two hours! Lessons were scheduled on Monday evenings in Saunders' home, usually beginning around 8:30. I was always his last student of the night. In retrospect I realize there was purpose to his generosity. My mother would drop me off about 8:15 and come back for me somewhere between 9:00 and 9:15. She stopped doing that after the third week. Mother simply got tired of waiting! She told me to call when I was finished. Eleven o'clock was not unusual! Saunders was a heavy smoker, a drinker of many cokes until the student prior to my lesson was finished, and then the Wild Turkey came out!*

*I played; he drank! He was elated during my senior year when he was informed of my upcoming Marine Band audition, although he did have connections with the Navy School of Music. Most of my lessons were entertaining, especially as he sipped the Wild Turkey; however, his teaching and discipline techniques with the high school band were anything but entertaining. He prepared me well for my future career with the controlling, martinet director whom I would come to fear. Thanks to Saunders, I understood Schoepper as well!*

*Upon entering high school, I opted to pursue the business course rather than college prep. In my senior year I interviewed with a small chain manufacturing company in Lebanon and was promised employment as an apprentice accountant upon graduation. As I look back on a half century of professional musical performance, that's quite a contrast in careers! The company that had expressed an interest in hiring me eventually went broke within a few years, and to this day I've been curious as to where I would be and what I would be doing had I failed my Marine Band audition.*

*Much of my success was also due to Freddie's influence, particularly during the early part of 1956. He convinced me to work my ass off, due to the fact that there was going to be a vacancy in the Marine Band's trombone section that summer. This meant diligent work, practicing much more than I ever imagined, and relearning solos played for various competitions and an annual performance rating competition sponsored by the University of Pittsburgh, known as the Pennsylvania Forensic League. It also meant working on scales, which I detested! Interestingly, scales have never been included in any professional audition to my knowledge and, of course, certainly not in any Marine Band auditions I had ever heard as its principal trombonist.*

*The time passed quickly, and the whole preparation drill began to get rather laborious. Suddenly, my mindset went from serious to humorous, as I contemplated any realistic thoughts of passing a competitive audition for "The President's Own" United States Marine Band! In retrospect, I do feel there is something to the notion about taking things too seriously, and that such seriousness can work against the aspiring candidate.*

*There wasn't much this seventeen-year-old knew regarding professional auditions, and the only matter of substance that was required as far as I was concerned seemed to be a demonstration of decent sound and technique, i.e. high, and fast! I am a firm believer that my good fortune has much to do with Robert Towne's famous quote, "Most people never have to face the fact that at the right time, in the right place, they're capable of anything." Fortunately, Freddie's timely and loving concern for me was actually the truism of that well-known quote and I am forever grateful to him.*

*Freddie had driven me down to Washington, D.C. to the Marine Barracks, the headquarters of "The President's Own" on Eighth & I (Eye) Streets. That address always made me chuckle . . . the printed "Eye" was to delineate the letter of the alphabet. I suppose it worked for the postal service.*

## Shostakovich!

The audition was scheduled for May 11, 1956, at 11:00 a.m. Since Jim's father had not permitted him to mention in his "request for an audition" letter that

Freddie was his brother, Jim was asked: "Are you related to Freddie Erdman?" This amused Jim, considering that he and Freddie were not the first or last set of brothers in the organization. Perhaps they simply took it for granted, although Freddie, to Jim's knowledge, had not informed anyone prior to that day.

Upon arriving for the audition, Jim was introduced to the assistant director, Dale Harpham. (Around this time, Congress had changed the titles of "first leader" and "second leader" to "Director" and "Assistant Director".) On his occasional weekend trips home, Freddie had described in thorough detail to the family his experiences regarding the band's first director, Captain Albert Schoepper, giving Jim a forewarning of things to come. As just a kid myself, I can remember sitting around the table, spellbound, by their stories of the man they called Schoepper.

### Jim:

*I wasn't looking forward to exposing what talent I had to this man! There was cause to relax after having been introduced to Harpham and being told he would hear my audition. He had been, of all things, a trombonist in the band prior to his appointment. In addition, Irving Fuller, the band's literary genius and publicist, would also be listening. Fuller was the program annotator for the Marine Band's weekly radio show, NBC's "The Dream Hour," which aired from 1931 until 1954. That was the audition committee: an assistant conductor and a musicologist to listen and judge—or so I thought. Harpham was very good at making my moment in history as painless as possible! It gave me the opportunity to draw a nerve-settling sigh of relief. He also invited Freddie to stay and listen.*

*I remember like it was yesterday, Freddie telling me to have prepared a march, a solo or two, and some sight reading. Uh-oh, sight-reading was my nemesis! The actual audition consisted of the "dog fight" of Sousa's "Stars and Stripes Forever," and that came off rather easily. Next was the theme of Sibelius's "Finlandia," another easy tune. Another request followed, this one for Julius Fučik's "Florentiner March."*

*I obviously had done well, because Harpham inquired of me how I managed to know that march. I explained that my Dad was a fine conductor and a genius at programming, always giving his audiences their fair share of marches, such as "Florentiner." In a three-hour-long carnival or church picnic gig, you never played the same march all summer long, with the exception of Sousa marches, as they reigned supreme. They still do!*

*The final piece selected was the shocker, and for good reason. Placed in front of me was a manuscript arrangement of the final movement of Shostakovich's "Fifth Symphony!" Who was Shostakovich?*

*To make matters worse, it was in the key of E major! It makes for a humorous story now, but not then. Every C, F, G, D, played over the first page was interrupted by, "No, that's a C-sharp, an F-sharp," and on and on. It was torture, extremely embarrassing and seemingly unending. There was some humor, and I realized I was the butt of it. My lack of sight-reading ability had always been troublesome, and this particular moment didn't do much to boost what little confidence I had gained to that point.*

*A few moments passed, though not without some hilarious discussion among Harpham, Freddie, and Fuller regarding my obvious problems with key signatures. I think it was more of a respite for them than a break for me! Harpham looked at me and asked, "Have you prepared any solos for us?" I offered Pryor's "Blue Bells of Scotland," "The Little Chief," and finally, Rimsky-Korsakov's "Concerto for Trombone and Military Band." The latter had been resurrected in the early 1950s and featured two show-off cadenzas edited by David Shuman. These included high E-flat and notes. High school students didn't fare too well on these ranges back then, although in today's professional trombone literature this is common practice!*

*The cadenzas both went okay, although after the sight-reading problems, I didn't feel I had accomplished much of anything. Shuman, incidentally, was a close friend of my trombone teacher, R. Leslie Saunders. It was Saunders who coached me on its performance during those school years. Many years later, Tom Knox, one of the band's arranger, and I collaborated and wrote two new cadenzas; I desired to put my own stamp on the piece instead of Mr. Shuman's edition. Cadenzas tend to be rather personal, so I hope Rimsky-Korsakov doesn't mind too much.*

*A few minutes after finishing the Korsakov, we heard the authoritative voice of the leader—the dreaded Captain Schoepper—fresh from conducting the chamber orchestra at a White House function. As he walked into the room, Harpham told him, "We're in here listening to Erdman's younger brother, Jim, taking an audition."*

*"Well, let's hear something," he replied. "What solo do you know?" Harpham replied for me, "The Korsakov." I later discovered that Schoepper was extremely fond of it. He requested that I play the first movement. I did as I was told, and it went rather well. Then he requested the final cadenza. I nailed it! He asked if I knew the intro to Pryor's "Blue Bells of Scotland." "Yes," I answered, and played it well, too. I was familiar with the rubato style of the late 1800s, thanks to both Saunders and my father's teaching of it.*

With a chuckle and grin to Harpham, Schoepper blurted out. "I'll buy that! Would you like to become a member of the Marine Band?" My immediate, emotional, and nearly choked reply was, "Yes!" He barked back with a very abrupt, "Yes, sir!" "Yes . . . sir!" I complied.

"Sign him up. We'll have two Erdmans in the band," he said with a laugh. "On tour they can room with the Saverinos!" On the way home I mentioned to Freddie that Schoepper made me think of Melville's classic, "Moby Dick" and the obsessive Captain Ahab. Experiencing life under him, I ended up appreciating and respecting him. To this day, I still do.

I feel compelled to add at this point a word about the arts and the integral part they played in many of that era's students' lives. Think for a second about the training and genuine support of our nation's public school systems, provided by the local school board, administration, and most importantly, the teachers. Had it not been for them, many of our greatest performers—be they in music, dance, theatre, or arts and letters—would have not succeeded, for there would have been no personal interest, nor funds to bankroll them.

My generation owes a huge debt of gratitude to the educational system that not only supported but also required the study and student participation in the liberal arts as a component of the curriculum, from the elementary through secondary schools. In many schools today, this sadly is virtually nonexistent. ❖

# Chapter 9

# How Do You Request Mast?

One early afternoon in June 1956, the Marine Band, including Schoepper and Harpham, along with troops of the barracks, stood at parade rest on the parade deck. They were dressed in khakis, awaiting the Inspector General (I.G.) for the periodic "I.G. Inspection." It was 1:30 p.m. and the temperature had inched above 90° F. When the general conducting the inspection finally arrived, Drum Major DeMar called the band and orchestra to attention. The general recognized the presence of Schoepper, Harpham, and DeMar, then proceeded to inspect the troops first, followed by the band.

Walking the line, he randomly picked out a Marine, firing a question about a particular Marine Corps regulation. Since Marine Corps regulars were expected to know everything by the book, nothing less than the right answer was expected. Quoting a regulation as if it were Scripture, the troops almost always delivered the correct answers.

Then came the band's turn. Its members had never been schooled in Marine Corps regulations, mainly because Marine Band members never experienced boot camp, where these regulations became part of a Marine's brain structure. Strolling by and peering over several of the band members who were standing at attention in formation, the general stopped in front of Bill Lubis, one of the band's long-time clarinetists and its assistant librarian.

"What do you do in case of fire?"

"I don't know, sir," Lubis said lamely. "Call the fire department, I guess."

The general stared in disbelief, as if addressing a creature from another world, then moved on.

### Freddie:

*What a comedy! I remember thinking after hearing Bill's answer. After looking over and passing several more of us, the I.G. stopped in front of George Parker. George was a big, strong teddy bear of a guy, and a little overweight by Marine Corps standards.*

*The General stood motionless, staring at George's belly.*

*"Got a pretty big pot on ya there."*

*"I like my beer, sir," said George.*

*After staring at George for a few seconds without any change in his facial expression, the General turned once again and moved on, stopping now to pause in front of clarinetist Don Carodisky, a quiet, unassuming fellow.*

*"When did you come into the band?"*

*"Nineteen-fifty-five, sir."*

*"How do you request mast?"*

*"I don't know, sir. I'm not Catholic."*

*Carodisky's answer was delivered with all the innocence and sincerity of the humblest of saints.*

*We could hardly keep from laughing. Stunned by his answer, the General slowly turned to his right and along with his aides made his way to the gate, leaving the premises and probably wondering what he had just heard.*

*Don's answer was the coup d'état. Nobody remembers that general ever interrogating another Marine Band member. He is probably shaking his head to this day.* ❖

# Chapter 10

# Second Brother

*Jim Erdman performing a solo on the old Watergate Barge, 1957.*

The time had come for Freddie's younger brother, Jim, all of seventeen years old and wet behind the ears, to make his official entrance into the Marine Band.

*Jim:*

My first day on the job was Wednesday, July 11, 1956 after arriving in Washington two days earlier. Ironically, the day of my enlistment almost found me on my way to Parris Island, South Carolina for basic training. A little-known fact, even among Marines themselves, is that members of "The President's Own" are not required to take basic training. Such a waiver allows the band to obtain the crème de la crème of musicians throughout the country, or for that matter, throughout the world. Going back to 1798, the year of the Band's founding, its roster has evidenced a host of foreign nationalities.

There is no doubt that we three brothers have the greatest respect for those who do endure the Marine boot camp and are without a doubt "a few good men!" Nothing exists quite like that affection for and dedication to each other and the Corps. We are sincerely proud of the title and privilege to wear that most famous of military uniforms, "United States Marine!"

After I was sworn in by the commanding officer of the Marine Corps post at the Philadelphia Navy Yard (remember, the Marine Corps is officially a branch of the United States Navy), I was invited to leave the building and wait while my parents, grandfather, and little brother Tim had a brief conversation with the officer. Walking down two flights of stairs and out the door, I was confronted by a Marine wearing the traditional drill sergeant's hat. He ordered me to line up with some other young men. I didn't know at the time they, too, had just enlisted. I stood there for a moment and questioned him as to what he was expecting of me, asking quite simply, "Why? Go where?"

Imagine a Marine Corps drill sergeant being asked "why!" He could have dressed me down right then and there, but instead sternly replied that they were loading up for the trip to Parris Island. In retrospect, I wondered: what made him think I had enlisted? I had no luggage with me, none whatsoever. Of course I was young, innocent looking, and I suppose it was natural for him to think I was fresh fodder! It remains a question unanswered to this day.

That moment seemed interminable and worrisome. The sergeant was clearly getting irritated. I remember his second remark so well: "All right! It's time to load up!"

At that precise moment, out the door walked my parents, Tim, my grandfather (for whom I'm named) and the colonel who had administered to me the oath. "Are you having a problem, Sergeant?" he asked, looking at the drill sergeant who seemed puzzled at my reluctance to board the bus.

"No, sir. This young man says he enlisted, but doesn't understand that we are leaving and he should board the bus."

"*This young man is not going with you, Sergeant. He is going to Washington, D.C. with his family, as he has just enlisted for duty with 'The President's Own' The Marine Band.*" *He seemed prouder during that moment than I was! I was in fact anything but calm. It almost triggered a catastrophic event in my intestinal system!*

*I've given thanks several times for that particular moment, the one beachhead the Marines were not as successful in landing on in an otherwise gloried history. Lucky me! I'm sure that, had I followed that order to board the bus to Parris Island, my future would have been an entirely different one. The comfort zone would have been a far cry from the one waiting for me later that day, as I headed to Washington, D.C.*

## Friday the 13th

His actual first day as a performing member of "The President's Own" began with a 9:00 a.m. rehearsal on Friday, July 13, 1956. It was another one-of-a-

*In this 1956 photograph, Jimmie Erdman is being sworn into the United States Marine Corps. From left to right, an admiring little Tim Erdman, Grandpa Jim Erdman, the Marine Corps colonel administering the oath, Jimmie, Dad and Mom. (Photo courtesy Department of Defense)*

kind moment, not only in how it happened, but why. "Remember," notes Jim, "that I was the tender age of seventeen, and had absolutely no professional experience. Today, the feat of passing such an audition and my acceptance into this famed organization would most likely never be repeated! Times have changed so much!"

He was sitting in the band hall in his civilian clothes, as he had yet to be issued the standard summer-weight khaki uniforms and red coat with blue trousers. His time was pretty much his own at this point, and he decided to observe the rehearsal.

*One cool cat to another; one of Jimmie's favorite tour photos. Ralph Moeller stands behind.*

*Jim:*

*I had chosen to pull a typical male teenager position by hanging one leg over the row chair in front of me—you know, the smart-ass slouch look. Not that that was my intent. It just happened. I must have accidentally pushed the chair with my leg, causing the chair leg to vibrate loudly against the floor. Or maybe it was some other kind of noise. Whatever it was, it caused Schoepper to turn around, stopping the band in the middle of rehearsing Rossini's "William Tell Overture."*

*Seeing me, he snapped, "Do you sit like that at home?"*

*"No," I replied.*

*"No what?"*

"No."

"No, sir!" he corrected me, and with the kind of authority dispensed only by God Himself.

"No, sir!" I repeated.

"What are you doing sitting there?"

"I'm listening to the rehearsal . . . sir."

Schoepper turned around and resumed rehearsal, worked with the clarinet section for a few seconds, then stopped conducting and turned around to me again.

"Why aren't you up here with the trombone section?"

"I don't have my uniforms yet, sir."

"The uniform doesn't play. Get your horn and get up here!"

Thank God I had my trombone with me! To this day, I have no idea just how far this would have played out. One fact had been established: Someone was in charge! Thank God. That could have been my first—and last—day on the job.

Walking up to the section, I took a seat provided me by one of the bass trombonists, Willy Gray. Willy became a very good friend and died a self-induced death years later while still a member of the band. The trombone section consisted of Robert Isele, Donald Hunsberger, Thomas Ellwein, Donald Bechtold, Willy, Lawrence Tichenor, and myself.

As I sat down, Schoepper was still at it with the reeds. I looked at the music in front of me, a second part. It had this strange-looking thing on the staff lines.

"What's that little thing on the staff?" I asked Bechtold.

"A tenor clef," he whispered.

"What's that?" I whispered back, dumbfounded. I never had heard of the thing.

Bechtold looked at me incredulously. "You don't know what a tenor clef is?"

"No, I've never seen one."

"Well, to put it simply, your middle C is now on the fourth line."

"No, it's not," I argued. "It's on the first line above the staff!"

The words that came next from Bechtold are stored forever in the farthest recesses of my brain.

"Not anymore it isn't!"

This was an entirely new experience for me: transposition—reading different clefs, seeing things I've never laid eyes upon—and only my first day on the job! Transposition was an entirely new experience for me. What was I to do? It reminds me of that wonderful movie, "Christmas Story," at the moment when Ralphie steps on his new glasses, breaking them, and all is lost—no Red Ryder Repeating BB gun for me! Try to imagine: someone auditions and is accepted into the world's foremost symphonic military band, yet can't read *various clefs. He's like a pilot flying at ten thousand feet who doesn't know how to read his instrument panel.*

Rehearsal threw no more roadblocks at Jim, who by now was learning by instinct how to keep a low profile and stay under the feared leader's radar. For weeks afterward, Schoepper didn't say much to him. The other bass trombone player, when learning of Jim's plight during a coffee break, escorted Jim into Harpham's office.

**This 1958 photo shows a portion of the band's trombone section: left to right, Willie Gray, Al Johnson, Jimmie and Bob Isele. Photo courtesy Department of Defense)**

Jim:

*We talked a bit, and Harpham remembered from my audition that I knew something about marches. He suggested that, if I knew the melody lines, I should visit the music library, check out the solo cornet parts to a dozen Sousa marches, then have Larry Tichenor play his bass trombone part as I played the melody, reading the cornet part as a tenor clef part. In essence, instead of learning tenor clef as an interval change, I simply learned it as a new clef.*

*The session was good therapy, and it worked. Good thing it did, for at the next rehearsal that following Monday, Schoepper went down the line, bypassing the great Isele, of course. When my turn came, I did a good job of faking, although I'm sure I didn't kid anyone! But I never got caught like that again. It took a weekend of diligent practice . . . and also taught me a valuable lesson: Be Prepared!*

*The same lesson would come to me many years later. After tour, we were given "compensatory time" of ten days, meaning we didn't have to show up for any work or at the barracks. A few days prior to returning to work, I took my horn out and started practicing. My wife asked me why.*

*"I've got a funny feeling," I said.*

*True to my suspicions and my knowledge of his ways, as he entered the hall for our first gathering since tour, Schoepper looked over toward me and stated rather loudly, "Erdman . . . AIDA!" He was referring to the emotional aria sung by the opera's character, Radames. At that moment, I looked at the books on the stand and noticed the single microphone, and realized he was going to record it right then and there, no warning, no rehearsal.*

*"Ritchie, we're ready!" It was a command, not a question.*

*The recording went quite well. After the morning's workout and more impromptu recordings, I had decided to go ask him for the Aida aria we had just finished recording, since waiting for it without him interceding would have taken months. When I walked into his office with the request, his comment was, "I caught you with your pants down, didn't I?" I replied, "No disrespect, sir, but I think I caught you with yours down!" He gave a hearty laugh, called the recording studio, and ordered it done for me before I left for the day. As I thanked him and was going out the door he said to me, "Jim, great job!" And, it was!* ❖

# Chapter 11

# Tour Grind

*Packing for tour. Left to right, Jimmie, Bud Malsh, Arthur Lehman. (Photo courtesy Department of Defense)*

## Look And Listen:

# United Nations Marine Band Shows Much Musicianship

### BY JOHN VOORHEES

A great deal of musicianship — and an equal amount of pleasure—was provided by the United States Marine Band, conducted by Lt. Col. Albert Schoepper in its matinee concert Sunday before a full house at the Opera House.

A second program, nearly sold out before curtain time, was presented in the evening.

It was a real treat to hear the famed Marine Band at the Opera House. For the first time we were hearing it as it should be heard, with every musical nuance made clear. It showed that the band is made up of first-rate musicians and that Lt. Col. Schoepper is a knowing conductor, equally at ease with classics, marches or popular tunes.

AS MIGHT be expected, it was those marches that were programmed as well as those that served as encores that drew some of the loudest applause. It would be difficult to imagine "The Stars and Stripes Forever," or any of the other marches played, being performed with more precision, snap or fervor. A march played by the U.S. Marine Band can certainly make one's blood tingle as well as making one both proud of the U.S. Marines and the Marine Band.

But most marching bands are like comediennes who want to play Juliet or comics who dream of Hamlet—they want to play serious music, too, even though oftentimes it would be better left to a symphonic organization.

NEVERTHELESS, the program included several symphonic numbers ... the Prelude to Act III of Wagner's "Lohengrin," Paganini's "Perpetual Motion" and Liszt's Fourteenth Hungarian Rhapsody. While all were played meticulously, such band transcriptions fail to do complete justice to the music.

More in keeping with a band's potential (or, to put it another way, music that suffers less from a more balanced instrumentation) were several popular selections — Morton Gould's appealing "Cowboy Rhapsody," several Arthur Sullivan tunes rescored for the ballet, "Pineapple Poll" and pop tunes by Jerome Kern and others.

And in some cases, they are even more musically rewarding for the listener than music created for the band—Arthur Pryor's "Thoughts of Love" may have been a good vehicle for the virtuosity of trombonist James Erdman but the musical result was far prettier when he turned, again as soloist, to the ballad, "When I Fall in Love." Similarly, baritone William Jones' performance of an aria from Rossini's "Barber of Seville" was less enthusiastically received than his performance of "I Hear a Rhapsody" and a spiritual type song that served as encores.

BUT THERE is no denying the abilities of the musicians, handsome in their red, white and blue uniforms. In addition to the band as a whole, there were impressive examples by the clarinet section in the Paganini work and Rimsky-Korsakov's "Flight of the Bumble Bee," and the cornet section in Leroy Anderson's likeable "Bugler's Holiday."

As long as an organization as fine as the U.S. Marine Band programs a goodly number of stirring marches, however, one can allow it whatever else they want.

Jones also served as commentator for the program and both programs were presented by the Seattle Police Drill Team.

MENTAL NOTES ... Well-known Seattle architect Paul Thiry is set to design the sets for the Western Touring Opera Company's December production of "Hansel and Gretel" and singers interested in being chorus members are invited to a rehearsal to be held at 8 tonight in the Fischer Studio Bldg., 1519 3rd Ave. Dr. ... W. E. R. Stanner will present a complimentary lecture on Australian aboriginal art at 8 p.m. Tuesday in room 56, UW's Johnson Hall.

*Note the headline in this Seattle Post-Intelligencer review. A literary gaffe like this one was always great for a much-needed laugh on tour.*

**B**ack in those days, our Sunday evening concerts at the Watergate Barge, played in full dress uniform with white trousers, were followed by the same program on Wednesday evenings at the Capitol Plaza, this time played in dress blues and white trousers. In terms of sequence of the same concert played twice, the band performed at the Watergate first, then the same program at the Capitol a few days later. At the start of the 1956 summer concert season, Sunday evening concerts began at 8:30 p.m.; while the following Wednesday evening Capitol Plaza concerts started at 8:00 p.m. Somehow, Freddie thought the Capitol concerts also began at 8:30 p.m. On the first concert at the Capitol Plaza, following the preceding Sunday opening concert of the season, observing the rule of thumb of arriving for a concert one-half hour before start time, he approached the entrance to the Plaza parking area at 8:00 p.m., just as he heard the band playing the opening measures to the Star Spangled Banner! Terrified that he had been late after all, he made a U-turn and headed out the parking lot for home, knowing full well that he was in for a session of hell by Schoepper the next morning.

Except that the dressing down never came.

Realizing that Freddie somehow got his times confused, Chuck Erwin and his assistant had the presence of mind to remove one chair from the cornet section, hoping that Schoepper wouldn't notice Freddie's absence. Did he or didn't he? No one knows for sure.

In late summer 1956, Schoepper called Freddie into his office and declared that he wanted his young star cornet soloist to perform the Staigers "Carnival of Venice" at every Sunday matinee on the upcoming Midwest tour. Freddie would be spelling off Chuck Erwin, who was otherwise the daily matinee soloist. On the Sunday after Labor Day, just like the previous year and with the same personnel, the tour band left the Marine Barracks by bus for Kennett Square, Pennsylvania for another grueling sixty-three consecutive days of two concerts a day and no days off, getting on and off the bus ten times every day, and still getting a *per diem* of about $12 a day.

Freddie played the Staigers nine times that tour.

When the tour band came back, Schoepper appointed Chuck Erwin to play the solo cornet chair. Erwin, who established himself as Mr. Power and Reliability when it came to any soloing or playing lead part, replaced Bob Dehart. Bob was a player known for his beautiful, lush cornet tone, but whose chronic drinking habit appeared to be finally catching up with him. As the band's solo cornetist, Erwin would go on to occupy the principal cornet seat for the next seventeen years.

## The Year of Turning

"In the 1950s, Americans had never been happier," wrote *U.S. News & World Report* in 2007, adding that steady paychecks, intact nuclear families, and not one but two cars in a new garage all contributed to a period of contentment. "Yet looming over all was the threat of global nuclear war." The Soviets' launch of Sputnik caught the country by surprise and spawned what became known as *the space race*. In Little Rock, Arkansas, racial tensions were bubbling to new highs. Accompanying this was the advent of the sexual revolution and introduction of the birth control pill. "Modernity was creeping in," said the weekly news magazine, citing the Ford Edsel as the year's most noted marketing example. A former adman named Dr. Seuss revolutionized the way kids learned to read.

"Remarkably, it all happened in 1957."

On New Years Day of that year, the band marched up to the Commandant's house to play the traditional "Surprise Serenade" for General Pate. A few days later, Captain Schoepper resumed sight-reading and recording sessions. After taking daily morning roll call, the drum major announced White House jobs, patriotic openers, and funerals, all of which were posted on the bulletin board. Reading the bulletin board was like a lottery in reverse. If your name was posted, it meant you probably had a funeral to play later that morning or during the afternoon, or perhaps a patriotic opener at one of the area's hotels.

This usually meant hanging around the band hall all day—unless you lived nearby, because then if you chose, you could go home and come back later. If your name wasn't posted next to a job for that day, the time was yours to do as you pleased. For some this meant playing golf, if the weather was cooperative, or attending classes. Some band members, it seemed, managed to stay off the bulletin board, using their spare time to obtain their doctorate degrees at Catholic University. In any case, our neighbors and friends outside the band tended to think we had odd hours.

Compared with other members of the military, we *did* have odd hours. But what those friends and neighbors didn't know was that our training at the time was at our own expense, for taxpayers were not responsible to pay for our continuing education. While that has changed over the years, band members took advantage of the many fine educational institutions in the D. C. area to advance their professional status. Few knew also that band members rarely lived in military housing. First, such housing was scarce as hen's teeth in the Washington area. Second, civilian housing subsidies made it especially attractive to band members with families.

Whether we had the day "off" or not, all of us were on twenty-four-hour call, seven days a week. That meant you could never plan on scheduling anything with 100 percent certainty, unless you were on leave from the band (everyone, regardless of time served or rank, had four weeks "leave" or vacation time).

The band's winter concert series would begin in February. Weighing in at 170 pounds, Freddie resumed his weightlifting at Arthur Lehman's house. Meanwhile on the national scene, President Dwight Eisenhower was inaugurated as President for the second time. It was Freddie's first presidential inauguration and inaugural parade. Everyone was required to play except Claude Pedicord, the harpist.

*Claude Pedicord. (Photo courtesy Department of Defense)*

*Freddie:*

*We left the barracks at 8:30 a.m., arrived at the west side of the Capitol, and began setting up on the platform located just beneath the immediate staging where the oath of office would take place. The actual festivities began around 9:30 a.m., with the Marine Band playing several selections as VIPs arrived. The temperature was crispy cold, but the sun came out, making conditions tolerable. For some reason, I found I was warmer when I was playing than when I wasn't!*

*A publicity photo taken of "The President's Own" under the direction of Albert F. Schoepper. (Photo courtesy Department of Defense)*

By July 1957, the Marine Band had one leader, Major Schoepper; and two assistant conductors commissioned by Congress for the Marine Band, Captain Harpham and First Lieutenant King. In anticipation of the upcoming nine-week tour in New England, Schoepper would lead the band on all evening and Sunday matinee performances. King would conduct all weekday and Saturday matinees. Once again, Schoepper asked Freddie to perform the Staigers *Carnival of Venice*, not just on Sundays as before, however, but every day. He would perform as the tour band's daily matinee soloist, or "matinee idol" as the guys liked to say. Schoepper also asked Jim to perform as matinee idol. Jim would be playing Arthur Pryor's *Thoughts of Love*. Jim by now had proven his own solo mettle, having soloed at many of the summer's Capitol plaza and Watergate concerts.

*Jim:*

The possibility of a solo career never entered my mind until the end of the 1956 winter concert season. Schoepper had called me into his office and asked me outright how I would like to be one of the soloists for the upcoming tour. What was I to say? I do remember being shocked and extremely nervous, simply replying, "Yes, sir." At the age of seventeen and with limited experience, did I have a choice?

The 1957 matinee tour programs were my introduction to professional soloing, including the grind of the constant traveling, loss of sleep, and poor dietary habits. In spite of all that and much to my surprise, the soloing went rather well. This gave both sides— Schoepper's and mine—ample time to experience the value, if any, of the decision.

*This tour publicity photo depicts a young Sergeant James Erdman, who went on to become the youngest ever master gunnery sergeant in the Marine Corps. (Photo courtesy Department of Defense)*

A situation worth mentioning ultimately led to my position a few years later as principal trombone. We were playing the March from Paul Hindemith's "Symphonic Metamorphosis," and I was playing the second trombone part. Midway through the theme's recapitulation, there is an accented slurred note connection written for my part. Schoepper was cuing me rather strongly, and I reciprocated just as strongly. This caused quite a bit of concern by a few players nearby regarding my interpretation of the measure, and as much as I attempted *to ignore them, their voiced objections became rather nerve-wracking. Understand: I was an eighteen-year-old surrounded by experienced professionals.*

*A few weeks of this caused me some embarrassment and worry. I did respect them, but by the same token, I simply didn't know how to solve the problem. One day, Schoepper inquired how things were going, how was I getting along, and whether was there anything troubling me.*

*Curiously, this was the only personal interest in me he had shown so far. I mentioned the problem with the Hindemith, and his very curt reply was, "Who's conducting?"*

*That settled that!*

*Ten days after returning from tour, we had our first rehearsal. Prior to beginning our morning's work, Schoepper announced a number of chair changes, including Jim Basta to principal horn and me as Robert Isele's assistant. Many years later, after Schoepper's retirement, we saw each other quite a few times. During one of those occasions of shared remembrances, I inquired as to why he gave me the position of assistant principal to Robert Isele. Schoepper's reply was curt and on point: "The Hindemith. You did as you were told."*

*I owe a debt of gratitude to Mr. Hindemith.*

## Asian Flu and Other Afflictions

Bill Jones would again serve as the band's baritone vocalist and concert moderator for both the matinee and evening concerts. For the evening performance, Schoepper assigned a cornet trio to perform Walter M. Smith's *Bolero*. All his principal musicians would make every tour—another Schoepper edict, which meant that Freddie and Jim, along with the rest of the principals, could count on being away from home for nine weeks every fall.

Five days into the tour the band was exposed to the Asian flu. Several musicians had become ill and were sent back to Washington. Flu shots were ordered for the entire band. To accomplish this, the band made a quick stop at the Naval medical facilities in Cape May, New Jersey, en route to a matinee performance while making its way up the East Coast.

There was one other so-called "affliction": missed notes in the cornet trio. The constant erratic performances moved an increasingly nervous and restless Schoepper to (a) assign Freddie as evening soloist, and (b) switch the cornet trio over as the matinee brass feature.

*Freddie:*

*By the second week of tour, the playing of anything programmed for every day and every night had become pretty much automatic, be it a solo or otherwise. Upon my introduction to the audience, I never failed to get a small attack of butterflies. Once the button was pushed, however, the experience of soloing from one day to the next was like being a machine—the horn would just play itself. Just attack the first note and away I'd go.*

*Throughout my boyhood, I often fantasized about being a featured cornet soloist with a professional concert band, such as the Goldman Band in New York. Now, that fantasy had turned into a reality. And with what better band than the Marine Band, "The President's Own."*

## A Young Man with a Future

*"The outstanding feature of the concert was the trumpet solo by Fredric Erdman, only nineteen years old, whose name did not appear on the program, as he was substituted for a cornet trio, because of his remarkable performance in the afternoon concert, and a request for a repetition. This young man has a technique that is unbelievable. This writer has heard all of the great cornet soloists such as Jules Levy, Arbuckle, Liberatti, and all of the other stars who were famous in his time, but never has heard a performance on a trumpet equal to that given by this young man at this concert. He will certainly become one of the great stars in the musical world."*

*—Benjamin F. Teel, Bandmaster, Public Forum, Cape Cod Standard-Times*

The band continued its tour up and down the New England states of Connecticut, Massachusetts, Vermont, New Hampshire, Rhode Island, and Maine. The scenery was breathtakingly beautiful, the foliage turning into a stunning array of colors. Attendances at the concerts were consistently good, and halls were sold out everywhere. Day after day, night after night, the act of playing with such a world-class organization filled Freddie with awe. He was especially impressed with the performance of the extraordinary Bill Jones, whose rich, deep baritone voice and beautiful diction lent so much professionalism to the stage.

*Freddie:*

*We were going into our fourth week and it was Saturday afternoon. Our concert site was not too far from the United States Military Academy at West Point. With Army football in high gear, it looked as if we wouldn't have much of an audience for the day's matinee. In fact, I didn't see more than 100 people in the audience. Bill Jones got sick with the Asian flu and was sent back to Washington, forcing King to announce all the numbers in addition to conducting. We were down to our final number, and it was time for him to announce the selections we were about to play from the Broadway musical "My Fair Lady." After naming each selection one by one, King got to the last one, "I've Grown Accustomed to Your Face."*

*". . . and, "I've Grown Accustomed to Your . . ."*

*Long pause.*

*During the next few seconds, King's mind went blank. It must have seemed to him an eternity.*

*". . . Face.""*

If King's memory had failed, as it sometimes did, so occasionally did the precision of the band's performances and the morale of its members. Freddie remembers Schoepper jumping on people for all sorts of reasons: a missed note, paying the hotel bill late, failing to get a haircut, or God forbid, not boarding the bus on time.

*Freddie:*

*None of us wanted to be caught in the elevator with this guy. Little did I realize when he took over the band in 1955 that his leadership would begin an era marked mainly by fear and intimidation.*

*We were now into the fourth week of two concerts a day, getting on and off the bus ten times a day, traveling an average of 200 miles a day. As my brother Jim has said, it was a job unequaled in its challenge to perform to the best of your ability under extremely difficult playing conditions—from gymnasiums to old art deco movie theaters, barns, gardens, opera halls and concert halls, from the school auditorium in Moab, Utah to Symphony Hall in Boston, Massachusetts. Our audiences numbered from twenty-two (in Rutland, Vermont) to twenty-five hundred. Occasionally we'd have a real crowd—twenty-five thousand at both matinee and evening performances.*

One evening, after several of us had dinner, we walked from the restaurant towards the theater holding the performance, about 200 yards ahead. We noticed something on the marquee that immediately hit our collective funny bone. It read: "The United States Marine Band and The Taming of the Shrew."

In the Marine Band you are expected to perform, regardless of how you feel. It doesn't matter if you're tired, sick, or bored. Somehow, you have to get yourself up for that next concert.

By the third-to-last day of tour, I felt lousy, yet I knew I still had to play both performances. On the following day I was running a fever; I could feel it. I played through the matinee and the evening performance lay before me. Arthur Lehman had a thermometer and began taking my temperature at intervals. I definitely had a fever. At the start of the 8:00 p.m. concert, I felt really hot. After being introduced to the audience, I could sense my resolve waning and the fever burning. But the show had to go on. Playing through the "Carnival of Venice," everything clicked, however, and my performance was solid. But all I wanted to do after the concert was sleep.

Once back at the hotel, Arthur walked me to my room. He took my temperature again and told me to get to bed pronto, since my temperature was now reading 103° F. After he left, I was asleep within five minutes.

On the last day of tour, Arthur paid my hotel bill and helped me with my luggage, carrying it to the bus. We were now on the road to the site of our last two concerts. Meanwhile, Arthur had spoken to Schoepper about my condition, and Schoepper agreed that I should stay in bed all day long—no matinee and no evening concerts for me. Arriving at the hotel, Arthur carried my luggage as we checked in and went up to my room. Immediately, I went to bed. Arthur promised to return after the matinee to check on me. I hadn't had anything to eat all day.

After checking on me briefly at 4:00 p.m., Arthur returned an hour later, this time with a very generous and delectable dinner from the hotel kitchen. Man, was I ever hungry! The meal was quite enjoyable. So was the long and deep sleep I fell into shortly after.

At 10:30 p.m., Arthur returned to my room and awakened me. He took another temperature check, and this time it read 98.4°—normal! Once again, he assisted me with my luggage and even carried my cornet. We made our way down to the lobby and out the door toward the bus, except that this time, I wasn't boarding any bus. Instead, I would be stepping into a car with Jimmie and his future wife, Kathy. Since we didn't have to report back to duty for the next two weeks, we were not taking the bus back to Washington, but driving instead to our hometown of Lebanon, Pennsylvania, which was only seventy miles away.

Two nights later, Jimmie and I were sharing a bedroom with twin beds in Grandma and Pop's house. It was the middle of the night and Jimmie was fast asleep. I was reading a novel about William the Conqueror. As I began reading what I remember as a pretty spooky part, I dropped off to sleep with the light still on.

Something was creeping up inside of me. I felt fear. Now I seemed to be running. Was I chasing somebody or something, or was something or somebody chasing me?

More fear, more tension. The fright gripped me. Suddenly, I bolted straight up in a flash, turned myself to the side of the bed, stomped my feet rapidly on the floor while letting out a bloody scream. I raced across the hall to the kitchen, grabbed onto the refrigerator door handle then just stood there in place, panting as I tried to catch my breath. God! What had happened to me!?

This was terribly embarrassing since, of course, it woke Jimmie, Grandma, Pop, and probably the rest of the neighborhood, too! When I went back to bed, I knew that it would be awhile, probably weeks, before I'd sleep without a light being left on.

It was then that I realized just how much pressure I had been under when performing those solos every night for the past sixty-two nights—the Staigers, followed by an encore, Jimmy Burke's "Runaway Trumpet." I think the pressure had just accumulated to the point where it had to explode.

The rest of the night passed peacefully, thank God!

When I awoke and arose the next morning, I remember thinking, "Boy, it sure is nice knowing I don't have to get on that damn bus this morning. And I won't have to until next September." In spite of the pressure of soloing, I did enjoy my fellow musicians and the music we played on that tour. The year had been a good one for me, the best in terms of my playing since I had joined the band. And there was also Jim, who did himself and the band proud through his performances as the afternoon's featured trombone soloist."

*Jim:*

Marine Band tours, of which I made nineteen (1957 through 1975), are legendary, particularly compared to today's traveling artists. As I remind myself of those trips, our per diem was a paltry $12.84, from which we were responsible for our hotel bill and food! Our tour manager, Oliver W. Trapp, was very business-oriented, extremely tight with a dollar (he typically re-sharpened his razor blades), and entrepreneurial, wielding great influence upon the leaders. He set the fees audiences were expected to pay to hear us, working with sponsors such as Rotary, Lions, public schools, churches, and other organizations, then *dividing whatever profits there were among the leader, band members, and him. There was a pecking order for any bonus pay: tour manager, director, assistant director, soloists, (vocalist first because he performed two roles—commentator and vocalist—twice daily) principals, and section performers. One year I received nearly $1,000! Business, after all, was still business, military or not! My guess is that the average band member's bonus was between $300 and $400. Much to the Marine Corps' credit, those policies have changed drastically.*

*Trapp's management and influence were quite obvious to me during the first few weeks of my second tour in 1958. For an encore I was playing Jimmy Forrest's great blues tune, "Night Train," made more popular by the big band trombonist, Buddy Morrow. It was Buddy's theme song, opening with a pounding rock beat and followed by a loud, screaming high C smear, then evolving into the blues. It was a huge success with young audiences. I was a very young nineteen years old and looked even younger (I was carded in bars well into my twenty-fifth year). Since matinee programs were intended to be educational, the leaders usually requested particular solos, and the soloist usually had free license on encores.*

*Or so we thought. Harpham, being the conductor for the weekday matinee concerts, had quite the personality for a younger audience. As they clapped for another bow from me after two or three, he would reply, "You may not have him, we're keeping him!" O.W. couldn't bear such "looseness" anymore and discussed it with Schoepper. After two weeks of great success, "Night Train" was replaced with a much more subdued "Why Do I Love You" from Jerome Kern's "Show Boat." O.W. came up to me few days later and offered a mild apology for the change and suggested I be more careful in the future about using anything that could be considered controversial for "The President's Own."*

*A Tribute to Robert D. Isele: The World's Greatest Trombonist (U.S. Marine Band—1937-1961)*

*Jim:*

*On an old 1940s NBC broadcast recording of Bob Isele performing "Elegie," he is introduced by the Marine Band's announcer in the following manner: "'Elegie,' by Robert Massenet." The announcer meant to say, "'Elegie,' by Jules Massenet, as performed by Robert Isele." The unintended mistake showed strong evidence of the love and respect this kind and gentle man engendered in "The President's Own" and all who worked with him. To my knowledge there has been no trombonist by the name of "Robert Massenet."*

Bob was the definitive example of the good guy, the lone ranger, the go-to guy, the best there is, unequaled in his profession. Each generation has its best, and on occasion there may be a repeat of greatness. But not in the case of Bob Isele.

For the brass player of any era, Robert Isele will go down in the books as one of a kind. His natural phrasing and musical application defied description. However, for those interested in hearing the quality of this man's musicality, a search of the Internet for the Marine Band's Bicentennial ten-CD collection, available commercially, would yield a satisfying sampling.

I had the distinct pleasure of working with Bob as his assistant and student, moving up beside him in December of 1957. This happened shortly after we returned from my first tour only weeks before. That move influenced me as a person and professionally more than anything else during my musical career. "Laddie, just listen," he said to me within a few days of being moved next to him. He wasn't referring to himself, just advising me to pay attention to the job, what it is, what it does, and how it affects not only those performing, but also those listening.

Great advice, useful in so many walks of life! Simply put, I learned how to play my horn and, in a manner of speaking, how to live my life. At no time can I recall during those five years observing and listening to Mr. Isele did he ever advise or suggest how I should play a particular part or phrase. All I did was follow his lead and yes, I idolized him.

Surprisingly, I didn't even know who Robert Isele was until an evening concert in 1955, the year before I joined the band. My parents had taken me to hear Freddie perform in Media, Pennsylvania, on his first tour. Although I was thrilled to hear him perform, I was riveted by one of the first selections, including the little solo excerpt opening of Robert Russell Bennett's popular arrangement of "Oh, What a Beautiful Mornin'" from Oklahoma. Guess who was playing that solo? Bob Isele, whose sound and expression were so descriptive of those famous lyrics that something stirred my inner being. I still hear it in my mind and wonder if that may have been the inspiration that awakened whatever talent I possessed.

If there was ever a question as to this man's innate ability to come across as "the only way any phrase should be performed," that question was answered for me upon my first hearing of Bob's playing. That was the first of two memorable performances.

The second, Samuel Rousseau's "Piece Concertante," was recorded live and unedited in 1959, and was to be Bob's final solo recording. I was privileged to have been there. It is the finest example of complete control, sound, interpretation, technique, and musicianship I've ever heard on our instrument. This is not the common, ordinary performance of a solo, or just a performance by an ordinary soloist. The music itself may not be the epitome of *composition. It is what this man makes of it: human presence, eloquence, sheer artistry. It is as though one would ask the great Pablo Casals to do a command performance of the Bach cello suites, and each would come off perfectly!*

*A closing word about my mentor and dear friend: Robert Isele's greatest attribute was that he was more about character than reputation.* ❖

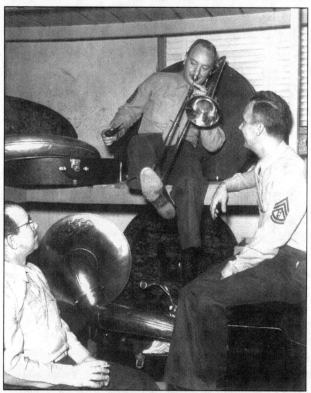

**Bob Isele's artistry ranged from head to toe, literally. Following his main solo, a chair would be brought onstage. Bob would sit down, tie his shoestring to the trombone's slide, and proceed to play his encore, Alexander's Ragtime Band, using his right foot to move the slide. (Photo courtesy Department of Defense)**

# Chapter 12

# Lip Problems

*Bill Jones at the microphone in Sheboygan, MI.*

I n the summer of 1958, Schoepper called upon Freddie to perform Hermann Bellstedt's cornet solo *Napoli* every night on the upcoming Midwest tour; and Jim, in the role of daily matinee soloist, to perform Arthur Pryor's trombone solo *Annie Laurie*. Throughout the summer concert series, Freddie and Jim, along with other soloists, were featured at the East Capitol plaza and the Watergate barge concerts. As fall arrived, Schoepper once again prepared himself and the tour band by going through the same rehearsal routine that he started back in 1955. The tour would consist of the usual grind: two concerts a day, traveling to a different town every morning, and getting on and off the bus ten times a day for sixty-three consecutive days.

*Seattle Times 1959 newspaper clipping of Fred and Jim Erdman, both appearing as soloists with the Marine Band.*

The schedule was rigorous and pressure-packed, starting with the bus ride, which could stretch from 125 miles to 350 miles a day. A train would have been far more restful, but that was a pipe dream. Haircuts were top priority; anyone who wanted to avoid Schoepper's wrath had to get one at least once every ten days, depending of course on how fast one's hair grew. Then there was the added pressure of soloists and principals playing under the dictatorial taskmaster. To understand tour, one had to factor in what were sometimes extremely difficult conditions such as buses and halls and gymnasiums that weren't air-conditioned during the dog days of September, stomach virus "epidemics" that sometimes ran throughout the band, occasional food poisoning, bug-infested rooms, and temper flare-ups.

And being underpaid at $12.84 a day.

Daily NEWS Photo

LOCAL MUSICIANS — Frederic Erdman (left), cornetist, and his brother James A. Erdman 2nd, trombonist (right), talk with Lt. Col. Albert Schoepper, director of the U. S. Marine Band, during intermission Monday night at the Lebanon High School, where the famous band presented a concert under the sponsorship of the Annville-Cleona Kiwanis Club. The Erdman brothers are sons of Mr. and Mrs. Fred J. Erdman, 709 N. Third Ave. The band also gave a concert in the afternoon.

*In this Lebanon Daily News clipping, Fred and Jim Erdman*
*share a light-hearted publicity moment with Schoepper.*

> *Freddie:*

> *One simply had to experience it. By the time the sixth week rolled around, some of us musicians were getting on each other's nerves. Tempers were frayed, and we found ourselves counting the number of days left. There were times when we felt so close, yet so far, from the end.*
>
> *By week seven, Bill Jones, Jimmie, and I continued to solo daily and nightly. On our way to the evening concert, we were riding through midtown Cincinnati. Joe Leo, serving out his time as a veteran and one of the most brilliant clarinetists I've ever heard, was on my bus. As we passed a store in the middle of town, some of us noticed a large wooden Indian standing inside the window, wielding a huge tomahawk.*
>
> *"Him have baton," Joe blurted out. On tour, the best humor could only be dark.*

## The Kudos Keep Coming

*"Fredric Erdman, the cornet soloist, has to be heard to be believed. Erdman plays with marvelous control; he plays soft, clear, clean, bell-like notes which are almost always separated and never seem to overlap or slur. He has an uncanny ability to play the most technical passages easily and without seeming to flourish."*

—Leonard Randolph, *The Daily Record*, Stroudsburg, Pennsylvania

## Civvies on Tour

The year 1959 rang in the old with the new, starting with the band's annual march up the arcade to the Commandant's house for its annual "Surprise Serenade" for General Pate (no surprise there), and the usual spate of White House gigs, patriotic openers, funerals, sight-reading, and recording sessions. All resumed in full swing, as routine and predictable as a garden of spring perennials.

The "new," at least to Freddie and Jim, was the arrival of Vince Lombardi in Green Bay as head football coach of the National Football League's doormat Packers. As the football season progressed, the Erdman brothers and others who followed professional football found close similarities between Lombardi and Schoepper. Both demanded nothing less than perfection from their players. Both ruled with an iron fist.

It was as if their legendary orbits were crossing for the first time.

In June, Freddie re-enlisted, signing his life away to the Marine Corps for another six years in the world's premier symphonic band, under its Lombardi-like leader. For that, he earned a bonus of $2,000. As the summer concerts got underway, both brothers were once again featured as soloists. The fall tour—this time the Erdmans' first tour to the West—brought with it more change in the form of a decree issued by Schoepper: the band would shed its dress blues during bus rides and travel in civilian clothes only, the first time it had ever done so. Dress blues were still the order of the day for matinee performances, however.

Another change was the removal of chevrons, stripes of rank, from both the dress blues and full dress coats.

**Freddie:**

*After three weeks out, Schoepper noticed one of us out of uniform. The culprit whose name was "Clinton" was wearing his dress blues while traveling and living in them! In the hotel elevator after the matinee, Clinton and I were laughing with Schoepper about something that had apparently struck all three of us as funny. Then, just like that, Schoepper looked over at Clinton and, like a chameleon, suddenly changed his tone.*

*"I thought I said you will wear civilian clothes," Schoepper snapped.*

*"Yes, sir," Clinton replied.*

*"I want to see you in civilian clothes tonight before the concert."*

*"Yes, sir."*

*Clinton had to go downtown and shop for some civilian attire. He had only packed his uniforms for the tour.*

## A Modest Lad . . .

Promoting the Marine Band's appearance at the Zembo Temple in Harrisburg, Pennsylvania, the local newspaper played up Freddie's upcoming performance by saying:

"It is not often a young musician, just out of high school, is so talented that he qualifies for acceptance in the United States Marine Band. However, concert-goers will have a rare musical treat on November 12 at Harrisburg's Zembo Temple, when one of the youngest members of this world-famous musical organization will be featured at the evening concert in the Sarasate-Mendez brilliant solo for cornet entitled *Zigeunerweisen (Gypsy Airs)*."

The article went on to say that Fredric J. Erdman, cornetist, who had celebrated his twenty-third birthday in June, was an instrumentalist of unusual and exceptional ability, and that his style, tone, and technique had attracted notice long before he joined the famous military band. It noted that, during his high school years and under the tutelage of his father, also an accomplished musician and present bandmaster of the American Legion Band of Palmyra, the young cornetist had earned state superior ratings annually from 1952 to 1955. "In 1953," said the paper, "as a sophomore at Lebanon High School, he was selected as soloist at the All-Eastern State Band Festival and for two years was appointed first chair cornetist at the Southern District Band Festival at Millersburg. . . .

"Since joining the band, Erdman, a modest lad, has earned his place among the ranks of the band's outstanding soloists. Following his first solo presentation at the Watergate Theater in the Nation's capital, he received a standing ovation and 'bravos' that resounded for minutes across the Potomac River. Small wonder that Lieutenant Colonel Albert Schoepper, director of the Marine Band, selected Erdman as a soloist on the annual fall concert tour." The paper quoted Freddie as saying it was an honor and privilege for him to be a member of the oldest military band in existence. "This group surpasses all other bands I have heard," the quote continued. "Its tone quality is astounding. Its sonority and precision is amazing. I intend to make the Marine Band my career, and I hope some day to earn the position of first chair cornetist."

The promo was written well in advance of the band's appearance. Ironically, Harrisburg would not get to hear Freddie Erdman that year on tour.

*Freddie:*

*Here out west, by the end of the third week of tour, everything seemed to be in full flower. The scenery was gorgeous. The air was drier and we seemed to be closer to the clouds. Maybe in fact we were, since the elevation was higher out here than in a lot of places I'd been on tour. This schedule, though, was rougher, because the towns and cities were located farther apart from each other than on, say, an East Coast tour. That meant earlier morning departure times. In fact, we had quite a few 7:00 a.m. and some 6:00 a.m. departures. In case I neglected to mention, we were playing two concerts a day for 63 consecutive days, each day in a different town and no days off. This is the way it's been since John Philip Sousa took over the Marine Band back in 1880. The only difference between then and now is that back in Sousa's time, the band traveled by train. Now, it was traveling by bus.*

## Trouble Brewing

His soloing on this tour wasn't his best. Playing the Rafael Mendez arrangement of *Zigeunerweisen (Gypsy Airs)*, something just didn't feel right. Late in the summer, his sound was developing "wolf tones." In the middle and on the red part of his upper lip, a peculiar bump, or lesion, had formed. "The Colonel either didn't know that I was having some difficulty," said Freddie, "or if he did, didn't say anything to me about it." The band was into its third week on tour by now, and things weren't getting any better. "My execution in the higher register was suffering," Freddie remembered, "and my chops just didn't feel right."

*Freddie:*

End of third week, Saturday night: We're playing Mile City, Montana. Thirty minutes before we take the stage for the evening concert, I am warming up and to my dismay cannot play a note higher than a written "G," one note above the staff. Well, I can't perform like this! I decide to go into the Lieutenant Colonel's dressing room and explain to him what my problem is.

"Why didn't you let me know of this before?" he asks.

"Colonel, I did not know of this before fifteen minutes ago," I reply.

"Well," he grunts, "I think it is unprofessional of you not to have told me before this."

"I didn't know of this before fifteen minutes ago, Colonel!" (Emphasis on "Colonel"; I'm getting a little angry with him.)

"Well, just go out there and do the best you can."

"I always do, sir."

8:00 p.m. The concert starts. After a few selections, Bill Jones gives the audience my usual introduction. "I really don't want to do this," I'm thinking as I leave my chair to face the audience. The band plays the intro and I come in on a cadenza. Which starts on a low written A and carries up to a high F above high C. I get up to a G-sharp, one-and-a-half notes above the staff and three more to go to get to at least the high D.

I never reach it. Not even close.

My career as a soloist is not exactly soaring at this point. I am literally feeling it and hearing it slide rapidly downhill into the sewer! I struggle through the rest of this long and torturous solo, knowing that I'm not impressing anyone tonight and am probably embarrassing the band, too. At the completion of this battle, the audience applauds politely and I resume my position in the section. There is no encore tonight, and none is necessary.

The following day, Schoepper took Freddie off the program, both as a soloist and section player. He didn't want Freddie to play at all. The idea was to rest him for a short time in the hope that the lesion would disappear. Two weeks later the band arrived in Laramie, Wyoming. Like a defiant leech, the lesion clung to Freddie's upper lip. No more soloing—he was now confined to just playing in the section.

The lesion wasn't the only thing going wrong. To make matters worse, Freddie wasn't feeling well. That evening, he went to dinner in the hotel dining room but had no appetite, which was unusual for someone who was used to downing big portions. He didn't eat anything. Performing the concert later that evening, he was feeling worse by the minute.

After the band's first featured selection, Bill Jones, developed his own "lesion"—a mental block that occurred when he tried to remember which town the band was visiting that day.

### Freddie:

*There was the great Bill Jones, expressing thanks to the sponsors for supporting the concert. ". . . And we want to give thanks to the sponsoring committee here in ..."But Jones can't think of the name of the town we're in! There's a pregnant pause, then he looks down at Raoul Querze, clarinetist in the second row. "Where the hell are we?" he whispers in a low voice to Raoul. "Honolulu," Raoul answers.*

*Jones then looked over at Schoepper, who cleared his throat and muttered softly, "Laramie." ". . . Yes, we want to give our thanks to the sponsoring committee here in Laramie." Wearing a poker face for the audience, Jones never lost his composure during that moment of forgetfulness. Not long after, Raoul left the band, got a degree from the Manhattan School of Music in New York City, then won a position as E-flat clarinetist in the Philadelphia Orchestra.*

After the concert, Arthur Lehman took Freddie to a doctor where an x-ray showed pneumonia. He was put to bed immediately with medications but stayed on the road with the band. Trapp and Schoepper decided not to send him back to Washington. Arthur continued to check in on him twice a day and became Freddie's caretaker. Freddie was convinced that Arthur was a good man.

By week eight, Freddie had fully recovered and was well enough to play in the section. It felt good to be sitting in with the band again.

*Freddie:*

*We are making our way back east, having just departed from Las Vegas. We're riding in the middle of the desert, and we come to this gas station for a fifteen-minute rest stop. Ralph Moeller, barisax and band veteran, has lost all his money gambling in Vegas. All he has to his name is one silver dollar in his pocket. Since we are still in the state of Nevada, this particular gas station has a slot machine, with a jackpot of $500. Ralph wanders over to the machine.*

*"Ah, what the hell," he says. "Why not?"*

*He puts his last silver dollar into the machine and pulls the lever.*

*Clang! Clang! Clang! Clang! Clang! The unbelievable happens.*

*Ralph just hit the jackpot.*

## Library Duty

The lesion persisted. After the band's return to Washington that November, Schoepper suggested that Freddie try resting the lip again. Instead of playing, he would work in the band library during rehearsal hours. Hopefully, in a month or two, the lesion would go away.

On November 10, the Marine Corps celebrated its birthday. The occasion was marked by a worship service and performance of the Marine Band brass choir in the loft of the Washington Cathedral.

By January 20, 1960, Freddie found himself still working in the band's music library, passing out and collecting music folders, fending off boredom. Except for a frequent stroll into the recording lab to look down at the band while it was rehearsing, wishing he could be down there playing with the rest of his fellow Marine Band members, there was nothing else for him to do. He was also about to miss out on the trip of a lifetime: "The President's Own," as he learned, was selected to represent the United States at the VIII Olympic Winter Games in Squaw Valley, California. In fact, it would be the only band of its kind to perform.

In April 1960, cornetist Bob Dehart retired. Toward the end, he took his share of guff from the leader. "I want guaranteed notes!" Schoepper would bark, chastising Dehart about his missed notes. Bob drank a lot and died a relatively young man, just sixty years old. One couldn't help wonder if a certain leader drove Dehart to drink . . .

The band was rehearsing for its upcoming spring/summer performances at the East Capitol plaza and Watergate. After rehearsal, Schoepper, anxious to know the status of Freddie's condition, called him into his office once again. "How's the lip?"

"Things haven't changed," said Freddie.

"Well," said Schoepper in an uncharacteristically kind tone of voice, "let's take a chance and have surgery done on that thing. What d'ya say?"

Freddie nodded in agreement.

"We'll set up an appointment for you at Bethesda Naval Hospital."

"All right, sir."

*Freddie:*

## Cooksie's Creation

*It was June 1960 and, boy, was I in for an experience! I learned that the surgeon who would perform the surgery on me, Capt. Cooksie, was the same surgeon who took out Bob Isele's lesion twenty years earlier.*

*Sometime after reporting in and filling out the paperwork, I was given Demerol, then wheeled into the operating room on a gurney. After placing me on the operating table, I was blindfolded! A few moments later and being completely off-guard, I was suddenly stunned by the anesthetic needle just above my upper lip in the middle, and let out quite a guttural grunt. "Yeah, Erdman, we know it hurts," said the Captain. Cooksie's bedside manner left something to be desired.*

*I don't know how long this operation is going to take. But this much I did know—I could feel him tearing away at the tissues around and on my upper lip. I was a bloody mess. Several hours after the anesthetic wore off, I got to my feet and steadied myself, then wandered over to a mirror in the ward, just to see what I looked like.*

*Oh . . . my . . . God!*

*The entire upper lip looked like a golf ball with stitches.*

*"It ought to be interesting to see whether I'll ever be able to play again after this," I remember thinking, gazing at Cooksie's creation.*

*Two days later, I saw across the way in my ward some other patients playing checkers. I invited myself to play the winner. Now, I had learned from a checkers master long before I came into the Marine Band, and I could see that these guys really didn't know how to play checkers. Strange as it seems, I lost the first game!! But then I won the second one and never lost after that. We played some fifteen games that day. From then on, I played different opponents every day and never lost. About the third day into this, one patient who watched me play stated arrogantly, "I can beat this guy!"*

*He never did. I played him ten games and he finally gave up. I should have hustled him and made some money!*

Two weeks later, after being briefed by Capt. Cooksie, Freddie was discharged from Bethesda Naval Hospital. Cooksie's orders were plain and simple: no playing the cornet for one month. ❖

# Chapter 13

# Double Duty

One day in August, Freddie finally picked up his old friend. Placing his embouchure into playing position and wondering what if anything would come out of the other side, he took a modest-sized breath and blew into the horn. A medium-loud note actually came out—a G, the second line on the staff. "At least that's a start," he thought.

*Freddie:*

*By the end of the first week, I could play up to a C, third space on the staff. By the second week's end, I could play the G, one space above the staff. My roommates were commenting on the progress I was making every week. I still wasn't assigned to go on the road this year, but at least I could sit in the "home guard" band section, the part of the band that doesn't go on tour.*

*Over time, my playing got increasingly stronger, and I finally realized the lesion itself was a result of over-practicing. Case in point: I would play through a three-hour rehearsal with Schoepper, then go home, grab some lunch and practice another three hours with a straight mute jammed into the bell of the cornet. It was just too much for the lip to endure.*

*The 1960 tour takes the band down South. I hear that Jimmie is playing at the matinees "Atlantic Zephyrs" (we sometimes call it "Atlantic Zippers"), while an accordion soloist is featured at evening concerts, a highly unusual departure from the norm.*

*Jim:*

## Not-So-Accommodating Accommodations

*Full understanding of this story requires a more careful exploration of our moods and how they were affected by so many exceedingly nerve-wracking incidents.*

*The 1960 tour through the Deep South was infamous and the reason was simple: the hotels. Let's just say that hotel/motel accommodations back then were not what the general public has become accustomed to these days. Amenities like comfort, food, and cleanliness have come a long way. Especially cleanliness! But in 1960 and in prior years, the selection of many of the establishments housing the Marine Band overnight was based on cost. Economics ruled. It was plain to see, in more ways than one, that our tour manager was not interested in comfort—for himself or for us.*

*A daily routine thus took shape. After arriving in town and checking in at the front desk, we would perform a bug check. We'd check the room, bathroom, and bed sheets—especially bed sheets—for bugs of all kinds. How unnerving it was to look under the bed just after opening the room door, or pulling up the bed sheets and discover to our chagrin the nearly inevitable host of roaches, spiders, or other insects! None of this was uncommon. Night after insufferable night, we came to realize that creepy crawlers could make strange bedfellows.*

*Survival instincts kicked in, and some of us would proceed to book ourselves into another hotel. The practice was frowned upon and eventually verboten by Trapp, whose attitude didn't help much to maintain a high sense of morale. On the road for two-and-a-half months, morale was always a fragile thing anyway. Under these circumstances, relationships that could and would otherwise have remained congenial, instead began to break down.*

*Perhaps this was the cause of a very strange development. It involved the leader's attitude towards one of our evening soloists. Schoepper had made a rather interesting decision that was to make my solo responsibility even more laborious and nerve-wracking. This year, 1960, he had broken with a Marine Band tradition of having a brass soloist at each concert. Instead, he decided to feature an accordionist during the first-half evening's program. The previous 1959 tour had him particularly annoyed with both Freddie and me, beginning with Freddie's illness and his inability to play for weeks. It really bothered the old man.*

My problem during that same tour was with an arpeggio at the end of the opening intro for the "Annie Laurie" solo, written by Arthur Pryor and arranged by Robert Isele. I was informed that my inconsistency was not in missing notes, but with the intonation while going from a low B to a high C, a problem that became my Waterloo for some time. As a form of punishment, Schoepper relegated me to "matinee idol" for this Southern 1960 tour.

We were in our twenty-third day. The place was Austin, Texas. The leader and the accordionist-soloist seemed to be having personality differences. The tensions between the two had been increasing day by day, with no apparent solution in sight. If tempted to dismiss the accordionist, Schoepper had to be thinking as well, "Who is my immediate replacement?"

As we boarded the bus that night after the concert, there he was, awaiting my arrival. "Erdman!" he snapped as I stepped into the well of the bus. "I've sent him home. You're on tomorrow night!" My first reaction was silent and somber. Deep down, I was screaming, "Two a day!?!"

The experiment added immeasurably to the grind. Playing two solos a day, one at the matinee, the other during the evening performance, may have seemed like a good idea to Schoepper, but it certainly wasn't my idea of a good time, particularly under the pressure of the Schoepper dictum of "guaranteed notes." Still, I managed to pull it off, this form of double duty fraught with musical peril. When I think of the workload, my stock had gone up considerably and surprisingly well. The solo, Gardell Simons' smooth sailing "Atlantic Zephyrs," is nothing in comparison to Pryor's solos. Under these circumstances, however, doing "Three Blind Mice" could be challenging on some days!

And it lasted all of twelve days, ending the day we arrived in Biloxi, Mississippi on October 15. In the solo's cadenza, there is a high note. I missed it. No doubt, that note is still attached to the auditorium's walls, and I'm rather proud of the glorious splattered mess. (A fly swatter could not have done it better justice!) While walking off-stage for an intermission break, I felt the strong tap of a baton on my shoulder followed by the remark, "You're not good enough for two a day. Back to the matinee only."

Some might have received such words with doom and gloom. I embraced them with the calmness of a summer day's fresh gentle breeze. I was relieved. I was happy! Thank you, God!

Unexpected Gift: There was another bright spot to come out of those twelve days, in the form of a personal gift. The second day of my newly appointed "downward promotion," we had arrived in Waco, Texas. As I took a brief walk between concerts, I noticed a sign in the window of a pawn and junk shop that said, "Not for an age, but for all time." That sentiment is now engraved in my wife's engagement and wedding rings. Something good comes out of everything!

By October 1960, Freddie was placed back on full duty playing rehearsals, patriotic openers, White House commitments, and funerals at Arlington National Cemetery. One month later, John F. Kennedy defeated Richard M. Nixon in the national presidential election. On November 10, as the Marine Corps celebrated another birthday, the Marine Band brass choir, as it had in previous years, performed in the raised loft of the Washington National Cathedral for a Marine Corps worship service.

*Freddie:*

*On January 20, 1961, a brutally Arctic-cold day, the Marine Band, as tradition would have it, played selections at the East Capitol plaza prior to the arrival of the new president. Upon his arrival, we sounded the four "Ruffles and Flourishes" followed by the march "Hail to the Chief," and the ceremony was underway. In the middle of the ceremony, the Marine Band performed a selection with a vocalist, followed by John F. Kennedy taking the oath of office, after which we once again sounded "Ruffles and Flourishes" and "Hail to the Chief." The newly sworn-in president then delivered his memorable inaugural address, energizing the nation. At the conclusion and following an hour-long lunch break on the bus, we left the Capitol premises to line up for the Inaugural Parade. It was a long and cold workday.*

*In May, the new president challenged the nation to use its collective skills and dedication to excellence to put a man on the moon by the end of the decade.*

*The Marine Band performing in front of the United States Capitol during one of its weekly Capitol concerts in 1961.*

*September 1961: I was back with the tour band. The tour schedule hadn't changed. As always, we were to play two concerts a day for nine weeks with no days off and traveling to a different town every morning.*

*After his experience with me as a soloist back on the 1959 tour, the Colonel became a believer of safety in numbers, assigning six soloists to perform at once—a sextet, in other words, playing "Bolero." Jim was the brass matinee soloist. The tour would take us through parts of New England and the Midwest.*

*Publicity photo of the cornet section in 1961. Front row, l-r, Charles Erwin, David Flowers, Charles Kautz, Fredric Erdman. Back row, l-r, Robert Brackman, Johannes Rasmussen, David Johnson, unknown. (Photo courtesy Department of Defense)*

*Jim soloing during an evening tour performance.*

*Sunday, October 15, 1961: A Boston Clam*

*Under clear blue skies, we roll into Boston, Massachusetts, to play the Sunday matinee. As we take the stage, I sit and gaze into a capacity audience of three thousand, some of whom are all but hanging from the rafters. I catch sight of the two mahogany tiers, semicircular in design and rounding the hall from one side to the other. The main floor slopes downward toward the stage, crystal chandeliers glisten from above. In this magnificent old theater, the program begins and the concert proceeds without a hitch.*

*After a brief intermission, the second half opens with the "March of the Steelmen" which ends on a sustained high note, high D above high C, for the solo cornet player, Charles "Chuck" Erwin, a 99% clam-proof player ("clam is a term used by musicians to denote a missed or "chipped" note). Like most of us, Chuck is doing his usual heroic job as the first-chair (principal) solo cornetist, along with his very capable assistant and second-chair solo cornetist, Dave Flowers. The Erwin/Flowers tandem on the solo cornet book on this and last year's tour is unbeatable. Nowhere in the country, or the world for that matter, would you find two solo cornet players better or even as good and consistent as these two top musicians.*

*The "Ralph Vaughn Williams English Folk Song Suite for Band" follows. The first movement being omitted, we begin the soft and delicate Intermezzo second movement. Chuck starts off with a solo passage. Not having enough recovery time from sustaining the high D on the previous march, he chips the top note of an octave slur. Playing an octave slur without any overtones or "trash" occurring between the lower note of the octave and the higher note is very difficult to execute after having to blow in the very high register. Schoepper's basic musical training was as a violinist, so he does not understand this, nor is he forgiving of it.*

*Without another incident, we play our way to the final number of the program, Richard Wagner's "Overture to Tannhauser." Suddenly, as we reach the midway point of the overture, I feel a shock radiating throughout my body—I have come in on an entrance one beat too soon! A blaring mistake, not only noticeable to the band but the audience as well. God Almighty! I'm in for it now. Maybe he won't say anything to me, although I see that infamous facial gesture of vengeance.*

*The concert ends with rousing applause. I hold my breath as we depart from the stage. Backstage, I hear "Chuck, Dave, Freddie, Colonel wants to see ya."*

*Still attired in our traditional scarlet tunics, the three of us walk into the inner sanctum that is the Lieutenant Colonel's dressing room. We see him pacing back and forth in the black uniform of the Marine Band director. Standing there, facing him, I am immediately excoriated.*

*"Erdman!" his angry voice resonates throughout the room. He glares at me. "That's high school stuff." He then raises both his hands to his head and says, "Your mind, it seems divided." His voice is getting louder now. "You're schizophrenic. That's what you are. Schizophrenic! Get out!"*

*Stung by his acid tongue and upon exiting and shutting the door behind me, I eavesdrop against the door. I hear his demanding and forceful voice.*

*"Now, I CANNOT have missed notes. What happened in the Vaughan Williams?"*

*"Colonel," Chuck replies, "that's a very difficult passage for a brass player to play when the embouchure has had really no time to recover or readjust from holding onto a high note like the high D at the end of the 'March of the Steelmen.'"*

*Schoepper: "That's just an excuse. You must guarantee me ALL the notes."*

*"I can't do that," Chuck says.*

*"How about you, Flowers?" persists Schoepper. "Can you guarantee me every note?"*

*"I can guarantee you nothing, sir," Flowers replies.*

*Furious, the Colonel grunts, then says with disgust, "Get out."*

How in the world could I have come in on an entrance one beat too soon?—a beat that could possibly have been heard around the world! Not only did I know that Schoepper would be angry, I knew—with every fiber of my being—that I had just missed a moment in time.

What had happened?

Because of the arduous task of constant repetition each day, our sense of who and where we were could and did become frayed, even tattered, and temporarily dimmed from city to city to city—a blur of yesterday, today, and tomorrow yet to come—floating déjà vu versus real time. The same bus travel routine and performing the same programs daily for nine weeks without breaks can drain a performer to wordless depths—even to a temporary or momentary abyss within the spirit where time stops and reality is suspended—for just a second or two.

I remember as if it were yesterday the words that emanated from Shoepper's rage. Were they warranted? Perhaps. Could we guarantee those notes any more surely because of his outburst? Probably not. Music danced across the stage and throughout the audience on tour, but the price performers often paid was unseen and unknown.

And how did we all get through the relentlessness of those rigorous tours? With an abundance of humor and the powerful glue of camaraderie in sharing life on the road.

## A New Tandem

In the following spring of 1962, Dave Flowers left the band to become associate principal trumpet to Lloyd Geisler with the National Symphony Orchestra in Washington, D.C. Shortly thereafter, the Erwin-Erdman tandem would begin and remain for the next ten years.

"Building a professional relationship with Colonel Albert Schoepper was an extremely difficult task," noted Chuck Erwin. "From 1956 until his retirement, I was the principal cornetist of the U.S. Marine Band. This position was that of concertmaster, as well as solo cornetist.

"Colonel Schoepper was an accomplished violinist, but had no concept of the physical limitations that brass players experienced, particularly during long exhausting rehearsals and formal concerts. He simply could not understand why notes were "chipped" or missed. Many were the discussions between the two of us regarding the intricate muscle structure of the lips and mouth area, called the 'embouchure.'"

From the Marine Band prism as seen through Erwin's eyes, Schoepper's obsession with notes and corresponding dismissal of strain and fatigue was palpable. "In the time of absolute anger, he would stare at me and say, 'I have a five-letter religion: N-O-T-E-S!' The intense and stressful concert tours, which lasted sixty-three to sixty-seven days (with two concerts a day), brought out his worst level of comprehension in dealing with embouchure fatigue. Individual brass players and/or entire brass sections would be called into his dressing room during concert intermissions to make them confess their violation of his religious commandment. Target concert dates like Boston, New York, Chicago, San Francisco, would provide a perfect feeding ground for a mass collection of brass players to 'face the music.' I had a particularly intimidating after-concert experience in Boston. I couldn't promise to guarantee every note."

Still, Erwin had genuine respect for the man. "Despite Colonel Schoepper's creating unnecessary tension," he added, "the Marine Band musicians could always rely on his complete knowledge of the musical scores and preparation for any and all musical events.

"It was only after both of us had retired that we were able to have an occasional lunch together and reflect on our working duties. It was truly a test of physical and mental endurance to perform during his tenure as director of 'The President's Own.'"

## The Schoepper Tour

Pat Pulverenti remembers Albert Schoepper. A longtime member of the clarinet section, Pulverenti harkened back to the 1955 tour, when Schoepper first became leader and, according to Pat, seemed to be degrading everybody. Interestingly, Pulverenti still preferred Schoepper's leadership to Harpham's. "The band was tighter under Schoepper," he noted. In one respect the 1955 tour was like any other tour: daily bus rides, two concerts a day. Some say that tour was the worst ever, in large part brought on by Schoepper's unwavering attitude toward perfection.

## Life on the Bus

When traveling on tour from one town to the next, everyone was required to wear a coat and tie. No exceptions.

The tour way of life was a *bus* way of life. Some managed their bus life quite well. By his window and the first thing without fail every morning after boarding, first-part cornetist Kenny Emenheiser, who joined the band about a year after Freddie did, would open the stock market pages of a newspaper, pull out a bunch of loose-leaf binders, organize them on his seat and go right "to work" updating his stock portfolios. Those who knew Ken used to think that "bus-work" would eventually pay off handsomely in future years as a nice financial supplement to Ken's military pension.

Schoepper read his *New York Times* and checked ballgame box scores. His knowledge of baseball was encyclopedic. He was also exceptional at doing crossword puzzles, completing most of those in the *Times* with ease.

Some tour members read their paperbacks, others the girlie books. You could always find a *Penthouse* or *Playboy* lying around. A few played one of the four C's: chess, checkers, cards, and cribbage. Some gossiped and slandered. Marine Band members could be their own worst critics, as long as they were criticizing one another, either to their faces or behind their backs. In fact, backstabbing seemed to be more rule than exception. The band at times seemed a verbal-cutthroat gang of rogues. Some band members suffered through "tour divorce": they were great friends prior to tour and thus agreed to pair up as roommates. By tour's end, they were sworn enemies.

Albert Johnson and Dave Flowers were roommates. Dave liked to rib Al, a good ol' Texas boy with a slight twang in his baritone voice, who could take it and dish it out as well. Both had an occasional disdain for Schoepper, but it was Flowers who came up with a ritual that only Flowers could get away with. Every morning, Dave would make it a point to be the last person to board the smoker's bus. As he climbed into the well of the bus, he'd stand straight up and, right in front of Albert Schoepper, would look back at Albert Johnson, shouting, "Albert! You *sonavabitch!*" The rant was Dave's ingenious way of expressing his feelings toward Schoepper. And there wasn't a thing Schoepper could do about it.

*David Flowers. (Photo courtesy Department of Defense)*

Some were silent travelers. They sat and stared out the bus window, or just went back to sleep for the better part of tens of thousands of miles. Everyone breathed, smoked, read, slept, snacked, sneezed, coughed, laughed, cursed, and even cried on the bus.

East Coast tours were shorter in distance than their West Coast counterparts. Jim has a logbook of all nineteen consecutive tours from 1957 to 1975 that he made with the band, including nine on the west coast. The approximate total mileage was one hundred fifty thousand miles. Freddie did twenty-two tours.

Considering that all this could go on for tens of thousands of miles over a time span that in early September saw increasingly colorful autumn foliage completely gone by Thanksgiving, it was easy to understand why a short-tempered, illness-prone Marine Band member could be an unhappy Marine Band member.

*Al Johnson.*

On the other hand, anyone who liked to see the countryside from the roadway and didn't mind the rigorous schedule or getting on and off the bus a total of 630 times was considered an ideal prospect for tour. Other prerequisites included not missing the family too much. Oh yes, you also needed to have a thick skin with fellow band members, especially those who had high opinions of themselves. Egos in overdrive are commonplace among musicians, and those in the Marine Band were no exception.

The most important requirement, especially for the principal players, was a good set of playing chops that showed both skill and stamina, enough to "guarantee notes" for sixty-three consecutive days—or sixty-seven, depending on the year.

## Flaring Tempers Take Their Toll

The pressure of tour could set off the pettiest argument, resulting in neither party talking to the other for days, weeks or months. During the last ten days or so of the 1958 tour, Arthur Lehman and Jim Erdman got into a heated argument. As "bus commander" who was responsible for taking a seat count prior to every bus departure so that no one would be left behind, Arthur felt that Jim was getting too close to being late in boarding the bus and taking his seat. He expressed as much to Jim, in a tone that was thinly disguised as authoritative.

Stress-filled from soloing, Jim cracked. In a fit of temper, he slammed down his right hand on the top of the seat backrest and sobbed. Obviously in pain, he let forth a few choice words, then sat down, silent until the band reached its destination.

Soon after the incident, Jim had his hand examined. A doctor placed it in a cast. The spat was costly: Jim was now forced to solo the rest of tour encumbered by an injured hand he had always relied on to move his trombone's slide. Surprisingly, Schoepper didn't notice the cast until near the end of tour, with about five days to go.

"What happened to Jim's hand?" Schoepper asked Harpham.

"Oh, he was just scuffling with the boys."

The next day in Cambridge, Ohio, just before the evening concert, Schoepper called Jim into his dressing room and inquired into the reason why his featured trombone soloist was wearing a cast. After Jim told him what had happened, Schoepper called in Arthur and proceeded to reprimand him for unnecessarily needling his star soloist.

Everyday life on the road took on its own Schoepper-driven meaning. There were rules. Paying the hotel bill by a certain time before departure was one; another was getting a haircut once every ten days. Boarding the bus on time was yet another—on "on time" meant fives minutes before departure. And *missing* the bus? Don't even think about it . . . although it happened to one musician. Discovering the bus had left without him, trombonist Gary Greenhoe hurriedly rented a car and drove for the next town less than a hundred miles away. It really wasn't Greenhoe's fault: Schoepper actually had the bus leave five minutes earlier than announced, a nasty habit of his. Greenhoe was there to greet the buses, and reminded Schoepper of the announced time. Nothing more was said.

## Irish Pennants

John Schaeffer, who came into the band in 1970, a couple months before I did, was a bass trombonist who had previously graduated from the University of Michigan, John and I made two tours under Schoepper. "Many were the occasions," remembers John, "when the Colonel would become incensed by some small imperfection. The so-called 'Irish pennants' were a frequent distress. If he detected one of those white threads hanging off someone's coat that contrasted against our blue trousers, he was simply unable to take his eyes off it and often conducted straight at the offender until the problem was corrected. 'So-and-so, see me in my dressing room' was sure to follow. We must have looked like a bunch of monkeys picking lice during our pre-concert 'pennant' checks."

*John Schaefer. (Photo courtesy Department of Defense)*

## Clash of Egos

Flutist Les Hunt recalled a situation on tour one year that was very amusing to watch for anyone lucky enough to be in the vicinity, and who was savvy enough to realize what was going on.

Les recalls that the band was playing a concert on the campus of the University of Michigan in Ann Arbor; and Dr. William D. Revelli, the university's legendary conductor who had a reputation as demanding, if not more so, than Schoepper's, walked into the conference room that served as Schoepper's dressing room. Likely, Revelli didn't knock.

To begin with, the Colonel didn't like his pre-concert routine disturbed and he preferred to have control over when and how he met his audience, including local VIPs. Further, a "normal" conversation with Dr. Revelli did not exist. It was always a lecture. If there was anything the Colonel couldn't tolerate, it was someone in his face.

So, for several minutes, the scene was Dr. Revelli running his mouth while Colonel Schoepper desperately tried to keep the large conference table between them. The clash between these two monstrous egos was obvious—two alpha males stalking each other on one's territory and the premises obviously not big enough for both.

## In the Footsteps of Barnum

Between 1950 and the early 1970s, the Marine Band had two tour managers: Trapp and Robert "Bobby Goggles" Williams. Managing tour was a business, which meant that the tour manager was in business to make money. That's what the *Economics of Trapp* was all about. To do that, he had to put his money on the line while going around the country and promoting his band—in this case the most famous band in the world—then pony up the necessary dough to fund the tour. The successful manager needed some P.T. Barnum savvy in his blood to do this.

Most importantly, he had to cover his expenses. He had to guarantee the sponsor a certain "take," and if he didn't sufficiently fill the house, he'd have to "eat" his guarantee and still pay the sponsor. The tour manager didn't always come out on top. The worst-case scenario actually happened in New Rochelle, New York, where in 1975 the band had to cancel two straight evening concerts due to no-show audiences. Imagine, going to the concert hall each evening, and no one—*nobody*—shows up for a concert by "The President's Own," the United States Marine Band!

It's a mystery as to how much the tour manager and conductor pocketed after expenses. Nobody had to: after all, it was the tour manager's money to disburse at his discretion. The important thing to realize is that such tours never cost the government a penny. The Schoepper-style tour lasted one year more after his retirement in 1972. After 1987, Marine Band tours were coordinated by the Marine Corps. Even today, if you want to hear a concert by the Marine Band in your town, it costs you nothing. ❖

*Jimmie Erdman soloing in Beaumont, Texas.*

# Chapter 14

# "Be Ready."

*Freddie:*

*Mid-December 1961: The annual Christmas tree lighting takes place on the Ellipse on a very cold evening, with music provided by the Marine Band. It's just a bit difficult playing a wind instrument when you are shivering.*

*Late Spring 1962: I hear that a cornet player has just played a rather impressive audition for the Marine Band.*

*June 1962: The cornet player is playing the first part cornet stand as the summer concerts begin. I'm still playing second part. "What gives?" I ask myself. "What can he do that I can't?"*

*August 1962: I go into Colonel Schoepper's office. I want to know why the new guy has been put up there on first part. "I have served you, Colonel, for six years. And yet, this neophyte, who just came into the Marine Band three months ago, is given a chance at the first part second stand before me."*

*"Yes, well. Ha! Let's see how things work out now," Schoepper replies, "and we'll talk about this after tour." Obviously, he didn't really answer my question.*

**White House Christmas quartet: left to right, Kenny Emenheiser, Freddie, Jimmie, Larry Tichenor. (Photo courtesy Washington Post)**

*September 1962: Chuck Erwin is playing the solo chair as he has been since 1958. I'm still playing first chair-second part, while the new guy has been assigned to play first trumpet on this tour. Brother Jim is being featured everyday on the matinee as trombone soloist, playing Arthur Pryor's "Thoughts of Love." He has also been playing principal trombone since Bob Isele's retirement in July 1961.*

*This is a West Coast tour and this year, the tour will be sixty-seven days long instead of the usual sixty-three due to appearances at four West Coast Marine Corps bases. Schoepper puts the band through his usual rehearsal routine prior to the tour's opening day at Longwood Gardens.*

*The matinee at Longwood is hot and the evening concert is cold. Some of us will probably get sick the next day. The same old guys are doing the same old things—playing two concerts a day, alighting to and from the bus ten times a day, and playing a different town every day for sixty-seven consecutive days, with again no days off.*

*The daily schedule for a West Coast tour is even more rigorous than other regions of the country because of the longer distances between towns. On many mornings, that would mean departure times of anywhere from 0600 to 0800.*

*Third week, Tacoma, Washington: Chuck Erwin is called back to Washington, D.C. to attend to an emergency with his wife. Chuck's assistant, who is not Dave Flowers this time takes over the solo cornet chair. As the days roll by, the Colonel is becoming increasingly displeased with this assistant's playing. Since knowing him from the very first day I joined the band, I've known all along that he should never have been put up there on the solo stand. He is missing too many notes for the Colonel, his intonation is not good and his tone sounds amateurish to me.*

*Two weeks of this have gone by.*

*Week five, Redding, California: After playing the matinee and putting my cornet back in its case, I am standing backstage. It is very dark back here. Suddenly and unexpectedly, I feel two taps on my left shoulder. "Be ready," says the Colonel in a low voice.*

130

*I know what he means. I tell the librarian to bring me all three solo cornet folders: the daily matinee, evening, and Sunday afternoon programs. I must stay behind and play through all of the solo passages and other non-solo passages to make sure I am reading and playing all the notes precisely.*

*6:00 p.m It has taken me three hours to play through all of this, at a nonstop pace. But—I'm ready.*

*I must now call for a cab to get me back to the hotel and try to grab a meal before I have to board the bus for the evening concert. The cabbie gets me back to the hotel. I head straight for the dining room and I'm in luck: the waitress comes over to me right away and takes my order. I've gotten to eat and have one-half hour to relax before boarding the bus at 7:30 p.m.*

## Musical Chairs

*Next day, Saturday afternoon: During the matinee, the Colonel is frowning and scowling at the assistant solo cornet player who has been playing the solo chair for the past two weeks. The conclusion of the matinee is followed by an announcement from the Colonel. "Cornet section, report back on stage in seating order after you've changed. Everybody else, back on the bus."*

*As I change into civilian clothes, I know what is about to happen. The Colonel warned me yesterday.*

*We return to our seats on stage and the drama unfolds. The Colonel comes out and steps up on the podium. "Get up the Hadley," he orders succinctly. (Henry Hadley composed the overture Schoepper is referring to, titled "In Bohemia.")*

*He conducts us through the opening section and then stops.*

*"No! That's out of tune there!" he barks out to the solo chair player.*

*At this point, the janitor is running a vacuum cleaner on the floor of the auditorium. Schoepper turns around and yells to the janitor "Get out! Can't you see I'm conducting a rehearsal here?!"*

*The janitor darts out of the auditorium like a scared gecko.*

*The Colonel resumes the "rehearsal." He takes us through a few more passages of the overture and says, "Not good enough." He picks out another piece. We play through several bars when we come to a solo passage for the solo cornet player, who gets about halfway through the passage when the Colonel stops. "No. No! You're missing too many notes! I can't have that!"*

*The solo cornetist says, "Well, I'm not getting much support up here, sir."*

*"Excuses. Excuses. I don't want excuses," Schoepper snaps. "Notes are what I want! It's the only religion I have!" Schoepper pauses, then resumes. "I can see where I put all my eggs*

in one basket with Erwin up here. All right. I'm going to try something different. Erdman, you come on up here. You two trade places," he finishes, pointing to the solo cornet player and myself. So now, I'm sitting on the solo chair, coming up from the second part. The one who had been playing the solo chair is now sitting back where I was and playing the second part.

One after another, the Colonel takes us through seven or eight selections, which have solo passages in them, including all three folios. After being satisfied with my playing of those solo passages, the Colonel says, "All right, we're going to try this seating arrangement tonight. "That's all."

After we are dismissed, we board the buses where the rest of the band has been waiting for the drive back to the hotel. The usual anxiety and apprehension sets in as I have dinner and it's getting close to bus time. As we arrive at the hall, the apprehension grows. I am going to be playing the solo chair tonight.

I'm excited. Butterflies are activated!

8:30 p.m. The concert begins. Feeling very tense, I play everything, not just the solo passages. But I'm playing up to my standards. If I'm matching my own standards, I know the Colonel has to be pleased with my playing—when it comes to notes, my standards are every bit as high as his.

After the concert, I am relieved of the tension and the Colonel says that we will keep this seating arrangement for the rest of the tour.

Upon boarding the bus, the former solo chair player and myself trade seats. He offers me his, which is a double seat for principal players near the front of the bus. And he takes my seat, which of course is also a double. The difference is that it is in the middle of the bus, and he has to share it with someone else. I now have a double seat all to myself. I also get a single room.

Five days later: I am satisfied with the work I'm doing on the solo chair. Bud Malsh, our solo clarinetist, is called back to Washington because of an emergency with his wife. Another change has occurred: the first-chair trumpeter has been taken off first trumpet and put on the third cornet part. On the Sunday matinee of four weeks ago, he missed an eight-bar trumpet solo, which occurs in the "Jerome Kern Fantasy." For eight entire bars, all we heard were the rhythmic brushes on the snare drum. The Colonel, of course, spent his wrath on the trumpet player. A replacement from the Home Guard band in Washington was then sent out to cover the first trumpet part.

Arthur Lehman has a short cadenza in Liszt's "Liebestraum," which takes place in the middle register of the euphonium. On the descending passage and for some reason unknown to Arthur, he has trouble controlling the notes. Happens to the best of us.

Schoepper tells harpist Claude Pedicord to play Arthur's part for the remainder of tour.

Tour Of 1962

| | | | | | |
|---|---|---|---|---|---|
| Sept. | 16 | Kennett Square, Pa. | Oct. | 22 | Stockton, Cal. |
| | 17 | York, Pa. | | 23 | Petaluma, Cal. |
| | 18 | Johnstown, Pa. | | 24 | Castro Valley, Cal. |
| | 19 | Steubenville, O. | | 25 | Oakdale, Cal. |
| | 20 | Zanesville, O. | | 26 | Barstow, Cal. - Marine |
| | 21 | Newport, Ky. | | | Corps Supply Center |
| | 22 | Seymour, Ind. | | 27 | Santa Ana, Cal. - USMC |
| | 23 | Mt. Carmel, Ill. | | | Air Station |
| | 24 | Charleston, Ill. | | 28 | Camp Pendleton, Cal. - |
| | 25 | Springfield, Ill. | | | Camp Pendleton Marine |
| | 26 | Hannibal, Mo. | | | Corpd Base |
| | 27 | St. Joseph, Mo. | | 29 | San Diego, Cal. - Marine |
| | 28 | Raytown, Mo. | | | Corps Recruit Depot |
| | 29 | Paola, Kans. | | 30 | Yuma, Ariz. |
| | 30 | Topeka, Kans. | | 31 | Needles, Cal. |
| Oct. | 1 | Lindsborg, Kans. | Nov. | 1 | Las Vegas, Nev. |
| | 2 | Hays, Kans. | | 2 | Cedar City, U. |
| | 3 | Goodland, Kans. | | 3 | Price, U. |
| | 4 | Denver, Colo. | | 4 | Grand Junction, Colo. |
| | 5 | Craig, Colo. | | 5 | Salida, Colo. |
| | 6 | Vernal, U. | | 6 | Colorado Springs, Colo. |
| | 7 | Ogden, U. | | 7 | La Junta, Colo. |
| | 8 | Pocatello, U. | | 8 | Garden City, Kans. |
| | 9 | Twin Falls, Ida. | | 9 | Wichita, Kans. |
| | 10 | Boise, Ida. | | 10 | Joplin, Mo. |
| | 11 | Grangeville, Ida. | | 11 | Springfield, Mo. |
| | 12 | Spokane, Wash. | | 12 | Jefferson City, Mo. |
| | 13 | Ephrata, Wash. | | 13 | St. Louis, Mo. |
| | 14 | Seattle, Wash. | | 14 | Metropolis, Ill. |
| | 15 | Tacoma, Wash. | | 15 | Bowling Green, Ky. |
| | 16 | Longview, Wash. | | 16 | New Albany, Ind. |
| | 17 | Corvallis, Ore. | | 17 | Maysville, Ky. |
| | 18 | Medford, Ore. | | 18 | Ashland, Ky. |
| | 19 | Redding, Cal. | | 19 | Charleston, W.Va. |
| | 20 | Grass Valley, Cal. | | 20 | Elkins, W.Va. |
| | 21 | Anguin, Cal. | | 21 | Harrisonburg, Va. |

67 Cities...67 Days...17 States...10144 Miles
Albert F. Schoepper, Director

*The Longwood Fire Company*

PRESENTS IN CONCERT IN ITS
12th CONSECUTIVE LONGWOOD APPEARANCE

*The*
*Presidents'*
*Own*

*Sunday, September 16, 1962*

LONGWOOD OPEN AIR THEATRE
KENNETT SQUARE, PENNSYLVANIA

LT. COL. ALBERT SCHOEPPER, *Director*

*October 22, 1962: Tension in Stockton, California*

*By mid-October, the Cuban Missile Crisis had everyone scrambling at the prospect of a nuclear holocaust. In an address to the nation, President Kennedy announced the discovery of Russian ballistic missiles being installed on the island of Cuba. We were in our holding room that had a TV set hanging from the ceiling when JFK came on the screen. We all listened and watched. Tension was in the air. The matinee was delayed one-half hour. After the concert that night, I commented to Marty Piecuch, my roommate and brilliant alto sax player, how inspired the band seemed to feel or sound playing our national anthem. I know I was. Marty replied, "Yeah, I don't think it was ever played more fervently." As irony would have it, the band had played at Castro Valley, California just a day or two earlier.*

Freddie maintained control of his newly appointed position as the Marine Band's solo cornetist. It was the best he had played since 1957. As the band entered its fifth week of tour, the pressure shot up, in no small way exacerbated by the Cuban Missile Crisis. Freddie recalls, "Everybody was wondering how long we would have to live if this thing didn't get resolved between the U.S. and the Soviet Union. It got pretty scary. We lived day to day, following the goings-on at the White House and the United Nations."

Meantime, the band performed at the four Marine Corps bases in California: Camp Pendleton, Barstow (near Twenty-nine Palms), San Diego, and El Toro—rainy, dreary, depressing—and all but deserted, while Marines, who had recently embarked in amphibious ships, were standing by off the coast of Georgia. Thirteen days later, thanks to JFK and his brother Bobby, Nikita Khrushchev blinked—or at least we believed he had. While it appeared that the United States had bested the Soviet Union in the Cuban confontation, we learned later that secret negotiations resulted in the removal of NATO missiles from Italy and Turkey in exchange for the dismantling of the Cuban missile sites. Political machinations aside, the crisis was over. We could breathe again.

Freddie:

*November 1962, one week before Thanksgiving, the tour band returns to Washington. Due to the continuous daily pressure of playing the solo chair, I have lost twelve pounds on this tour.*

*Monday morning, December 10, we go to Howard University to record for the funding of a new "cultural center for the performing arts." Each of the four service bands in Washington is to make a recording on vinyl disc to help fund the center that would someday become known as the John F. Kennedy Center for the Performing Arts.*

*After our morning arrival at the university, Schoepper tells the engineers: "There will be no stopping of the tape while we are being recorded." The Colonel does not believe in splicing.*

*He then rehearses the band in what he plans to record. We begin recording an hour later and are out of the building in less than three hours.*

## Only Used Fifty Tapes

*"The Marine Band led off the recording sessions on Monday, December 10, 1962. Its impact on Herman Diaz [producer from RCA Victor recording company] was remarkable. Earlier, he told me that he judged the military band musicians to be 'government hacks,' with only modest musical qualifications. 'Obviously', he said, 'if they had better qualifications, they wouldn't stay in military bands.' For that reason he brought 200 tapes to the recording sessions on the assumption that he would have to ask the bands to repeat parts of what they were playing in order to improve the quality of the recording and that, later, he would have to do a lot of cutting and splicing of tapes to gain from them something he could be satisfied with. While I had heard the military bands many times, and knew they were made up of excellent musicians, Diaz had made recordings of the finest musical organizations in the world. Who was I to argue with him about quality?*

*"However, soon after the Marine Band started recording, Diaz leaped off his stool in the recording room in a wild move to adjust the sound dials. After he had to do this a number of times, he exclaimed: 'These guys are fantastic, precision musicians!'*

*"Amused by his behavior, I pointed out that the military musicians play their music year in and year out, and, with good leadership, they get their performances down pat. Diaz shook his head in wonderment. I also remember that, at one point, when the U.S. Army Band was performing 'The Battle Hymn of the Republic,' Diaz' wife, who was with us in the control room, started crying. When I asked if she was all right, she replied that the music was so stirring that it brought tears to her eyes.*

*"As further proof of Diaz' dramatic change of opinion regarding the quality of the bands, he told me some days after the recording sessions that he needed only fifty of the 200 tapes he brought with him. Moreover, when he returned to New York, he gave his RCA Victor superiors a glowing report on the musicianship and snap of the bands. That judgment proved critical to me. Some weeks later, I was officially advised that RCA Victor had reversed its earlier decision against joining in the promotion and marketing of the recordings. With the center's approval, the company said it would promote and market them throughout its U.S. and foreign outlets. Obviously, I agreed. The RCA*

*Victor decision helped answer one of my nagging concerns, namely about how in the world the center could manage stocking, housing, selling, and distributing thousands of recordings."*

—Jarold A. Kieffer, former Executive Director of the National Culture Center

**The Marine Band records a vinyl disc to promote the Kennedy Center of Performing Arts. (Photo courtesy Reni News Photos.)**

## Going Down the Line

In January 1963, the full band resumed its regular duties: White House functions, patriotic openers, funerals, reading sessions, and concerts. Schoepper began something new called "Young Man's Band" in which he gave time off to his principals and soloists while taking the newer, younger, and less-seasoned players through two weeks of reading sessions. Young Man's Band gave the newbies a chance to prove their mettle, especially on the more exposed solo-part stands.

Meanwhile, Freddie remained as Chuck Erwin's assistant.

## Young Man's Band

*"Usually after the fall tour and at some time during the winter months, Colonel Schoepper would schedule special rehearsals for what was called "Young Man's Band." All the first chair players, along with other experienced players were not required to report for these rehearsals. A special*

137

*folder of music was prepared and the Colonel had various younger players take turns sitting on the first chair. This way he could see how they did as the band played through the various works he had selected.*

*"The Marine Band at this time used the Sousa band arrangement of players—the cornet section sat at the director's immediate right with the first cornets just about three feet from his right hand. This made for a rather stressful situation when we younger cornet players had to occupy those first two chairs. We knew that the Colonel had little patience with anything and wanted 'guaranteed notes.'*

*"On one occasion a cornetist who had been in another service band for ten years was placed on first chair and I was placed on second chair. The other fellow was so nervous that he was actually shaking as we took our turn at the director's right hand. Fortunately, we made it through our time of testing without any major catastrophe.*

*"Another younger player was not so fortunate. While in his first enlistment, this cornetist, in order to improve his playing, began to study with the first trumpet player in the Philadelphia Orchestra. His teacher had suggested an embouchure change and the young cornetist was in the midst of this when the Colonel placed him on the first chair during a 'Young Man's Band' rehearsal. On this particular day, this cornetist had difficulty getting all the notes to come out as they should.*

*"The Colonel was furious. He stopped the piece we were playing and told the young man, 'Pick up your instrument and get out. You don't deserve to be in the Marine Band!' Then, while we were all sitting there and you could hear a pin drop, the young man had to pack up his cornet and walk out of the hall.*

*"When he was gone, an even more stressful 'Young Man's Band' continued as others were moved to the 'hot seat.'"*

—Neil Holliker, U. S. Marine Band, cornet/trumpet, 1964–1968

*Freddie:*

*Once in a while, during a reading session, the Colonel would "go down the line." If he saw that a particular solo cornet solo passage or clarinet solo passage might be a challenge to the rest of us in the section, he'd make each player in the section play that passage one by one. Whoever "survived" without incurring a Schoepper tongue-lashing might have worn a tee-shirt that read something like, "I Survived 'Going Down The Line.'"*

*September 1963: The Colonel rehearses the tour band and I am going. This year's tour takes us through the Midwest. Jim is called upon to perform John Morrissey's "Concerto Grosso" for brass trio (Chuck Erwin and Bob Isle) on the evening program. I am performing in the sextet "Bolero" on the matinee.*

*The Marine Band packs a field house for a 1963 tour concert in Muscomb, Iowa.*

*President John F. Kennedy addresses a sea of photographers and onlookers. (Photo taken by White House photographer Cecil W. Stoughton.)*

## Performing for a Slain President

On November 22, 1963, President John Fitzgerald Kennedy was assassinated in Dallas, Texas. In mid-afternoon, while teaching trumpet at a nearby school, Freddie, along with the rest of the band, were contacted by phone to report immediately to the barracks. Meanwhile, as Lyndon B. Johnson was taking the oath of office aboard Air Force One, in the rehearsal hall, Schoepper began to take the band through the somber music it would be playing while in the funeral procession: Kenneth Alford's march, *The Vanished Army*; Joseph Pecham's *Our Fallen Heroes*, a march written especially for use as a funeral dirge; and Beethoven's *Funeral March*. Upon her arrival back in the capital that evening, Jackie Kennedy informed the Military District of Washington, D.C., that she wanted "his band"—the Marine Band—to lead the procession.

*Freddie:*

We fronted the procession, which started at the west end of the Capitol and stopped at Lee Mansion in Arlington National Cemetery, where we stood at the graveside.

We played a hymn, followed by "Taps." We stood right in front of and facing Jackie and her two children, Caroline and John-John. During the playing of "Taps," the Army Band bugler missed a note.

Sometime later, I heard someone comment to the bugler (an excellent trumpet player, by the way).

"You must feel pretty bad about missing that note in 'Taps'."

"No, I don't feel too bad about it," replied the bugler. "After all, if I hadn't missed that note, nobody would ever remember me." ❖

# Chapter 15

# "A Performance That Bankrupts the English Language"

By September 1964, the battle against the Viet Cong in Vietnam was becoming a matter of increasing concern to the country. Senator Barry Goldwater spoke of defoliating the jungles of Vietnam and standing up to the Russians. The very popular president Lyndon Baines Johnson used such loose talk to pin the "warmonger" tag on Goldwater, raising the possibility of nuclear war if the Arizona Republican were elected into the White House. The nation, apparently in no mood for a full-scale war, especially with the dreaded Russians, elected Johnson in a landslide over Goldwater in the national Presidential election.

At Eighth & I, Freddie was once again assigned to go on the annual fall tour, this time to the West Coast. There was a new tour manager in town: Robert "Bobby Goggles" Williams, small in physical stature but a competent promoter. What didn't change was the same old sixty-three-day grind. Freddie would be featured either in the *Bolero* cornet sextet by Walter Smith, or John Morrissey's *Concerto Grosso* brass trio on the matinee.

*Robert Williams, the band's tour manager.*

*Freddie:*

*January 20, 1965: Lyndon B. Johnson is sworn in as President of the United States on a very chilly and rainy day, the most miserable inauguration I have ever played!*

*Spring 1965: Recording Session, 0900*

*Schoepper wants to record Mark Hindsley's transcription of Richard Strauss's "Don Juan" tone poem, which has a running time of nearly 18 minutes. He follows his customary self-imposed rule of recording: no splicing. Into the microphone, Schoepper calls for Ritchie, the recording engineer.*

*"Ritchie?"*

*"Yes, sir. Ready."*

*The START button is pushed. The tape is rolling and the Colonel gives the downbeat. We are a quarter of the way into the piece when somebody makes a mistake. The Colonel stops the band.*

*"Ritchie?"*

*"Yes, sir."*

*"Beginning."*

*Ritchie rewinds the tape for take two. After about thirty bars, the trumpet player misses a note.*

*The Colonel stops the band.*

*"Ritchie?"*

*"Yes, sir."*

*"Beginning."*

*Ritchie rewinds the tape.*

*"Ready, sir. Take three."*

*We are halfway home, when one of the horn players misses a note. The Colonel stops.*

*"Ritchie?"*

*"Yes, sir."*

*"Beginning."*

*Ritchie rewinds the tape.*

*"Ready, sir. Take four."*

*Now we are one-third of the way through when someone else misses a note.*

*The process repeats itself as either a horn or trumpet player misses a note. After about the seventh take, I'm beginning to think we're never going to make it through this thing.*

*"Yeah, we were all sitting there wondering how long this would go on," recalled Les Hunt years later.*

*After the fifteenth take, Chuck Erwin stands up.*

*"Colonel," he speaks with respectful authority, "I think we've had enough for now. Why don't we take a lunch break and be back by one o'clock to resume?"*

*Schoepper agrees.*

*At one o'clock, we are all back in our seats. The Colonel comes through the entranceway, through the back of the percussion section and up to the front of the band. He calls up to Ritchie to begin rolling the tape. He then gives the downbeat and finally we make it all the way through the piece with nobody missing a note!*

*Sixteen "takes" were required to satisfy the Colonel. No splicing. Of course!*

## One More Time

*Following my warm-up, I take the solo chair seat, as Chuck Erwin is not here. He's either on leave; or Schoepper wanted, for some reason, only the upcoming tour band rehearsed. I'm about to find out the reason. After roll call and all matters concerning the band are dispensed by admin, Schoepper struts out, ascends the podium, and calls out, "Camille De Nardis—Universal Judgment." Something rings a bell about this piece. I don't recall ever hearing it performed. I know I've never played it.*

*"Ritchie."*

*"Yes, sir," replies Ritchie.*

*"Ready."*

*"Okay, sir." Uh-oh! We're going to record this!*

*The intensity mounts, as I am sitting only three feet from Schoepper's right hand. The tour band cornet section comprises six cornets: three on first, two on second, and one on third, with two trumpets behind us.*

*"Universal Judgment." A true test for accuracy and endurance.*

*We did it in one take. No splicing. Of course!*

*September 1965: Tour rehearsals begin with the Colonel conducting sectionals and then the entire ensemble. As in past years, we open the tour at Longwood Gardens in Kennett Square, Pennsylvania. Capt. Dale Harpham is conducting the matinee; Jimmie is performing Arthur Pryor's "Annie Laurie" on the evening show; and yours truly is playing the solo chair because The Colonel has allowed Chuck Erwin to stay home during this nine-week tour of the nation's Midwest.*

One of the longest tenured lead players in the history of the band, Chuck Erwin had played the solo cornet (first chair) since 1956 and would go on to hold it for a total of seventeen years. Dark-complected and sporting coal black hair, with dashing eyes and a square jaw, Erwin was one of the Marine Corps' poster boys. When the Corps needed a model for one of its uniform displays in a Marine Corps recruiting brochure, Erwin was the chosen one. Blessed with Hollywood looks, he was the George Clooney of his day; actually, better-looking! His personality on the surface was gentlemanly and chivalrous. He saved his less-than-pleasant side for the younger members of the band, who for whatever reason happened to be on his bad side. He could and often did impose his will on even the most recalcitrant.

During a tour in the early 1970s, a number of band members were well within earshot of certain sounds emanating from the hotel room of the first chair oboist. After each and every matinee performance, the oboist habitually marched back to his room from the bus, closed his door and began retooling his reeds.

There was nothing wrong with such a practice, especially since pros like this one considered the retooling necessary in order for the reed to respond properly at the next performance. But this ritual always took place in the middle of the afternoon, a time when some liked to nap in preparation for the evening show. Instead, they were treated to a steady diet of a the same squawking arpeggio—oboists call it "crowing"—that could be heard over and over again, the result of gouging and shaping, scraping, drying out, soaking, and aging the same cane many times in one afternoon, day after day.

After receiving complaints from one of the band members—namely, Jimmie—Schoepper called Bob on his room phone and gave him the word: "No more squawking. My men need their sleep." Now this particular oboist didn't take kindly to orders, even when they came from Schoepper, but to his credit, he complied, though not happily, adding that such preparation was necessary for good performance.

A few weeks passed, then the squawking returned. One evening just before another performance, as the band members were warming up in the hall behind stage, Erwin pulled aside the third-chair cornetist Kenny Emenheiser and, whispering in his ear, gave him some instructions. The two then walked over to a corner, stood behind a back stage pillar so they couldn't be seen, and waited for the oboist to approach. The plan worked. As he walked around the corner, out sprung Erwin and Emenheiser, their cornets blaring away in his face, the very same arpeggiated notes that had been heard *ad nauseam*. The plan worked, and those reeds were never heard from again, at least during that time of day.

## Universal Judgment

During the 1965 tour's evening performances, the Marine Band performed *Universal Judgment* every night. This proved to be an endurance challenge for the brass section.

Freddie:

As week three began, Arthur Fiedler, legendary conductor of the Boston Pops, attended a concert. The first half no sooner wound up with "Universal Judgment" than Fiedler was seen walking backstage to meet Schoepper and was heard saying, "When I get back to Boston, I don't want to hear any complaints from my brass section about endurance."

As the 1965 tour ends, I swear that after I retire, I will never again step onto a bus!

On January 1, 1966, the Marine Band played its annual "Surprise Serenade" for General Greene, the Commandant under whose command the Corps had expanded to 300,000 Marines. That July, Freddie learned that the Colonel had placed full confidence in his solo chair work by allowing Erwin off tour again. This would be a West Coast tour, with Freddie playing the solo chair again, and again performing the old chop-buster *Universal Judgment* every night for sixty-three consecutive nights.

Marine Bandsman solo cornetist.

**The caption for this 1966 promotional photo of Freddie reads, "Marine Bandsman solo cornetist." (Photo courtesy Department of Defense)**

Freddie:

*October, 1966, Las Vegas*

*Following the evening concert, we all head back to the gaming tables. I am at the blackjack table and not doing too shabbily. I'm up to $75. About 11:00 p.m., it is really crowded in the casino. I see Ed, tuba player and buddy of mine, strolling along with the Colonel behind me. I hear Ed say to the Colonel, "Freddie's a good blackjack player."*

*"He is?"*

*"Yeah," says Ed.*

*I see the two approaching. Uh-oh! Here it comes. The Colonel is going to want me to play a few hands for him!*

*Sure enough, the Colonel hands me a dollar bill and commands, "Here! Play for me!"*

*My luck is good, as I manage to build his winnings to $15. I haven't lost a hand yet.*

*"Do you want to keep playing?" I ask him.*

*"No," says the Colonel.*

*I cash in the chips and hand him the fifteen dollars. As he and Ed stroll away, I call to the Colonel and say, "Does this get me a rate?"*

*I get no answer. I have been put out with him for the past three years, because I was expecting a rate (promotion) soon after I rescued him on that 1962 tour. Because of two people playing politics, I did not get the promotion. I got screwed! I am still pissed off and have hardly practiced for the past three years because of that.*

*Next morning: Another early leave time—0600. This is a very demoralized band, as most of us have lost money at the casinos. I made out okay, walking away with $155 added to my wallet. Me, a big spender from the Eastern metropolis of Lebanon, Pennsylvania! Ha-ha!*

*The bus is very quiet as we ride through the desert on our way to Provo, Utah. After we've been on the road for six or seven weeks, we really don't much care where we are. Sometimes a stranger will ask us where we've been and/or where we're going. "I don't know where we were yesterday, where we are today, or where we will be tomorrow," one of us answers. "And furthermore, I don't give a damn!" These strangers must think we're crazy, not knowing where we were yesterday. They just don't understand when they see us pulling out our itineraries to check where we were.*

Vietnam commitments continued to escalate. Just around the time the Ninth Marine Expeditionary Brigade was putting boots to the ground at Da Nang, Freddie, Jimmie, and their bandmates were landing in two of Nevada's— and the world's—most famous neon cities.

Reno and Las Vegas are, of course, the highlights of any West Coast tour, as Freddie noted. "But after we leave Vegas, it is a deadly dull and silent five-hour ride into Utah! Everybody is depressed!"

*Freddie:*

*From here on out, it is nothing but a grind to get on the bus every morning, ride a couple hundred or more miles, get off the bus, check in at the hotel or motel, grab some lunch, get back on the bus, ride to the concert hall or gymnasium, get off the bus to play the matinee, get back on the bus, get off the bus, relax for two or three hours, get dinner, get back on the bus, ride to the concert site, get off the bus to play the concert, get back on the bus and ride back to the hotel or motel, and*

147

*finally get off the bus. Ten times on and off the bus in one day, and then the next day, it starts all over again. Same drill, same routine for sixty-three consecutive days.*

## Resurrection

In late spring, 1967, as the spring concert series resumed, Schoepper called Freddie into his office during the band's fifteen-minute rehearsal break.

"You wanted to see me, Colonel?"

"Fred," Schoepper said with a smile, "I need a good, strong cornet soloist for tour this year. How about playing *La Mandolinata* for the evening program?"

"All right, sir."

"Fine. Let's schedule you to play it sometime during the summer concerts."

"All right, Colonel."

Walking out of his office, Freddie remembered thinking, "Gee, we're going to have to start practicing again. We haven't done that in three years. I've been resurrected as a tour soloist."

Freddie:

*August 1967: My first solo performance in over two years goes well and is favorably received by the audience at the East Capitol plaza.*

*September 1967: Lieutenant Colonel Schoepper conducts sectionals and the full tour band. This year's tour will take us up through New England and as far west as Minnesota. As usual, Bill Jones will be the vocal soloist and concert moderator for both matinee and evening shows. Jimmie will be featured in a trombone quartet for the matinee and I will be the featured cornet soloist for the evening show.*

*For at least as long as I've been with the Marine Band, the soprano brass section (cornets and trumpets) play B-flat cornets and B-flat trumpets only. We never have played or used any of the higher pitched trumpets, pitched cornets, or flugelhorns, nor were alto horns used in the brass tenor section like a lot of the European bands do. Sometimes I think it would be nice to use some of these instruments; but I guess either the budget would not allow their purchase, or the directors do not see any need for them.*

Higher pitched instruments like the E-flat cornet or piccolo trumpet are played in order to more easily execute passages written in the high register, which would otherwise be more difficult and demanding to play on a regular B-flat instrument like Freddie's cornet.

*Freddie:*

*First Sunday after Labor Day 1967: We start the tour at Longwood Gardens and proceed through some of New England. As I solo every night, I am not satisfied with most of my performances, but the audiences like them.*

*September 25: This morning, Arthur Lehman, our bus commander and legendary euphonium soloist, steps on board the bus five minutes before we take off for the next town. He is carrying three or four copies of the morning's newspaper and, as I take my seat, he stops by and hands me one of them. It has a review of last night's concert. The critic praises me but criticizes the Colonel's conducting. Arthur has been collecting reviews ever since Trapp assigned him to do so; now, every time he finds one, he sees to it that I get a newspaper copy.*

## The Critics Speak

Writing for the Manchester *Guardian*, John Gruber had this to say: "Frederick [*sic*] Erdman, cornetist, provided the highlight of the evening last night, as the United States Marine Band offered the second of two concerts in Bailey Auditorium, sponsored by Manchester Community College. The personable bandsman displayed absolutely phenomenal technique, as well as impeccable tone and intonation in Bellstedt's *La Mandolinata*, a composition designed to display virtuosity, but of very limited musical value."

His review went on to report on two other featured soloists: Francis Cocuzzi, who offered a "marimbaphone" [*sic*] version of Sarasate's *Gypsy Aires*; and Bill Jones, whose powerful baritone voice "was heard in the 'Soliloquy' from *Carousel*, the Rogers and Hammerstein hit of some seasons back."

"Neither was as outstanding as Mr. Erdman," wrote Gruber. "Cocuzzi and Jones both had to cope with a heavy-handed accompaniment, while the trumpeter was on more equal terms with the background provided by Lieutenant Colonel Albert Schoepper, who directed."

Arthur Lehman would always stand near the front of the bus and read aloud such reviews to everybody. One in particular was pretty wild and drew laughs from everyone within earshot. "Presented in a solo role was cornetist Fredric Erdman," wrote Les Zachels for the *Cedar Rapids Gazette*, "who played a spectacularly smooth yet electrifying interpretation of Bellstedt's old classic for cornet, *La Mandolinata*."

Zachels added that the work was a *tour de force*, abounding in "triple tonguing and dizzy arpeggios. A member of the band since 1955, this youthful virtuoso practically melted the pistons on his instrument. In fact, his performance was one that bankrupts the English language."

Then there were these words penned by a director of bands for the Brainerd *Dispatch* in Brainerd, Minnesota. "Perhaps the highlight of the concert was the cornet soloist of the evening, Fredric Erdman. This young artist gave a dazzling rendition of the well-known *La Mandolinata*. Breathtaking technique, a lovely sound and amazing control characterized Mr. Erdman's virtuosity." The writer, D. P. Trzpuc, reported that such artistry received the biggest ovation of the evening, and rightfully deserved. ". . . Mr. Erdman's performance was the gem of the evening."

*Freddie:*

*I love football and have become an avid fan of Vince Lombardi's Green Bay Packers. We are in the middle of our tour and the Packers are in the middle of regular season play. They are going for an unprecedented third straight NFL title, but right now, they are hurting. The entire starting backfield is out with injuries including Bart Starr, their starting quarterback.*

*To say Jimmie is an avid fan of the Packers would be a huge understatement. He has had a passion for that team since the late 1940s.*

**Freddie soloing with the band on tour, 1967.**

*A visit to Packerland. Standing in front of Bart Starr's home are, left to right, Freddie, Al Johnson, Bart Starr, Jimmie, Fred Case, Ed Simmons and Roger Stoner.*

*November 1967: Tour is over. Green Bay defeats the Los Angeles Rams 28-7 for the Western Conference Championship after regaining their starting backfield and having been proclaimed by the sports writers to be "over the hill."*

*December 23, 1967: The Green Bay Packers defeat the Dallas Cowboys in what is called "The Ice Bowl" to win a third consecutive NFL title, and go on to Miami where they will play the Oakland Raiders in Super Bowl II. My year is complete.*

*New Year's Day 1968: We play the "Surprise Serenade" for the new Commandant, General Chapman. The Green Bay Packers defeat the Oakland Raiders 33-14 for their second straight Super Bowl title. Vince Lombardi retires.*

*The band's regular duties resume and Lieutenant Colonel Schoepper continues to feature Jimmie and me as two of the many soloists on the spring concert series at the Departmental Auditorium downtown and at the East Capitol plaza and on the Watergate barge during the summer.*

*The Tet Offensive begins at the end of January, continuing in various mutations until the end of that summer. The Marines win every battle in successful defense of Vietnamese citizens.*

151

*Spring/Summer 1968: Rev. Dr. Martin Luther King is murdered in Memphis, Tennessee. Powerful reactions rush across the country like fiery waves. Only two months later, Robert Kennedy is assassinated in Los Angeles. Again, the nation is stunned by the violent loss of a young, charismatic leader. The tumultuous Democratic Convention in Chicago in August marks 1968 as a cultural turning point in American history.*

*September 1968: This month opens with the usual routine, with the Lieutenant Colonel holding sectionals before rehearsing the full tour band.*

*Sunday after Labor Day: It's Longwood Gardens time again. From there, we head for the West Coast, repeating last year's tour programs. Jimmie and I are performing the same pieces: Jimmie in the trombone quartet on the matinee, me on the evening concert playing "La Mandolinata" every day and night, respectively.*

*I think I'm playing "La Mandolinata" better than I did on the 1967 tour. The opening cadenza is cleaner. I had just a little bit of trouble with that last year.*

*October 1968: The Colonel has caught somebody paying his hotel bill late!*

**The band on tour, 1967. Right to left, Col. Schoepper, Chuck Erwin, Freddie, Kenny Emenheiser.**

*As has been the Colonel's policy, hotel bills are to be paid at least one half-hour before departure time. Everybody will be on board five minutes before departure time. Anybody who is late paying his hotel bill will be "sentenced" to having to board the bus one hour before departure time.*

*The Colonel has been known to sit in the lobby as early as five or six o'clock in the morning, just waiting to pounce on a latecomer. And now, he is dressing down the poor guy in full view of the entire lobby, a very severe and audible tongue-lashing. Watching, I recall Arthur Lehman coming to my own rescue, when I came awfully close to not only failing to pay my hotel bill paid on time but also being late for the bus. If it had not been for Arthur, I might still be showing scars from Schoepper's vicious wrath!*

*We had only three or four days left on tour when, after the evening concert, John Wright and I had a few drinks while playing checkers up in my room. It was about three in the morning when we decided we'd better get some shuteye. After John left the room, I went to bed. The next thing I knew, the phone was ringing. I picked up the receiver. It's Arthur. "Freddie, are you up?" "Yeah," I answer sleepily. Suddenly, I felt a shock course through me. I knew I was in trouble—I'd overslept, and departure time was 7:00 a.m.*

*"It's twenty minutes to seven, Freddie. I've paid your hotel bill. When you come down, do not go out to the bus through the lobby. You can sneak out through the back entrance, but get on that bus now! The Colonel is chewing out six guys right here in the lobby for being late, so you don't want him to see you, okay?"*

*"Okay, Arthur. Thank you." Geez! "You can hear him all over the place," exclaims Arthur. I made it to the bus at ten minutes to seven. As far as I knew, nobody but Arthur knew I was late, and that included Colonel Albert F. Schoepper. I've always said Arthur is a great friend!* ❖

# Chapter 16

# Schoepper

*Colonel Albert F. Schoepper, 1965.*
*(Photo courtesy Department of Defense)*

We were rehearsing the *William Tell* overture. In the opening, slow section. a musical dialogue occurs between the English horn and flute. For some reason, the flutist didn't quite execute the musical passage to his liking, or Schoepper's.

Schoepper stopped the band and pointed at the troubled flutist. "What's wrong?" he asked

"I guess I'm just nervous," replied the flutist.

"Well then, just relax, godammit!. RELAX!"

The whole band broke into laughter. Schoepper laughed along. It was one of those rare moments that revealed the man's humane side.

*Freddie:*

*Playing the solo cornet chair under Lieutenant Colonel Schoepper is indeed a high-pressure job. As I play with a high degree of intensity every night, I must and do demand of myself the best of which I am capable. Anything less is not acceptable to me. The B-flat large bore cornet has been my whole life. Accuracy on every note is always my objective. It involves intense concentration. The demands I place upon myself have enabled me to survive under Schoepper's dictatorial reign.*

"Before joining the Marine Band, I had heard that the band played with amazing technical prowess. The 'Machine Band' was a common term used to describe us . . . what amazes me to this day is the way we played together as an ensemble under Colonel Schoepper. Notes were precisely the same length, trills were played as if one man was pushing the buttons and everyone else's buttons were connected together, tempo changes were made in precise unison, dynamics changed like an organist pushing a single pedal. The man was in charge!"

—John Schaefer, bass trombone

Flutist Les Hunt joined the band in the late 1960s and remembered Schoepper's unique style:

*Les:*

*"Tyrannical conductors usually come in two categories: (1) The real purists such as Arturo Toscanini, whose tantrums were born of an intense desire for perfection, and (2)*

*the calculating, dictatorial personages whose life slogans were variations on "Who can I trap today?" Fritz Reiner and George Szell were sterling examples.*

*". . . The earliest thing I remember being told upon my arrival in 'The President's Own' was, 'The Colonel runs this band with an iron fist, and henceforth, for as long as you are here, everything is 'Yes, Sir' and 'No, Sir.' Do not forget it. He has the personal ability and authority to promote you tomorrow——or never, as the case may be.' One of Colonel Schoepper's modi operandi to keep us on our toes (or to keep things stirred up) was the 'reading rehearsal.' Particularly in non-concert seasons, folders would be made up of old 'chestnuts' in order to expose newer members of the band to the repertoire. Sometimes the first-chair people were there, other times not, and a lot of times the resulting exposure was of new members under the gun. The tension would be unbelievable. The notion of 'Who can I trap today?' was in constant evidence.*

*"Sometimes players were asked to play passages individually, and the results could be anything from good to disastrous. If a player was obviously in command of the part, he was left alone, but if there were problems of any sort, he was asked to repeat the passage, perhaps several times. Some players were traumatized by this, to say the least, and it could have long-term implications.*

*"There were also times when new players were asked to prepare a solo to play with the band, and a solo folder was made up. You never really knew what to expect until you were standing there. The solo might be of your own selection or possibly of Colonel Schoepper's, and all it took for a first-time effort to really hit the skids was to have something like a tempo or other interpretive difference that you didn't expect.*

*"My own experience was like that. After many hours of preparation of a solo that he had selected, my time came to play. It wasn't long before I realized that he had some ideas of the piece that were quite different from mine, and I really started to sweat. I felt as if I had absolutely no grip over what was coming out, and it became an exercise in damage control and survival rather than any type of artistic experience.*

*"When, after what seemed an eternity, the end of the piece came, I started to let go a bit, and was entertaining thoughts of 'Okay, it's in the can, to hell with it, let's go down to the staff NCO club and have a beer or three and forget about it.' Then Colonel Schoepper looked at me and said, 'Not bad. RELAX! Let's do it again.'"*

*Jim:*

Albert F. Schoepper could be described as a martinet—tyrannical, picayune, demeaning, frightening, untiring, impatient, authoritarian, stubborn. He was the Fritz Reiner of the symphonic band world. He almost always employed the best and expected the best. He tested every nerve in your body, for he wanted to know just how much pressure you could take under the worst of playing conditions. Most of those "worst" playing conditions were his doing. This book title is not without reason and no doubt the proper description for him, regardless of how we felt about him. A quote from the "Bicentennial Collection" recording says it all, and most deservedly: The Marine Band was "at its finest under his direction."

**Les Hunt. (Photo courtesy Department of Defense)**

Traveling with Schoepper was an experience. Upon the retirement of our esteemed vocalist, William Jones, Schoepper had me assigned to the seat directly across from him and behind the driver. Not much legroom! The Colonel was interesting, well-read, a good history buff, and more than humorous! He was a New York Times reader whenever one was available, and excelled at the Times' crossword puzzles. He would begin doing them as we left each town, and it was rare when he didn't finish by arrival at our destination. Schoepper was not an "open book," but each musician had to be incredibly unaware if he didn't know where he stood with the man. I always found him to be true to his word, good or bad. He held many of his intimate feelings about his personal life and immediate family close to the chest. If there was any excitement that would reveal an aspect of his home life, it was when he described in glowing terms his two grandsons.

Albert Schoepper gave me my career, and I am forever indebted to the man. Three months prior to an audition for "The President's Own," I was a seventeen-year-old who

*had just been hired as an apprentice accountant to begin work upon graduation from high
school. But, I never arrived for that employment. Semper Fi!*

## Bigger than Life

Of all the conductors of the premier Washington, D.C. service bands, Albert
Schoepper was to the Marine Band what Reiner was to the Chicago Symphony
Orchestra, or Toscanini to the NBC Symphony Orchestra—a mercurial dicta-
tor with a razor-edge tongue whose mannerisms and manner of rule stayed,
roamed, and dominated inside the heads of his players long after a rehearsal or
performance had ended. Blessed with cunning, a quick wit, and stature bigger
than life, Schoepper could deliver his barbs like "smart bombs" that traveled
with precision to the heart of the matter, verbal darts efficiently delivered, words
that could launch from the podium and destroy a career in seconds. Even in
"ordinary" conversation, his sentences could move along like a slithering king
cobra, threatening to sting his victim any second, and with lethal-like injection.
His voice had a rich but lean quality. Coated with an edge of loftiness, supe-
riority, and aristocratic bearing, it had a certain casualness of tone, a dead-on-
the-mark fluidity. As Jim Erdman and John Schaefer have observed, such lethal
fluidity left the listener with no doubt as to who was in charge.

Standing tall and fully erect while flaunting a Napoleonic bearing, he per-
sonified the arrogance of power. When he spoke, his delivery was smooth as
black ice.

On mornings when the 8:45 a.m. rehearsal was about to begin, "The Sultan
of Musical Swat" would enter from the back door of the John Philip Sousa
Band Hall. The banter circulating throughout the band as it was warming up
would abruptly stop. Silence would accompany his every stride to the podium,
purposeful, imperial. Once there and amid the generally fearful stillness, he'd
put on his reading glasses, announce the composer of the selection (instead of
the title) and survey the band with eyebrows raised, engaging each player's eye,
as if to say, "I expect nothing less from you than *guaranteed notes.*"

The baton would then drop and the music begin. From that point, the
Marine Band became Schoepper's band, the former young violinist now exud-
ing a Patton-like military bearing with precision conducting, overshadowed by
the harsh, unrelenting demands for perfection, "even beyond," noted Mary Jo
Tarrants, a close friend of Freddie Erdman during the Schoepper days (and
today his wife).

In today's military, a watch-phrase is "rigid flexibility." Schoepper was all rigidity. There was nothing flexible about his insistence on excellence, an attribute to those who revered him and seismic defect to those who deplored him. "He was a tyrant of towering proportions," remembers Tarrants. "The memories of his excellence and abuses, all at the same time, are rekindled from generation to generation." He had little-to-no tolerance for the smallest mistakes, even during rehearsal, always refusing to settle for anything less than the sound of perfection and excellence he heard in his head. To Albert Schoepper, mediocrity could be worse than cancer, and he despised it to no end, be it rehearsal or recording session, to say nothing about performances.

*Jim:*

*From young to old, the band had a wide range of ages during Colonel Schoepper's reign. Few if any of us knew anything of his past. Much of the complexity behind the façade of an iron-fisted ruler had to do with his childhood. His father died after being having been hit by a cab. As if that wasn't enough, he arrived home from school one day to discover his mother dead, sitting on a porch chair. He shared both of those losses with me during his final tour in 1971 while we were playing in Rochester; our travel route had taken us directly by the cemetery where both parents were buried. His voice was quiet, calm, and thoughtful, compared with his usual abruptness, as he told me, "I will not be coming this way again."*

## An Impressive Pedigree

"The Colonel was born in Rochester, New York, in 1913," cites an old press release, "and at the age of seven began his musical training under the guidance of violinist Alfred Perrot."[1] After graduating from high school, Schoepper entered the Eastman School of Music to further his studies with the late Gustav Tinlot. A likeable Frenchman, Tinlot was concertmaster for the Symphony Society in Manhattan, led for a brief period by guest and legendary conductor Bruno Walter. Under Walter's baton, Tinlot performed Rimsky-Korsakov's *Fantasy on Russian Themes*. Tinlot also played with the French American Quartet, a string foursome of some renown throughout New York City, and was a featured artist on a 1919 Disque Gramophone recording of Svendsen's *Romance en Sol* and Grieg's *Chanson du Solveig* from the *Peer Gynt* Suite. Schoepper also studied with

---

1    "Meet the Artists, Program, The John F. Kennedy Center for the Performing Arts presents the United States Marine Band, 11/25/71, p. B.

Andre Polah, who in turn studied with Arthur Nikisch, a lineage that might be more revealing about Schoepper's conducting prowess and his ability to extract the most from his players.

*Albert Schoepper, U.S. Marine Band, 1938. (Photo courtesy Department of Defense)*

The Hungarian-born Nikisch performed mainly in Germany but was also conductor of the Boston Symphony Orchestra from 1889–93, and later the Berlin Philharmonic Orchestra until his death in 1922. Nikisch, a leading interpreter of the music of Bruckner, Tchaikovsky, Beethoven, and Liszt, gave the premiere of Bruckner's Seventh Symphony in 1884. He is credited for having taken the London Symphony Orchestra to the United States in 1912, a first for a European orchestra.[2] Nikisch gets credit for another pioneering venture, that of conducting the Berlin Philharmonic in a complete recording of Beethoven's *Fifth Symphony*. It marked the first time that a commercial recording had ever been made of a complete symphony.

Worth noting are some similarities between Schoepper and the one-generation-removed Nikisch. Both were accomplished violinists. Nikisch played in the orchestra at Bayreuth when Richard Wagner conducted *Beethoven's Ninth* for the laying of the foundation stone of the Festspielhaus. Schoepper played in the Marine Band orchestra, performed as a violin soloist at the Pan American Union, and frequently soloed on network radio programs and in concert performances. He performed with the Marine Chamber Orchestra as first chair violinist before many foreign heads of state.[3]

Nikisch could mesmerize his musicians, projecting a personality of warmth and charm. Fritz Busch, considered one of the twentieth century's great

2    "Arthur Nikisch," Answers.com, www.answers.com/topic/arthur_nikisch
3    "Meet the Artists, Program, The John F. Kennedy Center for the Performing Arts presents the United States Marine Band.

conductors,[4] was a member of the Concerts Colonne Orchestra in Paris that Nikisch guest-conducted. He was obviously impressed with Nikisch's charisma. Busch writes that as he entered, Nikisch smiled at the horns and winds "with such charm, that when he stepped up . . . the whole orchestra was already on its feet and had broken out into enthusiastic applause . . . the orchestra would have died for Nikisch."[5]

Schoepper could also mesmerize his musicians, but that is where the similarity ends. Schoepper projected intimidation. Plus, it is impossible to imagine anyone "dying" for Schoepper simply because they loved him. Because, of course, they didn't.

In terms of efficiency, his beat was precise and authoritative, even though his downbeat was ahead of the band's response by nearly a half beat, meaning that the band would only respond to the downbeat after the baton would reach the middle of the following upbeat. (This also was known as The German Beat.) This was especially true on slow beats such as would occur in a slow movement. It may have been confusing at first to any newcomer who had never played under his direction before. All one had to do was follow the band, however, and in no time it would be understood exactly where his downbeat landed, or rather, "occurred." The band's precision never suffered on account of its delayed response; somehow, it always hit the first note with unquestioned uniformity of attack, as if it were directed by God Himself.

---

4    "Fritz Busch," Maestro Marucie Abravenel, web site, www.maurice-abravenel.com_Busch_english.html

5    "Arthur Nikisch," Answers.com, www.answers.com/topic/arthur_nikisch. During a visit to Leipzig where Nikisch was conducting the Leipzig Opera in productions of such works as *Die Walküre* and *Tannhäuser*, Tchaikovsky observed Nikisch in conducting action and wrote home, saying, "[O]ne only gains a true idea of the perfection to which an orchestra can attain under a talented conductor when one hears the difficult and complicated scores of Wagner played under the direction of so wonderful a master as Herr Nikisch."

*A 1958 publicity photo of Albert Schoepper. (Photo courtesy Department of Defense)*

One of the very first pieces of music I ever played under Colonel Schoepper's baton was Aaron Copland's *El Salon Mexico*. When I saw all the meter changes, I exclaimed, "Oh my God! What's this?" Jim Underwood and I were sharing the second cornet stand that morning. Jim, who went on to play principal trumpet with the Columbus Symphony until his untimely death from salivary gland cancer in July of 2006, leaned over and whispered in my ear, "Tim, just relax and play with me. I'll get you there." I listened to Jim, played as softly as I could, and managed to escape Schoepper's wrath, at least for that morning's rehearsal.

## The Schoepper Sound

From 1955 until his retirement in 1972, the Marine Band sound was Schoepper's sound, forged from intimidation, sheer will, and unrelenting determination on the part of both musicians and leader. One did not have to be an audiophile or have a discriminating ear to appreciate the Marine Band's organ-like, operatic sound. A Schoepper-led band had one sound; the same band led by someone else (usually an assistant director or guest conductor) had another, and always less in terms of tightness, intensity, and passion. Schoepper had given the band

163

its precise, virtuosic, symphony-sound identity. As soon as he left the podium for someone else to rehearse, that same identity was lost, replaced by a thicker, less disciplined sound.

Les Hunt describes the psychological difference.

*Les*:

> *"There were occasional instances where one of the assistant directors would have a reading folder and the rehearsals would have an atmosphere that was totally different.*
>
> *"One morning, assistant director Jack Kline was on the podium and we were quite 'at ease.' The usual tension was far away and we were making the best of spending the morning rather routinely going through some repertoire.*
>
> *"Then, suddenly, this unmistakable voice came from the back of the hall: 'Jack, go back to letter F and do that again.' We had no idea the Colonel was even on the premises, much less in the room! You could feel the sudden change in the air and the rush of adrenalin. It was a topic of discussion later in the locker area how the mere presence of one person in the room could have such an effect."*

## A Matter of Survival

In addition to being the Marine Band's twenty-second leader and director, Schoepper was also recognized as "supervisor" of all Marine Corps base bands. Few if any of us in the Marine Band really knew what that position meant. Schoepper a "supervisor?" That would be like calling Idi Amin a "manager." All we cared about was surviving another rehearsal, another concert, another tour. Most of us seemed to appreciate his wit, as long as it was directed toward someone else and not one of us.

Mood swings were predictable. Everyone expected them from "the old man." The problem was, you didn't always know which way a mood would swing. In nanoseconds, he could go from a smile to a glare and a grunt. For some, it was better to know he was already in a foul mood than to witness his bright side and be on edge, wondering when everything would transform into dark shadows.

## No Way to Be Fully Prepared

*John Schaefer:*

> *"I think they like to make sure that every new man's first job was a Schoepper concert—all part of the attitude adjustment. Bear in mind that I had come from the University*

*of Michigan and been in William D. Revelli's band for four years. WDR was no soft touch, to say the least. Fear of the old man on the podium was well ingrained.*

*"I had heard some Schoepper stories, but there was no way to be fully prepared.*

*"Muster was called at 0845 and, during the reading of daily assignments, a hush fell over the room. The door of the band shell had opened and in strode a very pompous man with a baton under his left arm and a small stack of scores in his right hand. He sported a smirk on his face as he glanced from side to side, as if looking for prey. Al Johnson nudged me and with a head nod indicated without words that I should be on guard. The reading of assignments was quickly and nervously completed; and the admin staff scurried off like rats from a sinking ship, disappearing through the nearest hatch.*

*"Colonel Schoepper laid his scores on the conductor's stand and he called out the first selection. I was expecting him to open his score—which never happened. Why he brought his scores is beyond me. I soon found that he rarely opened them, preferring instead to be on the lookout for a victim.*

*"Ffwitt!*

*"Down came the baton almost before the words of his announcement had finished echoing through the band hall. I scrambled to get my horn up with my left hand and open the music with my right.*

*"Before the first note finished resounding, ffwitt! A cut-off.*

*"The Colonel was now chewing out some new man near the front of the band for not being prepared for a downbeat. I had dodged a bullet. Being in the back of the band has some advantages. June, it seems, was one of Schoepper's favorite times of the year—fresh new blood in the band, easy pickings. The old guys couldn't lie back, though. There was plenty to go around. Schoepper could quickly identify weakness and seized every opportunity."*

## Gridiron, Alfalfa, and Carabao

Though his humor frequently surfaced at the expense of his players, he could and often did see other funny parts of life. His quick wit may have been honed in part over the years through all the hours he spent as the *music director* for three distinct "dinners" held annually from January to March, in the posh quarters of Washington's Shoreham, Willard, and other downtown hotels. Known as the Gridiron Club, Alfalfa Club, and Military Order of the Carabao, these elitist organizations counted as members those belonging to the inner circles of Washington, D.C. Formed to meet once a year over food, drink, cigars, and banter, their mission was primal and playful, a venue for the political and military establishment to revel and let its proverbial hair down. Such gatherings gave the Washington elite a chance to let its hair down in self-deprecating style and tone, taking and throwing verbal slings and arrows at each other. Clubs like the Gridiron, Alfalfa, and Carabao also provided longtime political foes with a unique and rare opportunity to enjoy a certain chumminess with one another, if only for the evening's duration. Up until the Ford presidency, these clubs were male-only.

Schoepper was always in heady company around this time of year, especially when so much of his time was being spent in an organization as dark-humored as the Gridiron Club. Its membership today is about sixty-five and includes those from major newspapers, news services, news magazines and broadcast networks. Known as the city's "oldest and most prestigious journalistic organization, going back to the days of Benjamin Harrison," the Gridiron Club has entertained presidents as well as politicians, generals, diplomats, and artists. The club got its name from a cooking implement used for grilling, and spoofing and roasting one another were seemingly good reasons for establishing the Gridiron over 120 years ago.

Every spring, those in the journalism profession and their guests would gather for an evening of food and alcohol and cigars while trading potshots with one another. The affair was underscored by an appearance by the President of the United States. Since its founding in 1885, presidents have attended Gridirons, the one exception being Grover Cleveland, who was "openly hostile to the press." Wrote Henry Graff in his *History of the Presidency*, "Cleveland remains the only president who refused to attend the annual dinner of the Gridiron Club, the insider association of Washington journalists founded in 1885, where the president and the press, attired in white tie and tails 'singe but do not burn' each other with more or less good-natured sallies."[6]

Walking into the room to the strains of "Hail to the Chief" played by the Marine Band, the President would then go on to enjoy his "fifteen minutes" of comedic fame. "Speechifying" was the order of the day, and no Gridiron soiree would be complete without frank and off-the-record remarks by the President, along with more laughable nonsense from each political party's chosen representatives. Presidential aspirants had their chance at some short-lived stand-up comedy as well. A one-liner in 1958 from a certain presidential aspirant is memorable. "I have just received the following wire," said then-Senator John Kennedy, "from my generous daddy: 'Dear Jack—Don't

6      Graff, Henry, A History of the Presidency, http://www.presidentprofiles.com/General-Information/A-History-of-the-Presidency.html

buy a single vote more than is necessary—I'll be damned if I'm going to pay for a landslide.'" [7]

*Ladies man? Left photo, Colonel Schoepper escorting First Lady Jacqueline Kennedy during a gala event in Washington, D.C.; right, dancing with one of President Lyndon Johnson's daughters.*
*(Photos courtesy Department of Defense)*

As musical director, Schoepper's Gridiron lineage can be traced back to the club's first musical director, John Philip Sousa, who wrote a march, titled appropriately enough, "The Gridiron Club," which has been played at each banquet by the Marine Band. Schoepper's band was a traditional mainstay. Wearing a broad, self-satisfied smile as the band came onstage to perform, he would direct the band through "The Gridiron Club," beaming with pride as he showed off his musical Crown Jewels before the evening's prestigious gathering of journalism's best and brightest.

Every Gridiron Club night was capped off with self-skewering skits, to the accompaniment of the Marine Band Orchestra and howling laughter. Amid the countless jokes and clunkers, the alcohol flowed and the smoke thickened. The skit, entirely satirical and seemingly cathartic, especially when participation

7    Address by Senator Kennedy before the Gridiron Club, Washington, D.C., March 15, 1958, from the John F. Kennedy Presidential Library and Museum, www.jfklibrary.org/

167

included members of both parties, was always good for provoking countless eruptions of room-filling laughter. The success of the night's merriment largely depended on Schoepper's ability and commitment to the music, and that it fit the skit's lampooning objectives.

Despite his close ties with the Gridiron Club, Schoepper never used the press to his advantage or that of the band in promoting the Marine Band as one of the world's first and foremost symphonic concert bands. That effort would come years later, under the direction of one of his later successors, John R. Bourgeois. Press-savvy and full of desire to have the band known far and wide, Bourgeois promoted the band like no leader had since Sousa.

Similar to Gridiron was the Alfalfa Club. Like Gridiron, Alfalfa staged an annual dinner each year. Alfalfa, however, closed itself off to the press. According to its web site, Alfalfa was founded in 1913, an exclusive Washington, D.C. club for the rich and powerful. "Its sole purpose," said an Alfalfa press release, "was to hold an annual banquet each January to honor the birthday of General Robert E. Lee. There are approximately 200 members, each eligible to bring up to two guests to the $200-a-plate diner. The club always serves filet mignon and lobster."

The *Village Voice* once had this to say about another elitist club called The Carabao. "This Saturday, more than a thousand of America's top military and government leaders and their guests are scheduled to gather at the Omni Shoreham Hotel in Washington, D.C., for a secretive tribal rite called the 103rd Annual Wallow of the Military Order of the Carabao. And they won't be singing *Kumbaya*.

... "One thing that fires up the bulls never changes: the bellowing of the Carabao anthem, *The Soldier's Song*. At the 2002 Wallow, the room was already thick with smoke—every place setting had been adorned with (forget that embargo) an authentic Cuban cigar—when a voice said, 'Gentlemen, please turn to your songbooks,' and the U.S. Marine Band, seated to the side, struck up a tune."[8]

The Military Order of the Carabao was founded in 1900 to counter and satirize the very pompous Order of the Dragon ... this idea for a lampoon was conceived by several Army officers one night at the Army-Navy Club in Manila during the Philippine Insurrection ... While the original spoof was real enough,

8    "The Empire Strikes Back. The Tribal Rites of America's Military Leaders: No wonder they're bullish on war" Urbina, Ian, The Village Voice, Jan. 29-Feb. 4, 2003.

the Carabao order came to epitomize the camaraderie that grows among members of the armed forces..."

If any commonality existed among all three clubs, it was that their members were male (with the exception of legendary journalist and White House gadfly Helen Thomas—she was a Gridiron Club member, and even its president), and they depended on Albert Schoepper to provide the music and supervise the comedic skits.

The Marine Band always appeared at each of these dinners, marching in ranks to center stage in front of the gathering and playing two or three selections, then marching back out. It's possible that Schoepper was one of a select few who were privy to the goings-on at all three clubs. In terms of a White House "chief musician," Schoepper was it. He either performed or conducted before Presidents Roosevelt, Truman, Eisenhower, Kennedy, Johnson and Nixon. Many in the Marine Band did not even know Schoepper was a music adviser to the White House.

He was not immune to criticism from high places. *The Washington Post* reported that Schoepper was criticized for dismissing all but four of a number of Marine Band orchestra musicians, preferring to use the small combo for President Lyndon Johnson's dancing entertainment. A *Post* writer noted a concern expressed by those "behind the scenes" that the ensemble was too small. More discord was struck when, on an earlier occasion, rain began to fall during an outside White House reception that was being serenaded by the Marine Band. Everybody retreated inside except for the band, which packed up its instruments and boarded the bus back to barracks. Johnson, unaware that the ensemble had disbanded, wanted the music to resume and ordered, "Strike up the band!" Not a note was to be heard.

Schoepper's celebrity traveled beyond 1600 Pennsylvania Avenue and outside the confines of world-class papers like *The Washington Post*. On Episode Number 663 of the popular television game show "What's My Line," he appeared alongside three other service band conductors: Lieutenant Colonel Hugh Curry (Army Band), Lieutenant Anthony Mitchell (Navy Band) and Colonel George Howard (Air Force Band). The names of the four guests were pre-signed on the blackboard.

Then the leaders entered the stage and placed check marks next to their names. All four wore their uniforms, so the panelists were blindfolded. The episode included comedian Joey Bishop as panelist and Hollywood celebrity Peter Lawford as the show's "mystery guest."[9]

### Freddie:

October 1968, Grand Rapids, Michigan: We have a packed house for tonight's concert in this huge convention hall. Looks like it seats about 3,000. Following our customary fanfare, Bill Jones as usual greets the audience and introduces Colonel Schoepper. The audience applauds. The Colonel struts up to the podium. He then hitches up his belt, using his arm with a motion that is misleading. If one catches it out of the corner of his eye, he might mistakenly believe it is the preparatory beat for the pickup notes which lead into the first bar of the "National Anthem," when in fact it is not.

And it happens! I hear a note coming from a cornet player behind me when nobody else has played yet! He has played one beat too soon. A very noticeable blunder indeed! At that moment, I recall getting suckered into the same situation six years ago on the infamous "musical chairs" tour of 1962. It happened one week after the Colonel put me up on first chair, solo cornet. He never said a word about it to me, probably because I rescued him from a possible breakdown in the cornet section.

As the first half of the program is progressing, we can see smoke coming fom the podium. While conducting (from memory, by the way), he is continuously looking beyond Chuck and me to the cornets behind us with, literally, tongue in cheek. This is known among band members as a "whammy." I can see him smoldering. His frustration is that he knows the culprit is either one of the second or third cornets. He just doesn't know which one. This is one of those rare occasions when I can read his mind: "I'll get him," he's thinking. "Goddamn it! Who is it!?"

The first half ends. Schoepper calls for the cornet section to report to a huge reception room in the backstage area. So, we walk in order of our seating arrangement: Chuck leads the way with the rest of us following behind.

We come to a discreet spot in the room and line up as follows: Chuck is to my left, Charlie Kautz is on my right (solo cornets and first cornet, respectively), followed by Jimmy Taylor, Joe Rasmussen, and last but not least, Ritchie Clendenin. After positioning ourselves in a relaxed at-ease stance, we notice that the reception committee or sponsors are setting up doughnuts and coffee. A moment later, Schoepper struts in with his baton.

---

9    CNET Networks Entertainment, TV.com, http://www.tv.com/whats-my-line/show/5501/episode_guide.html&season+14

*The people preparing this long table across the room, seeing him strutting towards us, scatter like a flock of birds and completely evacuate the room.*

*Schoepper is furious! Our lineup is curved to the right, so Ritchie Clendenin, being the last man in the lineup, is in full view of the Colonel. The Colonel stops at Chuck's oblique left, standing at attention and slapping his right leg continuously with his baton. "All right, who did it?!" he demands forcefully.*

*Looks at Chuck. "Erwin?"*

*"No, sir," answers Chuck.*

*Looks at me. "Erdman?"*

*"No, sir," I answer.*

*"Kautz?"*

*"Not I, sir."*

*"Taylor?"*

*"No, sir."*

*Schoepper is getting more agitated.*

*"Rasmussen?"*

*"No, sir."*

*Schoepper casts an evil eye at Ritchie, the last man in the lineup.*

*"Clendenin." (Was that a question or an answer?)*

*Ritchie is a very pleasant, casual sort of guy, very tall, lanky, and one hell of a trumpet player. With a mild smirk, Ritchie says, "Yes, sir."*

*"Well, why didn't you say so in the first place!!!" The Colonel is almost yelling.*

*Ritchie doesn't answer. He just stands there with that usual cool, relaxed stance of his and keeps looking at the Colonel, and the Colonel just can't stand it.*

*"You're a liar!" He's shouting. "That's what you are. A liar! That's all! Dismissed!"*

*As we make our way back, the Colonel remains behind Ritchie. Pointing his baton to the top of Ritchie's head of red hair, he says disgustedly, "And your hair! It looks like wires!"*

*Months before, after watching Clendenin, one of his best trumpet players, march on the parade deck, his shoulders drooped forward, Schoepper quipped, "Clendenin. Looks like a human question mark."*

*Week before Thanksgiving, 1968.*

*Nixon defeats Humphrey two weeks earlier.*
*Tour has ended. Ritchie Clendenin has made it home alive.*

For all his bluster, however, Schoepper did have an Achilles heel. Les Hunt found it.

*Les:*

*"During the yearly grind known as tour, mental and physical capacities were stretched to the limit. Further, there was only one concert folder for each venue, matinee and evening. This had two disadvantages,"* Les remembers. *"First, performances could become stale and wooden at times. Second, some pieces that worked fine in a concert hall might not sound so good in a gymnasium—and vice versa. The advantages were that after a few days you could just about play the concert without opening the folder and the ensemble qualities locked in very tightly—which, actually, could be a disadvantage at times. With the ensemble becoming that polished, the least variation could cause major issues with one person in particular. When there was a discrepancy in a performance, Colonel Schoepper would deal with it at his earliest opportunity, usually with disproportionate severity.*

*"On Schoepper's last tour in 1971, we played in Duluth, Minnesota, around the midpoint of the tour. The concert hall was the municipal auditorium in the downtown area near the waterfront and it was a 'walk day;' we stayed in a very nice hotel two blocks away . . . we welcomed days such as this, as we could be a little more relaxed about the schedule.*

*"The evening started out with promise; we found out there was wine and cheese set out for us in the backstage area for later and we kicked off the concert with the W. Paris Chambers march 'Chicago Tribune.' At the end of the march, one of the cornet players routinely put the first valve down and aimed for the high concert A-flat for the 'stinger.' And missed. Spectacularly.*

*"The displeasure on the Colonel's face was an easy read, but that one thing, in and of itself, was not the cause for a big blow-up. Things started to deteriorate in the next piece. There were some cameo solo passages among several of the instruments, including the flute, who was yours truly. The ensemble became, for reasons unknown, a little out of convergence, and the list of scores to settle began to add up.*

*"A couple more such things took place before intermission and we knew he would be loaded for bear. We played 'The Stars and Stripes Forever' for an encore at the end of the first half and you got the feeling that everyone was trying to figure out where he was going to be during intermission so he could be somewhere else. He took his bows and walked off stage right. The rest of the band walked off stage left.*

*"And I ran right into him. He saw me first and I subtly tried to turn and be invisible. To no avail. 'Hunt, goddammit, you watch me in the overture, goddammit, you're not the conductor, goddammit!!!'*

*"My first feeling was, okay, just stand there for a moment and take it then move on, but toward the end of the diatribe, I began to sense how totally irrational this scene was and started to crack up. I was certainly not prepared for what I then saw: He turned pale, his jaw dropped, and he walked away. Needless to say, I realized immediately that that was not the thing to do and I spent a lot of time thinking about whether in those few seconds I had just thrown my career down the river. It ultimately dawned on me, though, that I had found an Achilles heel: Apparently he was deathly afraid of someone laughing at him. I never heard about it again."*

*Whether anyone else ever discovered Schoepper's vulnerable spot, no one knows.* ❖

# Chapter 17

# Miracles — Major and Minor

**M**en on the Moon . . . and "Seventy-Six Trombones"

On January 20, 1969, the Marine Band played the inaugural ceremony and parade for President Richard M. Nixon.

On July 20, 1969, literally billions of people all over the world stopped what they were doing to watch three U.S. astronauts, Neil Armstrong, Mike Collins, and Edwin "Buzz" Aldrin, land on the moon. After a successful mission and a safe return to earth, celebrations, parades, and appearances were planned across the United States to honor the three men and their momentous achievement.

Of course, the Marine Band was part of the festivities. Flutist Les Hunt recounts his memories of the astronauts' first public appearance after emerging from quarantine—a state dinner held, not at the White House, but at the Century Plaza Hotel near Beverly Hills, California.

*Les*:

*"We flew there a few days in advance (in mid-August) aboard an Air Force C-141 and set up camp at a small military base near Long Beach. Each day before the event, we would go over to the hotel, rehearse a few things . . . and mostly wait around in classic military fashion while others worked things out. Finally, the evening came . . . We anticipated it not being much different from other White House dinners—at least in terms of what we*

had to do—but the sheer scale of it all was huge. And for one of the very few times in my experiences with presidential functions, the president was not the center of attention!

"When at last it was time for the astronauts to make their appearance, the response from the crowd was enormous. They came in from behind the main curtain individually and when Neil Armstrong, the first person to set foot on the moon, stepped into the spotlight . . . the standing ovation went on for several minutes. From our vantage point, one of the exciting things to do was see just who was there. Everyone but those at the head table entered through one of the big double doors right behind us. As we were able, we would look up every once in a while and keep mental score. Once I glanced up and realized that Bob Hope was walking right behind me. He nodded to me with a smile.

"This went on for the better part of an hour when something happened that made the evening uniquely special for me. We were in the middle of one of our pop music tunes when I heard our senior assistant director, Major Dale Harpham, yell out, 'Well, hello, Meredith!'

"I thought, 'You're kidding!' Sure enough, I turned around just in time to see Meredith Willson yell back, 'Hey, where's your flute?'

"So I got up, we introduced ourselves, he sat down in my chair (!), grabbed my flute, and asked, 'Okay, what's up?'

"Major Harpham called up 'Blue Tango' by Leroy Anderson and Meredith had a great time showing off while I made small talk with Mrs. Willson.

"Of course everyone remembers Meredith Willson for the great musical 'The Music Man' that included such hits as 'Seventy-Six Trombones' and 'Marian the Librarian.' He followed that a few years later with 'The Unsinkable Molly Brown.' Very few know that he played flute and piccolo in Sousa's Band in the early 1920s and in the New York Philharmonic under Arturo Toscanini later in the same decade."

*Freddie:*

*September 1969*

Colonel Schoepper holds sectionals and full tour band rehearsals as usual for the upcoming New England and upper Midwest tour. On very few occasions, we have a date we call a "walk day," meaning that the concert site is within walking distance. There are no buses provided for the concerts that day. Any given tour usually has only three or four walk days. Without those, we're talking about alighting to and from a bus 630 times within a nine-week period. The average nine-to-five worker who takes public transportation via bus, boards and disembarks from a bus in a nine-week period (with weekends off) 196 times.

*Sunday after Labor Day*

As always, Longwood Gardens is our first date on tour. Jimmie plays "Morceau Symphonique" on the evening concert every night. Every night I play "Carnival of Venice," this one a new arrangement by our in-house arranger, Tom Knox. It has the same variations, but with a different opener and interludes. In our second week on the road, I feel no longer comfortable with the cornet I have been playing for the past fifteen years. I had my Vincent Bach large-bore B-flat cornet refurbished two weeks before tour, and it just doesn't feel like the same horn anymore. The resistance seems to have changed. I tell John Wright, who is in the section on the road with us, about this. John offers to let me try his, which is also a Bach large-bore cornet. Before the evening show, J and I trade horns and I stay behind and practice with J's horn at the school. Man, do I like this horn! As the evening concert approaches, John kindly suggests I continue to use his horn for the rest of tour, since I have to solo every night. When we get back to Washington, we'll have the horns re-assigned. I am very grateful to John and shall always be highly appreciative of his very kind offer.

## More Tour Reviews

After our concerts in Providence, Rhode Island, on September 26, 1969, Ruth Tripp of *The Providence Journal* enthused: ". . .The musicians in dress uniforms made a splendid appearance. The program was excellent both in the quality of performance and in the selection of music. Skillful arrangements of symphonic works made the lack of strings almost unnoticed. . . .

"Soloists of a high order added variety to the program. James Erdman played a trombone solo, 'Morceau Symphonique' by Alexandre Guilmant, with beautiful tone and an excellent display of technique. His encore, 'By the Time I Get to Phoenix,' fitted into the program smoothly. His brother Fredric Erdman played a cornet solo, the old favorite, 'Carnival of Venice.' This was a technical display which will not be matched in a long time. I have heard the famous trumpet player Del Staigers play this number many times and have held to his performance as a model. This performance by Fredric Erdman exceeded it in skillful technique. The lovely tones of the cornet were displayed with the encore, 'Windmills of Your Mind.' Here the breath control was phenomenal.

"The finale was a medley of all the songs of the armed forces. . . There is nothing like a good band concert and the United States Marine Band certainly knows how to play one."

October 1969: Jimmie, having been a passionate Green Bay Packer fan since the late 1940s, has made contact with the team's star quarterback Bart Starr via letter on one or two occasions. As we are headed to play in Green Bay, Wisconsin, Jimmie, the diplomat that he is, arranges with Bart and his wife Cherry to let us (Jim, three others, and me) visit him *at his house in Du Pere, just outside Green Bay. Bart kindly gives us forty-five minutes of his time during our very interesting and exciting visit. Thanks to Jimmie, this day was, by far, the biggest day of the tour—no, correction—the biggest day of the year for the five of us.*

*January through April 1970: Bill Jones retires. Michael Ryan from the Army Chorus is our new baritone vocalist and concert moderator.*

Bill Jones' retirement marked the end of an era featuring one of the world's great operatic baritones. One of my fond memories attending Marine Band concerts as a boy was Bill's funny renditions of Mussorgsky's *The Flea*, as well as the operatic aria to Rossini's *Barber of Seville*. After Bill retired, he went to work as an insurance salesman for Metropolitan Life Insurance Company. He died soon after of cancer.

*Freddie:*

*February 1970: Roll call is at 8:45 a.m. Entering the band hall, I notice that a number of recording microphones are in place. Why are they here?*

*After getting seated, I look inside the folio to see what's in store for us with the Colonel this morning. Leafing through twenty-five or thirty pieces, I come across a composition that is in manuscript. I certainly have heard it before—the Bach Toccata and Fugue in D Minor—but never saw a transcription of it for band. I notice that Louis Saverino wrote the transcription. (In addition to being a composer and arranger, Louis was a phenomenal tubist who played four other instruments in the Marine Band.)*

*I look it over, not practicing it or thinking about it, just checking all the notes, then put it aside and warm up. Immediately after roll call and departure of the drum major, the Colonel struts through the band, ascends the podium, places his scores on the conductor's stand, and calls out, " 'Saverino! Toccata and Fugue.'"*

*He then looks down on his right at Chuck and me and chuckles. I can see he's excited about doing this piece. I was actually expecting him to rehearse it—"Okay," I'm thinking. We get up our parts.*

*The Colonel calls up to Ross Ritchie, the recording engineer.*

*"Ritchie?"*

*"Yes, sir."*

*"Ready."*

*"Yes, sir."*

*Oh boy! This is a surprise to all of us, since none of us had known he wanted to record this! We haven't even read this thing down.*

*In typical recording sessions, under the best of conductors, a piece as simple as the Star Spangled Banner can be rehearsed and rehearsed, then rehearsed some more, until it's completely sterilized! Then, and only then, will the conductor feel confident in recording it. On the other hand, a work as complex and nuanced as Bach's "Toccata and Fugue in D Minor" can require not just hours, but days of rehearsal on end. Even then, there's no assurance that everyone from the conductor on down will feel ready to record.*

*But, with the Colonel, nothing is ever typical, and certainly never over-rehearsed.*

*The stage was set, ready or not. We were going to sight read...and record at the same time!...the Toccata and Fugue in D Minor, without rehearsing so much as one-sixteenth note.*

*Nerves and chops notwithstanding, the Toccata is just a bit scary, as we on the solo cornet stand have to come in cold on a high concert A (the opening note), then follow that with the familiar descending passage.*

*"Take one," says Ritchie.*

*The tape rolls.*

*The Colonel raises the baton for the forthcoming forceful downbeat.*

*As the baton strikes the downbeat, Chuck and I nail the high concert A. There is no backing away. I feel intensity increasing from note to note, phrase to phrase. We're going for it! The entire ensemble is not only sight-reading this, but is in synch with each other, including the old man himself. As we play along, I become thrilled at hearing the technique of the reeds and the power of the low brass!*

*My confidence in not missing any notes swells as we near the end of the piece. When we come to the final chord, Schoepper holds the fermata for approximately six seconds . . . a feeling of relief and satisfaction . . . triumph! The Colonel releases the chord, followed by a moment of silence. "All right. Good!" says Schoepper with convincing satisfaction.*

*Amazing! First take. No splicing!* ❖

# Chapter 18

# Third Brother

*A very young Erdman Trio, circa 1955.*

*Freddie:*

*Spring 1970*

*Tim Erdman, our younger brother, auditions for Colonel Schoepper on cornet. I am standing close to the closed door of the Colonel's office. Tim is ripping through Raphael Mendez's version of the last movement to the Mendelssohn Violin Concerto. He is then taken through several sight-reading tests. When the door opens, the audition is over, and within a couple of months, Tim will be playing with us in "The President's Own."*

*Summer 1970*

*The three of us brothers are riding around together here in Washington one day and the subject of tour comes up. When Jimmie and I are trying to tell Tim about a Marine Band tour and its perils, Timmy just fluffs us off by saying, "Oh, I know all about tours. I did a couple with the Valley Forge Band."*

Four uniforms hang silently, attached to a closet door, the hangers bent from the weight of wool that's aged forty-some years. Two are of faded bluish-gray that I wore during the late 1960s at Valley Forge Military Academy. Another is my GI-green Marine Corps overcoat with red gunnery sergeant stripes on it. The last one is behind all the others but still manages to catch the eye: a red coat with brass buttons and white braid, accompanied by blue trousers with a white stripe down the middle, my well-traveled concert dress of "The President's Own" The United States Marine Band.

I wore it last in 1979, the year I walked away from the Marine Barracks at Eighth & I Streets for the final time as a member of *The President's Own*. With my family in tow, we headed back east. I was determined to prove there was life beyond the Marine Band.

About 35 years later I took the red coat off its hanger and tried it on. It was a laughable exercise in futility, about as pointless as trying to wrap a banana peel around a watermelon. Buttons would close to within six inches of their respective buttonholes and refused to move any closer, the pairings simply no match for a well-fed stomach.

So I asked a teacher named Roger to wear it instead. At twenty-one years of age, my then-skinny body type was the same as sixty-year-old Roger's is today. Whenever I gave an elemenetary class a presentation on John Philip Sousa, Roger would agree to don the scarlet tunic and blue trousers in order to show the kids how I once wore the Marine Band uniform. And every time I saw Roger in it, I was reminded of all those years and pounds ago, followed by nanosecond flashbacks of life as it was back then, spent with my two older brothers. . .

## The Erdman Trio

Morning roll call, Sousa band hall. Drum major reads off the names: "Erdman, F?"

"Here," replies Freddie Erdman.

"Erdman, J?

"Here," says Jimmie Erdman.

"Erdman, T?

"Here."

*The three Erdman brothers performing for the first time together,*
*Watergate, 1970, Washington, D.C.*

For me, being able to answer "here" had cemented a life-long dream: getting into the Marine Band with Freddie and Jimmie. Every kid back then had dreams, and I was no different. For a while, though, dreams were one thing and reality was another. If I wanted to join my two older brothers in the Marine Band, I'd have to practice my cornet and piano. Dad said so, many times.

This, sadly to my way of thinking, was easier said than done. Like other kids between the ages of eight and twelve, baseball was my grand obsession. Practicing was depressing. Summer is for sandlots, not music. And so I went into each summer afternoon, wearing my Baltimore Orioles cap and carrying bat, glove, and grass-stained ball, bypassing an old, beat-up, houndstooth-covered trumpet case along the way. About ten of us roamed the ball diamonds in the northeast section of Lebanon, "across the tracks" as our south-side's wealthier neighbors used to say. When they came up to bat, my Catholic friends would call themselves guys like Mickey Mantle (the obvious) and proceed to spray hits and hit home runs. I wanted to be the Orioles' Jim Gentile. He was my hero, and in his honor, I always swung as hard as I could, and usually struck out or hit dribblers.

The only attention my cornet got during those days was from the silverfish that crawled out from inside the case when I'd open it. When I saw the slimy little bug greet me the first time, I slammed shut the lid, and refused to open up the infested box for another six months.

## A More Mystical Pastime

There was another pastime. This one drew on more mystical proportions and took place inside the basement of my Grandmother Erdman's house, just across the driveway and across from the house in which I grew up. It was time for playing priest. That's right, my dream was to someday join the priesthood. Imagine that! Bedecked in splendid homemade priestly vestments my mother had sewn for me (let's see, I had an alb, berretta, stole, chasuble, and yes, even a cincture), I pretended to be a holy man. I fashioned a card table altar complete with a cardboard box tabernacle, and a chalice I made from a brass lamp pilfered from my Grandmother Schubert's bedroom, containing a few precious unconsecrated communion wafers, or hosts, that our parish priest would occasionally donate for the good of the cause.

Thus equipped, I would say "Mass." I was good with the incantations, although these would sometimes conflict with other "sounds" coming from the other side of Grandma's basement. These were the hard-hammered, staccato utterances delivered by none other than my big brother Freddie.

You had to be there. It was a setting of the absurd, the kind of scenario a Salvador Dali would have enjoyed describing with his legendary brush. Freddie was always a private person and never liked to show off his wood-shedding.

I guess a lot of gifted musicians are that way. During occasional visits home from Washington, D.C., he would walk across the driveway and enter Grandma's. I could hear him greet Grandma and Grandpa, trade a few pleasantries and laugh his customary, chisled greeting-laugh, and then descend into the basement, just as I was about to begin Mass. He'd give me a nod and a crooked smile with furrowed eyebrows, walk past my altar and over to the other corner, retrieve his cornet from case, rattle the valves a little, and stuff a rag and a mute in the cornet bell. For the next hour or so he'd run through his routines, doing acrobatic leaps of notes that perhaps only two or three other players on the planet could do. It was always an intense time. Freddie was a fiend for practicing ungodly intervals, slurring or tonguing widely-spaced notes at lightning speed, hundreds of them, over and over again. Sometimes he'd miss a note (remember, we're talking hundreds).

God forbid he'd miss it a second time. It was like going from heaven in one corner of the basement to Dante's *Inferno* in the opposite.

An expletive of the irreverent sort would erupt like a flash that, taken out of context, might otherwise have fit in nicely with my liturgical chants. With my hands folded in a saintly manner and my young and innocent eyes raised to the heavens, I'd intone "Dominus vobis cum," while Freddie, a volcano of disgust at that point, would exclaim "Jesus Christ!" or "Goddammit!" or just a plain, unadulterated, "God!" He was always hard on himself, and it was no different in Grandma's basement, where prayers and blasphemous epithets percolated into the upper reaches of space, then fell toward the floor, like some floating, twisting spiral of deranged verbal napalm.

Those were interesting "Masses." When Freddie lost his temper, I always prayed harder. I prayed in Latin, too (no wussy English for this priest). It was easy, picking up the dead language, especially if one went to Catholic school every day for eight years, where each school day was preceded by real Mass in real Latin. Those were the days when men were men, and Catholics were Catholics. Of course I didn't know what all those Latin words meant, but they sounded nice. Later in my life, the Mass went by the wayside as my life took different paths.

## Life with Brothers

My brothers were considerably older than me but still behaved brotherly. Freddie would give me an occasional cornet lesson and play card games and electric football. The lessons were essentially worthless. The stupidest thing, like a clumsily played note, especially if Freddie missed one, would set us off laughing and giggling for minutes on end, until our dad would come through the French doors to his teaching studio and say something stoic and with a poker face like, "Well, I can see that you two are hard at work." Of course, that would make us laugh even harder.

Electric football was cool. Freddie and I would line up our "players" against one another. Then he'd turn on the switch. The electricity would cause the "gridiron," a 2½ foot by 1½ foot steel plate painted to look like a football field, to vibrate, causing one of the halfbacks to move, a tiny cotton "football" stuffed in a clip soldered to the back. We'd take those games more seriously than some of today's Super Bowls.

Jimmie would send me interesting trinkets from tour—the farther away, the better and more interesting. Once he wrote me a letter on copper-strip stationery that he purchased while playing out West in what was apparently a copper-mining town. When it came to his little brother, Jimmie was a big spender. He bought me World War II model airplanes. They came with a stipulation: he insisted on "helping" me assemble them (I got to hand him the Testors model glue, paints, and decals).

*That's our brother Michael sitting in the high chair; today, he is an assistant radiation safety officer and a Senior Instructor in Radiology for the Pennsylvania State University Medical Center in Hershey, Pennsylvania.*

He looked out for me. When I recorded the cornet solo *Hungarian Melodies* with the Valley Forge Military Academy Band years later, he took the vinyl record and played it for the Marine Band's leader and feared conductor, Colonel Albert Schoepper. The conductor liked what he had heard. The record became my first "audition" for the United States Marine Band.

Jimmie was loaded with big-brother advice and still is. He told me to play "with heart." But then, he has a big heart, and he always has had a lot to say. Most of his advice has been right on the mark, though I didn't always pay heed. When I graduated from Temple University and was ready to join the Marine Band, Jimmie thought in the worst way that my first car should be a 1970 green Fiat Spider I fell in love with. I wished to this day I had followed that advice; instead, I bought a ten-year-old Buick Le Sabre convertible from our next-door neighbor, an oversize "Queen Mary" that drew a lot of "yuks" from the Band's more-hip members.

Freddie taught me ping-pong. On one of his weekend visits, he told me that he had played the table-tennis champion from Hawaii and "almost beat him." My father set up a table in our semi-finished basement, and the more we played, the better I became. I figured if I could beat Freddie, I could say to my friends that maybe I could then beat the ping-pong champion of Hawaii; by this time, my priestly days and dreams were over. For a while, ping-pong became my claim to fame throughout the neighborhood. In sixth grade I developed a lethal forward-hand slam that dominated every player that dared to play on my table. Eventually, I learned to beat Freddie. Jimmie wasn't bad, but beating him wasn't too much of a challenge. We'd play for hours on end on those too-rare Saturday afternoons when Freddie was home.

One afternoon in 1960, my mother called down and told Freddie to come upstairs for a phone call. It turned out to be from an old flame he dated in high school. That was the last afternoon we'd spend playing ping-pong.

Freddie married the caller. When he came home on subsequent weekend visits, his new companion and he were mushy and climbed all over each other in rampant public displays of affection. He was feeling great. I felt crushed and abandoned. Remember R. Leslie Saunders, Lebanon's dictatorial high school band leader? The "caller" was Mr. Saunders' daughter, Joanne.

## Christmas Quartet

Christmas was always a special time of year. For me, it meant that my two older brothers came home from Washington, and that if I practiced enough, our dad would take the three of us out into four or five strategic street corners in Lebanon and, as a family quartet—Freddie on first cornet, me on second, Daddy on third and Jimmie on trombone—we'd play Christmas carols under the street lamps. I literally couldn't wait for this to happen. I even practiced, silverfish or no silverfish.

We always started on the south side of town, where some of Daddy's well-heeled attorney friends lived, then worked our way back to the sidewalk under the street lamp outside our house on Third Avenue. A particular Christmas Eve in the late 1950s marked the one-year anniversary of a tragic suicide by a neighbor who resided directly across the street from us. My father was concerned about playing any carols in a manner that might be considered offensive to the grieving family, so he instructed all of us to be on our best behavior. Grandma Erdman was determined to save our performance for posterity and had us set up a small three-inch reel-to-reel tape recorder that had been given to me as a Christmas present. We placed the recorder on her front porch, just outside her door, then assumed our respective positions under that beacon street lamp that shone so brightly.

The carols were going fine. Despite the December night chill, Freddie was soaring and Jimmie was roaring. I played my second part as dutifully as I could muster, with Daddy playing the third cornet part.

As we continued playing, the cold night air had a knife's edge to it, enough to adversely affect the best of chops. When we got to "O Little Town of Bethlehem," Freddie blistered a high note. This was enough to set Jimmie off giggling, so much so that he had to stop playing. Aware of Jimmie's "distress," Freddie promptly caved and choked from laughter and he, too, had to stop. Like a house of cards, I joined in, laughing to the point that my eyes were tearing. And just like that, our sacred quartet was decimated, save our father, a lonely voice on the cornet, heroically playing the third part to utter and final completion, all by himself. After his final note, he lowered his cornet and said in his customary stoic manner, with more than a tinge of sadness and regret, "Okay, boys, I guess that will do it for tonight. We're finished."

That was the last time we ever played as The Erdman Quartet. We put away our instruments as if we were the string quartet that played for the Titanic as it sank. There was some muted giggling as we all sauntered off the sidewalk and back into the house, knowing full well that Daddy would never take us out again.

No one seems to know exactly where Grandma's tape recording is. I have an idea, but I'm afraid to go near it for fear it's haunted.

## "They Play for the President of the United States"

I was bullied growing up, mainly by a guy named Dwayne who always seemed to zero in during some of our pick-up ball games. Later, I used that experience to "protect" my younger brother Mike, who tried the cornet himself at a young age but never had the yen to pursue it; however, Mike, who helps run the radiation waste lab at the Pennsylvania State Medical Center in Hershey, Pennsylvania, knows more about music than the rest of us brothers put together.

I'm not sure when the real dream was sprung, the one about joining my two older brothers in what many regarded as one of the world's finest symphonic concert bands. Freddie entered first, in 1955; a year later, Jimmie went into the band. Both went in fresh out of Lebanon High School and became known as a "brother act." Freddie is twelve years my senior, Jimmie, ten. I grew up watching their stars develop, rising in the musical firmament of the concert band universe. I heard about both of them in demand as guest soloists and clinicians around the country.

By ninth grade, I had adopted their world-class performance level as my own musical measuring stick, not close to realizing just how far on that stick I had to go until any comparisons could be made. But my father told me I could be like them and do what they did, "if I practice hard enough." That was the trick. By this time I had accepted the idea that I had to practice, but the sports muses wouldn't go away. I still liked to go out and shoot hoops, play tennis, and go over to the diamond for a hot afternoon of baseball.

During those sandlot ball games, I never hesitated to brag to my friends, especially when we were losing: "You guys can have your Mickey Mantle," I'd tell my Yankee fan friends. "I have two brothers in the United States Marine Band. The President's Own.

They play for the president of the United States. So there!"

## Remembering the Watergate

The Marine Band's mission was the same then as it is today: To provide music for the President for every ceremonial occasion imaginable, inside or outside the White House, in performances numbering more than 200 a year, in front of monarchs, barons and statesmen and stateswomen of every ilk and color.

In summertime, the band would grace a sweltering city with its twice-weekly evening concerts: on Wednesday, at East Capitol Plaza, and Sundays, on a charming pontoon-like structure called the Watergate barge. That's right—long before the name "Watergate" was a political scandal, it was a wooden and steel barge moored just below the Lincoln Memorial. A gangplank-like bridge connected the barge with the street. I can remember my dad and I walking hand in hand across that bridge and being greeted by then-Captain Schoepper. "Well, another Erdman, heh?" he'd exclaimed with a slight chuckle. "Perhaps he'll join his two brothers in the band someday, eh, Mr. Erdman?" My heart would skip a beat. I had by this time overheard many Schoepper stories told by my brothers to my mother and father, and in his presence I could only stand still in awe and fear, a poor imitation of Lot's pillar-of-salt wife.

When the barge was removed in 1965, a stage was built in its place. That stage was damaged by Hurricane Agnes in 1972 and removed. A mile or two up the road from the site of that old Watergate barge, the Watergate Apartments and offices were eventually built. Towering above the nation's government town, those same offices a couple years later helped destroy a presidency, casting their shadow forever across the pages of history.

## The Valley Forge Connection

After my high school graduation and having experienced, as his lead cornetist, the dictatorial direction of R. Leslie Saunders, I attended Valley Forge Military Junior College. Three of the Marine Band's own: Charles Kautz, Don Carodisky ,and Terry Detwiler, had also attended the same military school located just out-side of Philadelphia, Pennsylvania. David Rorick came to the Forge a year after me, then a few years later went into the Marine Band.

My own connection to the Forge came through James May, who also attended Valley Forge. He was from Fredericksburg, Pennsylvania, near Lebanon, and one of Dad's star trumpet students. During his summers at home, he would come over to our house and tell me about what the Forge was like. "You should drive over and take a look at it, Tim," he urged. So, my dad and I, along with a fellow classmate and friend, Brian Kreider, drove over during a January blizzard that kept most other motorists off the turnpike.

The band's conductor, Dudley Keith "Duke" Feltham, was there to greet us that bitterly cold afternoon and gave me my audition. Duke was a British bandmaster who imposed his own strict regimen on cadets like me. He was a brilliant man and consummate musician whose band played alongside Eugene Ormandy and the Philadelphia Orchestra when the two groups would team up to play Tchaikovsky's *Overture of 1812*. Upon my first week as a plebe, Duke asked me to play Vincent Bach's *Hungarian Melodies*. The solo went well, and I became his concert soloist for the next two years.

Plebe life at a military academy like Valley Forge is a stressful existence. Here, I learned to excel on my trumpet despite the rigors imposed. Three months after coming to the school, Duke arranged for the VF band to play for the Union League in Philadelphia at the legendary Academy of Music. I was his cornet soloist that night.. I'll never forget the anxiety—and thrill—of getting up in front of thousands dressed in their tuxes and white ties and play *Hungarian Melodies*. A couple of days later in formation, Duke walked up to me and presented me with a congratulatory letter from the president of the Union League. "Here's a feather in your cap, Mista Air-dmon," said Duke in his typical Brit style, handing me the letter, which included complimentary remarks about my performance. I kept my chin "in" while Duke was talking—that was what VF plebes were expected to do when addressed by their tactical officer and bandmaster.

Later, Jim May and I would sit side by side in the Marine Band for a few years. The Valley Forge connection was palpable. Six of us—Carodisky, Kautz, Detwiler, Rorick, May and myself—played in both the VF band and the Marine Band.

Brian Kreider, by the way, took and passed his audition for Duke on the French horn. He and his twin brother Bruce today head up their own historic drama company, Kreider Productions.

*Tim Erdman as a plebe at Valley Forge Military Junior College, 1967. VFMAC was known for its concert band, and a number of alumni went on to become members of the U.S. Marine Band.*

On a cold day in January of 1970, I auditioned and was accepted into the United States Marine Band. Aside from the joy of joining my two brothers, passing my audition was advantageous in one other respect. Going into the Marine Band had saved me from going to Vietnam, which would certainly have happened otherwise, thanks to a newly re-instituted draft lottery.

The lottery took place in 1969, and it occupied the minds of every college and high school student who didn't have a draft deferment. Some of my friends had vowed never to yield to the draft; they would go to Canada instead, or fake their physical in order to obtain a 4F classification. I thought otherwise and had made up my mind: either practice hard for that audition and get into the Marine Band, or go to Vietnam.

The actual draw was conducted on December 1. A large glass bowl contained 366 blue balls, each marked with a different day of the year. Selected at random, each ball determined the order of induction. If your birthday fell, for example, on March 19, that meant that you were 200th in line to be drafted into the military for probable service in a land that saw more than fifty thousand servicemen and women killed. Those at the very bottom whose birthday fell on June 8 were designated Number 366 and did not have to worry about going.

Since my birthday falls on December 6, my draft number was "ten."

"A very dubious Congratulations to me," I thought.

One month later, in January, just like for Valley Forge, I took and passed my audition—except that this time it was for entrance into "The President's Own," the United States Marine Band. I was going into the band as a staff sergeant, assigned to duty as a member of the cornet section, becoming the third Erdman brother to have entered the band, and surrounded by some of the finest players in the world. ❖

## Chapter 19

# Impressions...Ras..."Truck's gone!"

"The Marine Band of the 1970s consisted of two distinct groups—the old career guys and the draft dodgers. There was little crossover between the groups. Some of the old guys seemed as old as dirt to the freshmen. There was one clarinet player I fully expected to need a hearse before the end of the day. New guys had to decide with which group to associate. I had never been much of an antimilitary type in college (and there were plenty of the latter in the band at the time), so I more naturally fell in with the old guys. Jim Erdman took me under his wing to shield me from Schoepper's intense dislike of the new rabble in the band. I suspect this action started me on the path that ultimately led to my decision to make a career out of the Marine Band. . .

"As the rehearsal continued, we eventually came to the vocal solo. Bill Jones was going to perform 'Grenada.' Jim looked over to me and said, 'Put your horn up to look like you're playing, but don't even think about actually playing a note.' Very strange instructions, I thought. Then, ffwitt! Ffwitt! Ffwitt! We were halfway down the page in what seemed like half a second. Where on this scribbled manuscript were we?! I glanced up over my stand and spotted Schoepper looking in my direction. He had a look on his face as if to say, 'How did he manage to not fall into a rest?' I discovered early on that, when in doubt, it was better to leave it out but look like you know what you're doing."

—John Schaefer, bass trombonist

### Freddie:

*September 1970: With the summer concerts ended, it's time to get ready for another nine-week tour and the same rigorous, relentless schedule it has always been—sixty-three—no, make that sixty-six—consecutive days of two concerts a day, no days off, and it's a West Coast tour.*

*The Colonel (he has been promoted to full Colonel in May 1970) is featuring us three Erdman Brothers on the evening concert (every night on tour) playing John Morrissey's "Concerto Grosso," written for two cornets and trombone. When Tim enlisted into the Marine Band this summer, it was a history-making event. That is, the Marine Band had, for the first time in its history, three brothers from the same family serving at the same time in this unique and traditional American institution.*

*This tour will mark my fifteenth since 1955; and Jim's fifteenth consecutive tour since 1956. It will be Tim's first.*

### John Schaefer:

*"Colonel Schoepper programmed the 'Finale' of the Tchaikovsky Violin Concerto on the 1970 tour to be played by the clarinet section. Every night for sixty-six days, Bud Malsh stood to play the opening cadenza and, on the last note of the cadenza, the entire clarinet section stood to play the rest of the movement. Coming from the University of Michigan band . . . I was blown away by the absolute precision of our clarinet section. It sounded like one huge clarinet. Perhaps it was the fear of being called out by the Colonel for a minor imperfection; perhaps individuals opted to "leave it out" when faced with a moment of indecision. Whatever it was, it was one of the most amazing experiences of my entire career."*

### Freddie:

*Denver, Colorado: We are in our third week out. I, as usual, have a single room, as do all soloists and first chair band members. Tim has asked me if he could room with me this one day, because his roommate's wife was coming out to stay with him. I said, "Sure."*

*The Colonel jokingly calls wives who come out to see their husbands "camp followers."*

*12:00 noon: We arrive at the Brown Palace Hotel in downtown Denver. We are starting our fourth week of tour. Tim and I get our keys to the room. We step on the elevator and as we are lifted up, Tim doesn't say a word. When we get to our floor, we make our way to the room. Tim opens the door, throws his suitcase down, flops across the bed lying spread-eagled in prone position and says, "Man, I'm ready to go back to Washington!"*

*Laughing, I say, "Whattaya talking about?! We're only three weeks out, man. We have another six to go!" While Tim lays exhausted, I wander over to the window. We have a room with a view, a spectacular vista of the Rockies.*

*As far as being in a partial solo role in the brass trio, this is relatively easy. The Morrissey offers little challenge in terms of technique. But it's a nice piece.*

*September 1971, Midwest Tour: We are once again getting ready to live out of a suitcase for nine straight weeks. The Erdman Brothers will repeat for the Midwest what they did for the West Coast tour—perform the "Concerto Grosso" every night.*

**The Three Erdman Brothers soloing on tour. This is a 1975
photo of L-R, Tim, Fred and Jim performing Morissey's Concerto
Grosso in Annville, Pennsylvania.**

By now it was winter in 1971, and I had now been in the band for about ten months with one tour under my belt. I sat next to Jim Underwood, who shared the second cornet part as we performed throughout the West Coast during the previous fall. The following February, Schoepper held his perennial "young man's band" and rookie solo auditions. Like the rest of the first-year players, I was expected to get up in front of the band and play a solo. I chose the popular Rafael Mendéz trumpet adaptation of the violin concerto by Felix Mendelssohn. This was an abbreviated version that consisted of the slower-moving theme followed by the presto-like second movement whose eighth and sixteenth notes were meant to fly like the wind, in a display of flashy technique.

I had never considered myself a technical wizard on the cornet like my oldest brother Freddie. However, two factors fueled my passion and inspired me to perfect this solo. The first was Freddie, of course, whose technical prowess had become my standard. The second was Mendéz—his amazing artistry had inspired a generation of trumpet players the world over. When I first heard Mendéz performing the Mendelssohn on a vinyl disc recording, I knew this was to be my signature solo, just like the Staigers *Carnival of Venice* was for Freddie.

Coming home after the 1970 tour, I practiced the *Mendelssohn Concerto* inside and out and played it so many times with the Mendéz recording that I practically wore out the record's grooves. When it was time for the solo auditions, I was eager and ready to step out from the shadows of my older two brothers and prove myself as a competent soloist in the United States Marine Band.

That morning, all of the seasoned band veterans were gathered in rehearsal formation, bringing to mind the veterans of an NFL team, poised to sample the musical offerings of rookies like myself. There was one difference, however. The football vets were reported to have liked to make sport of the "newbies" during training camp. Here in the Sousa Band Hall, things were more sobering. I could sense that no one sitting there and waiting to accompany us rookies was hoping we'd falter or fail under the intimidating baton of Albert Schoepper.

I don't remember who preceded me, but I can still feel the apprehension that grew as I sat in front of the second cornet stand, awaiting my turn.

Then it came.

"Mendelssohn, next! Young Erdman, you're up!"

Schoepper glanced over at me, as I arose and walked over next to where he stood on the podium. At that point, the nerves seemed to vanish. He gave me a wink and a hint of a smile.

"No music?"

"No, sir. It's all up here," I replied, pointing to my head.

"Hrmph!"

I played the solo from memory and nearly flawlessly. After ripping through the last arpeggio and up to the high C at the end of the solo, Schoepper exclaimed, "Well done, young Erdman.

"Let's do it again."

I remember thinking, *Okay, he wants me to prove the first time was no fluke.* So, I played it through one more time, and again almost flawlessly.

Afterward, I received hearty congratulations from many members of the band, some exclaiming that I was "the next Freddie." "You sounded just like Mendéz," others remarked.

Imagine the feeling that welled up inside of me, the exhilaration of knowing I had just faced one of the most demanding conductors in the business, and not once but twice. Returning to my seat, Underwood leaned over and whispered, "Man, Erdman, that was great. That's one solo I'd never tackle myself." To hear Jim Underwood say that in such complimentary fashion—and coming from one who himself went on to become a longstanding principal trumpet of the Columbus Symphony—was a compliment of the highest order.

After Schoepper retired, I played the *Mendelssohn* on a Wednesday night concert at the East Plaza of the Capitol with Captain William Rusinak conducting. Like Schoepper, Rusinak himself was an accomplished violinist. It was a hot summer night, and thousands had gathered on the steps of the Capitol. I felt okay about my performance, vowing to do better during the Sunday evening repeat performance.

That following Sunday, rain had forced cancellation of the concert.

I soloed in front of the band a few more times after that, occasionally stepping out from the Erdman Trio as its third brother. Unlike my brothers, I never attained distinction as a premier soloist. Such moments, however, taught me the value of the pursuit of excellence, and I am mindful of them every time I walk out to conduct my community concert band in Lebanon, Pennsylvania.

## The Man With Moving Experience

Joe Rasmussen had put on his share of miles driving the equipment truck. The truck contained cases of instruments and uniform trunks that were built in the 1930s. Wooden and painted black, the trunks had convex metal corners that allowed them to endure the day-to-day beating of a sixty-three-day tour.

Curmudgeonly, short and stocky, and a longtime veteran of the cornet section, Joe "Ras" was the band's stage manager, a job he won in 1952 (he had once worked as a mover and was experienced in moving furniture). No one messed with Joe, though he didn't have an unkind bone in his body. The man was simply built for the job: rugged, with the strength of a bull.

Joe had his share of near-misses. One was a pond of water into which his driver almost skidded while trying to negotiate a narrow path that led back to behind the stage where the band was performing in 1955. The path was unpaved and slick, flanked on its left side by the pond. "Go right. Go right!" barked Joe to his driver. "It was the scariest moment of my life," he remembered years later. "We came so close to losing $300,000 worth of instruments."

In 1955, when interstate routes were just coming off the drawing board, drivers like Joe had to content themselves with country roads. Chuck Erwin remembered when the buses approached an overpass and were too high to go under. "There was only one solution," Chuck told Freddie years later, "Let some of the air out of the tires—so we did."

But that wasn't enough. Everyone from the second bus now had to get off and get on the first bus, in order to further lower it. That worked. It got through. Now, we had to take care of the second bus and get it through. So, the full band got off the first bus, and this time climbed onto the second. The second bus' tires were deflated. Then, everyone got on it, lowering the bus just like the first bus.

We moved on.

Never let it be said that a military band can be too heavy.

*Joe Rasmussen. (Photo courtesy Department of Defense)*

Ras's work ethic was unmatched. It was a grinding routine that only a bulldog in uniform like Joe could perform consistently well from one day on the road to the next. After arriving at the concert site, he would instruct the stagehands exactly what had to be done and how to do it, while unloading and setting up the instrument trunks behind stage. After each concert, he'd scurry off the stage following the last round of applause, then quickly change from his red coat into a short-sleeve Marine khaki shirt and reload the uniform trunks and instrument trunks.

## "You're Not Going to Believe This!"

In 1971 in Linden, New Jersey, something peculiar happened. Following the concert that night, Joe and his assistant, Luke "The Greek" Spiros, the band's assistant principal euphoniumist, had the truck loaded in minutes with their usual efficiency. After pulling down and carefully locking the truck's rear sliding door, they went around and climbed inside the cab. Joe started up the engine and drove several blocks to a downtown Howard Johnson's Motor Lodge, where the band was staying for the night. After, parking the truck and securing it for the next day's trip, Joe and Luke decided to catch a meal at the HoJo's restaurant next door. Joe finished eating first, said good night, and left to go back to his room, while Luke stayed behind to finish his cup of coffee. "I'm going to re-park the truck in front of our room," Luke said to Joe as an afterthought. "Have a good night. Get some rest."

As Luke stepped outside, he instinctively looked up to see the truck where they had parked it only moments before. To his astonishment, no truck was to be seen. Luke turned his head, looking to his left and then to his right, then started walking briskly to the spot where they had parked it only moments ago.

Luke felt as though he had just been hit by a truck—except that in this case, *there was no truck.* The space in which it had been parked was now empty. He looked around the parking lot, searching in desperation for the familiar Ryder logo. No logo, no truck. The realization suddenly dawned: it was gone.

Luke turned around and raced back to his and Joe's room, "Joe," he yelped, opening the door, "you're not going to believe this. The truck's missing!"

"Ha!" laughed Joe. His roommate was known for pulling an occasional prank, and Joe wasn't going to fall for this one.

"Joe, listen to me," insisted Luke. "The truck's gone. It's not there."

"You've got to be kidding!" Joe uttered in disbelief in his typical gruff voice.

"I'm not. Go see for yourself."

Joe could see that Luke was serious.

Picking up the room phone, Joe called the state police, then said to Luke, "We need to let the Colonel know about this right now."

Joe and Luke went to Schoepper's room and rapped a few times on the door.

"What!" bellowed an irritated voice from inside. "What d'ya want!"

"The equipment truck is missing, Colonel," said Joe.

"Find it!" barked Schoepper.

199

## A Long, Long Night

In what seemed to be a rapid-fire sequence of events, the New Jersey State Police arrived, followed by agents from the FBI. Joe and Luke contacted the operations office back at 8th & I in Washington, D.C., who then began calling each of the tour members' wives, asking them to collect whatever uniform components they could get their hands on and bring them to the Marine Band office as soon as possible.

All during that night, the phone kept ringing from wives and significant others. Staff aides from the band office began checking in on a regular basis for updates. The news media began calling, first the local outlets, then the national desks. The truck heist had become a national sensation.

There would be no sleep for Joe or Luke this night.

## Breaking the News to "Goggles"

Schoepper called tour manager Bobby "Goggles" Williams. The world outside the band knew him as Robert Williams, a seasoned public relations man and thoroughly professional in all aspects of his job—but we knew him as Bobby Goggles, an affectionate moniker pinned on this kind-hearted man, small in stature, with a nose for money, and who wore spectacles with lens the thickness of rocks, quarter-size discs that could magnify his eyes so that a satellite in earth's orbit could zoom in on them.

Nobody knows exactly how Schoepper "presented" his tour manager with the bad news. One can only imagine, however, how it must have flooded the "Goggles" with an instant tsunami of panic. An annual Marine Band tour was the heart and soul of Bobby's pride—and income. People were paying good money, the price of admission to the concerts he spent six months scheduling and promoting. The equipment truck—gone? That would mean a heist of the band's uniforms, instruments, and music. Who could want such a "treasure?"

And, how could the United States Marine Band play concerts without its scarlet-tunic-and-blue-trousered uniforms, its world-class instruments, its historic treasure of music, much of which was original manuscripts?

Upon hearing Schoepper's words, Bobby's eyes must have popped wide-open like goose eggs, his pupils thick and soupy, peering trance-like through the specs, seeing in his mind's eye thousands and thousands of dollar bills tumbling in mid-air, one over the other into an abyss of bankruptcy, a rush of green

200

quicksand. How many concerts would have to be cancelled? How much money did Bobby Goggles stand to lose?

Hopefully, the wives would be able to respond quickly after getting that phone call from operations.

What about music? In that case, the library would have to react like lightning, copying scores and reassembling about ninety new concert folders, one set of forty-five for the matinee concert, and another for the evening.

Could it all be replaced? How long would it take?

## The Sleep-Deprived Road to Danbury . . .

Meanwhile, the word spread like wildfire throughout the band.

None of us could believe it. Shaking our heads, we began phoning our wives or friends at home late that night, requesting them to go into the band hall at Eighth & I the next morning and bring an extra set of uniforms, plus any extra instruments they could get their hands on, either there or what we had at home. All staff at the Marine Band office was contacted, as well as the "Home Guard" band personnel who were left behind back in Washington, D.C. (While part of the Marine Band went on tour, the Home Guard personnel stayed back in then nation's capital to continue carrying out its regular musical performances at the White House, funerals and other ceremonies.) All were directed to immediately proceed into the locker rooms, rummaging through lockers for regulation black shoes and more red coats and blue trousers, being careful to match shoe and uniform sizes to those of the tour band members.

At eight o'clock the next morning, the band boarded both buses and traveled to Danbury, Connecticut, the band's next stop. Joe and Luke were ordered to stay behind in case the truck was found. Back in Washington, D.C., by early afternoon, everything was packed on a C-130 Marine Corps transport plane, which was standing by for emergency take-off to Danbury. By this time, CBS News and other national television news networks were reporting the strange heist: "The equipment truck to the Marine Band has apparently been stolen," reported an anchor. "Police, the FBI and other law enforcement personnel are scouring the downtown area for a Ryder truck containing the band's uniforms, its instruments, and cases. The band is currently on its annual two-and-a-half month tour."

The matinee concert was cancelled, and more cancellations seemed likely. At 2:45 p.m., police discovered a Ryder moving van parked in a back alley, just two blocks away from the Howard Johnson Lodge. The door's lock had been forced open, but other than that, nothing had been disturbed. "Imagine the looks on those guys' faces when they discovered a moving van containing a bunch of black boxes and all those instrument cases," chuckled Joe.

Joe and Luke thanked the police, then took off for Danbury, trading off driving and going at top speed on the Jersey Turnpike. They felt they could make Danbury in time for the evening concert. Joe started out, then Luke took his turn at the wheel. While Joe soon fell asleep on the passenger side, it didn't take long before Luke himself began feeling drowsy. Neither had gotten a wink of sleep the night before. Reaching New York City, Luke made a wrong turn somewhere around the George Washington Bridge. To correct his mistake, he decided to make a U-turn on the Triborough Bridge. "If I had gotten caught, there would have been a very heavy fine," said Luke.

Joe, meanwhile, slept through the entire episode.

By just after six o'clock that evening, Joe and Luke arrived in Danbury. The band was enjoying dinner, relieved to see the truck once again. But for Joe and Luke, there was no time to eat. Apparently, the loading crew thought the duo wouldn't make it in time for a concert, so they never bothered showing up, which meant that our "Fearsome Twosome" now had to unload all the coat and instrument trunks by themselves—plus, set up the stage by placing podium, chairs, and stands in place, along with distributing all the music folios, without the benefit of the pushcart. Even with a pushcart, loading and unloading that equipment truck day in and day out was a backbreaking job and required the strength of yeomen like Joe Rasmussen and Luke Spiros.

Moments before the evening concert, the major media outlets reported a follow-up to the "Marine Band Missing Truck" story. "Today," in effect said the anchor, "CBS News has learned that the missing truck belonging to the United States Marine Band, the "President's Own," has been found, just a few blocks away from the hotel where the band was staying in Linden, New Jersey." ❖

# Chapter 20

# "The Greek" and Another Joe

fter the evening concert that night, Schoepper jumped all over Luke Spiros for hitting a wrong note. The old man showed no appreciation for Luke's unfailing work, the stress he was under in cooperating with law enforcement during the truck's recovery earlier, going sleepless that night, then having to drive a great distance the next day, and still having to get the stage ready for the evening's performance. Such behavior showed the height of Schoepper's unfairness and, most of all, a total lack of regard and compassion for his fellow troops.

## "The Greek"

No one in the band could embody talent, character, and luck—both good and bad—quite like "The Greek," as Freddie liked to call him. During his late teens, he worked as a "soda jerk" at a pharmacy in Brookline, Massachusetts. Aware of his interest in science, chemistry, and technology as well as music (Luke was already making a name for himself as a talented euphonium player throughout the Boston area), the owner of the drug store, a generous donor to the Massachusetts College of Pharmacy, discouraged him from going into the music profession.

But, "music was my first love," remembers Luke. "At that time, I was studying with Aaron Harris, the noted euphonium artist. Harris in turn taught

Ostrander, the bass trombonist with the New York Philharmonic." Luke also had close ties with Charles Colin, trumpeter, teacher, and famous music publisher in New York City who taught many top-notch studio players. "Because of that," noted Luke, "and the fact that I was in the musicians' union and playing with the then-famous Vienna Hoffbrau Orchestra at the age of seventeen, I knew all these guys. They were the all-time pros in New York."

While the bands he played in as a youth had solid reputations as good bands, Luke remembers one in particular that stood out. "In 1957, I heard the Marine Band when it was on tour." (Freddie was the evening soloist on that tour.)

## Marine Dream

"It was playing up around the Boston area. I was so awestruck by the band's sound, power, precision, and artistry. It became my dream to play in this band, the best concert band I had ever heard." While his goal was to make the Marine Band, Luke nevertheless wrote to all of the service bands for an audition. He also received a "letter of interest" from the West Point Band, which had listened to a tape he had sent of his playing.

In 1962 and intending to audition for each of the four service bands stationed in Washington, D.C., Luke arranged for a one-day trip to the nation's capital. Taking a Greyhound bus from Boston, he arrived at Washington's Greyhound bus terminal some hours later. "Here I was, a nineteen-year-old kid, hauling my euphonium and backpack, not knowing my way around and having very little money. I wound up spending the night above the bus terminal and discovered it was a whorehouse."

The next morning, Luke hailed a cab to the Washington Navy Yard, a few blocks down from Eighth & I's Marine Barracks. No one was there, however, to hear him in an official capacity. "So I walked up towards the Marine Barracks. On my way I encountered a musician from the Air Force Band." The musician asked Luke why he was walking to the barracks.

"To audition for the Marine Band," Luke replied.

"Oh, you don't want to work for that sonuvabitch!" exclaimed the Air Force bandsman (referring to Schoepper).

Arriving at the Marine Band office, Luke was greeted by then-Captain Harpham. After a brief and friendly exchange, the captain, who Luke was to learn was also the Assistant Director, initiated the audition.

"Is Art Lehman here?" Luke asked.

He knew of Lehman, the band's principal euphonium player and soloist who could play difficult virtuoso solos at breakneck speeds.

"No," answered Harpham. "He's on tour."

Luke played four solos, impressing Harpham, who then pulled out a hard-cover book on sight-reading. It was the Charles Colin etudes. Knowing Colin and having practiced many hours out of his etude book, Luke had all of the Charles Colin etudes memorized. Meanwhile, unaware of his ties with Colin or his etudes book, Harpham concluded that Luke was the best sight-reader in the world. "Let's wait until everyone gets back from tour, about four weeks from now," said Harpham, alluding mainly to then-Lieutenant Colonel Schoepper and Lehman. "But don't worry—you're already in, since you're Marine Band caliber."

There was no mention of boot camp. Luke was unaware that he, like other entering Marine Band musicians, was exempt from basic training.

## A Life-Changing Signature

Four weeks later, he auditioned again. This time, Schoepper officially hired him into the band.

A few days later, his life took a radical turn. At the Boston recruiting station and thinking he was doing the right thing, Luke applied for enlistment into the United States Marine Corps, signing a "combat" contract. The document he should have signed was a "non-combat" contract, in which it would have stated, "The enlistee is to do duty with the United States Marine Band only." By going right into the band, his rank would start at E-5, a fact that Luke relayed to the recruiter.

E-5?

The recruiter had never heard of anybody enlisting as an "E-5." That was the rank of a drill sergeant. In the recruiter's mind, it was unthinkable for any-one to enter the Marine Corps having the same rank as the drill sergeant, or DI (drill instructor) whose purpose, after all, was to make life for the new recruit a living hell.

So, as protocol would dictate, Luke took the oath and was sworn into the Marine Corps. Meanwhile, the recruiter learned that his new recruit was a musi-cian. What the recruiter failed to recognize was the difference between a Marine Corps band (of which there are several "base bands" located at San Diego and other parts of the country) and the United States Marine Band, "The President's Own." Thinking he was doing the right thing, the recruiter proposed to Luke a "110-day plan" which would include fourteen weeks of boot camp at Parris Island. After that, he could audition for a Marine Corps band.

This seemed to make sense, and after taking and passing a physical, Luke boarded a bus for Parris Island, South Carolina, along with other recruits, "fresh fish" as they were sometimes referred to by seasoned grunts. Six years before, Jim Erdman almost made the same mistake by being told by a DI to "board the bus" to Parris Island, but instead was "spared" at the last minute by the Colonel who swore him in.

This time, however, no one in any similar official capacity was there to "spare" Luke from life in the Marine Corps and not the Marine Band.

## Parris Island

As the bus pulled onto the parking lot at Parris Island's Marine Corps training facility, its engine simmering to a low idle, the door opened and Luke stepped out, wearing his distinguished black musician's frock, a cigarette dangling from his mouth. Immediately, he found himself face to face with a DI, who proceeded to swat Luke with a backhand swipe, knocking his cigarette to the ground. He then yanked Luke's coat off and threw it into a nearby trash receptacle.

The humiliation continued as Luke and the other recruits were ordered to strip off their clothes.

"There we stood," he grimly remembers, "all looking like prisoners from Auschwitz."

A few days later, Luke was standing in front of his bunk and locker for a "routine" daily inspection. The same DI decided to go after Luke again. Noticing this time that his belt was crooked, he punched Luke in the face and squarely on the mouth, knocking out two front teeth, which rolled onto the floor; and jarring loose another tooth, this one just hanging from his gum line.

Luke went berserk, lashing back furiously at the DI, hitting him with count-less punches, and nearly killing him.

The DI wound up in sickbay, detained there for two weeks.

The incident was hushed up. An agreement was made among the com-manding officer, platoon commander, the hospitalized and abusive DI, and Luke, who would be spared any punishment for wasting the DI as an act of gross insubordination, in exchange for his silence about the entire episode, in order to prevent any negative publicity that otherwise would have leaked into the press about abuse in Marine Corps training. The next day, Luke reported to the dental facility for repair work on his mouth, fully aware that a tremendous amount of remedial work lie ahead, not just on his mouth and embouchure, but in adjusting to a new way to blow his euphonium. Such an adjustment would have to be made, if he had any chance of realizing his dream of playing someday with The President's Own in Washington, D.C.

## The End of the Dream?

During basic training, each recruit takes an aptitude test in order to determine one's suitability for his or her field of work upon "graduation." Scoring the highest rating of his battalion, Luke's field was designated "cryptology," a high-security skill.

A few weeks elapsed before a letter from the Marine Band arrived. "Luke," the letter went, "what are you doing down there? You're supposed to be up here."

After consulting with the Commandant's office, the Marine Band received this reply: "We feel that Sgt. Spiros would better serve the Marine Corps as a cryptologist than as a horn-blower."

At the end of basic training, Luke was transferred to Pensacola, Florida; and later, to Hawaii, Korea, Hong Kong, and Vietnam, where he served as a cryptologist and radio operator in the Third Marine Brigade. "By this time," he recalls, "my dream of playing in the Marine Band was completely shattered.

"I was totally devastated."

## Prison Duty

After serving in Asia and Hawaii, he asked to be transferred to a base near his hometown to finish out his term. He was sent to Portsmouth Naval Prison Center in Massachusetts, a transfer that had him leaving behind the balmy 89°F. temperatures of Hawaii, back to a frigid 10°F. below zero in Boston—and ten feet of snow!

"Portsmouth was the only duty station in the Marine Corps available for my clearance," he says. "It was there that I learned to be a prison guard and how to treat the prisoners.

"The cruelty of treatment to these prisoners made the DI at basic training look like a puppy."

Inside one of the prison's bathrooms, Luke began practicing his euphonium. A sergeant major overheard him and retrieved a bass trumpet, handing it to Luke, with a special "order" attached.

"Since this station doesn't have a bugler," said the sergeant major, "I want you to play reveille and taps on this (the bass trumpet) every day and night."

It was during this time that Luke saw the hand of Divine Guidance.

"I was never cruel to any of the prisoners," he says. "When the authorities realized that I just didn't have it in me to treat them the way they wanted them treated, they transferred me to Camp Lejeune as a radio operator with the Second Marine Division," which was later informed that it was about to be "shipped out" to Vietnam. About that time, Luke encountered a Marine Corps major in the disbursing office. The major remembered Luke as a prison guard up in Portsmouth, when the major himself, oddly enough, was a prisoner (he was later acquitted). "He remembered me practicing solos and playing reveille and taps every day and every night," noted Luke.

"He also remembered how nice I was to him. He suggested that I get qualified for the 2nd Division Marine Corps Force Band at Camp Lejeune."

Ridiculed by the auditioners for even thinking of an audition, Luke stunned everybody with his playing and passed the audition with more than flying colors. There, he finished out his term of enlistment, a four-year career detour, from 1962 to 1966, from hell and back.

## From Low to High

"I was finally out, and I vowed never again to get involved with the Marine Corps," said Luke, who was by now back in Boston and undergoing more dental remediation. He took a teaching position at Brookline High School, tuned pianos, played as a resident soloist every Saturday morning broadcast with the Walter Smith's Gazebo Band over WBUR Radio, and wound up being reunited with the Vienna Hoffbrau Orchestra as a performer.

In 1968, the Vienna Hoffbrau Opera House burnt down. At about the same time, the Gazebo Band contracts ended, because Boston University no longer wanted to support the band. On top of that, Luke lost his girlfriend.

"It had to be the lowest point of my life," he remembers.

Fighting his way through a brief period of depression, Luke sent a tape to the Marine Band, playing as a soloist with the Gazebo Band. "I really didn't expect anything to come of it," he said. Months went by without any response. Then, in June of 1969, his phone rang.

"Luke, it's Major Dale Harpham. Remember that dream you had of playing with the Marine Band?"

"Yes."

"Well, the job is still yours, if you want it."

He could hardly believe his ears.

A routine audition was arranged. Meanwhile, Luke found himself crying his heart out in sheer gratitude.

"All I ever wanted my whole life was to play in the Marine Band," he says.

One month later, Luke Spiros enlisted into the Marine Corps once again, only this time it was, according to the contract, "for duty with the United States Marine Band only." He was strongly advised to make sure the recruiter handled things right. *Remember not to board the bus.*

Today and for the past twenty-plus years, "The Greek" wears two dentures: one for eating, and one for playing. On one guest solo engagement, Luke forgot his playing dentures, but played anyway. It is doubtful that anyone in the audience ever noticed. He retired from the Marine Band in early 1987.

**Luke Spiros.**

## Another Memorable Joe

*Jim Erdman:*

One of our excellent oboists and English horn players was Joseph Suchomel. Tall, dark, and handsome, Joe was reserved in personality. He was also one of those "party fellows" at times, especially when it came to the social nights when the Band worked the pit for the Alfalfa, Carabao, and Gridiron skits. These were prestigious gigs to play, and were quite different from our regular concert and White House performances. Prior to a regularly scheduled rehearsal one Wednesday morning, I had gone in to see the Colonel about a pass that was submitted earlier, but hadn't been approved. "See me during the break," said Schoepper.

*Walking into the hall and toward my seat, I noticed Respighi's "Pines of Rome" on the stands. Why? I wondered. After all, it wasn't on the program for that night's concert at the Departmental Auditorium.*

*A few minutes later, Schoepper strode in and immediately called it up. "Respighi!" We played it through without incident, including Joe's lengthy English horn solo, which went very well. Schoepper acknowledged Joe's performance then paused for a second or two.*

*"Lucky. Do it again!"*

*Schoepper's remark left us all dumbfounded. But—that was life with Schoepper. Playing it the second time around, Joe chipped a note.*

*"Not so lucky," quipped Schoepper. "Let's do it again, right this time."*

*This went on for what seemed like an eternity, and the Respighi was going nowhere fast. In disgust, a livid Schoepper threw the baton to the floor. "Take ten," he barked. "And when we come back, Suchomel, get it right!" On the way out, he turned around and said to me, "Erdman, see me now!"*

*"What did you do?" asked Dale Weaver, my assistant. I responded by telling him about my inquiry into the pass approval.*

*Hearing my knock on the door, Schoepper yelled, "Come in!" I found him seated behind his desk, toweling himself. "I got Suchomel, didn't I?"*

*"Why?" I asked back. "It's not even on tonight's program. Or the season, for that matter."*

*"I heard the Respighi on WGMS [the FM classical radio station] driving in. I was going to get him."*

*My pass was approved.* ❖

# Chapter 21

# Pretzels

*Jim:*

*Life with Schoepper was not always a grindstone or hammer. The man had a soft spot, if you were lucky enough to hit upon it at the right time.*

*Case in point: he was an extremely intelligent individual, an interesting and well-spoken man, a walking encyclopedia when discussing history, or his favorite subject, baseball. He knew absolutely nothing about football, and admitted during a morning bus ride that he had never seen a football game and couldn't understand the American public's attitude toward the game. When I asked him if there was any possibility of cutting an encore march, "New Colonial," from the matinee concert, with hopes that I could catch the last quarter of a televised Packer-Lions game, he did! The next morning as he stepped onto the bus, he looked at me sternly and said, "My God, what a bunch of cretins running up and down a field doing nothing!"*

*He actually had watched the final quarter!*

*The late 1960s and early 1970s brought many new and convenient gadgets to the world of travel, among them, insulation bags for storing food and drink and restrooms on the tour buses. Up to this time there was no such thing as "bottled water" as we know it today. And try riding non-stop for 100-plus miles without a "pit stop."*

*The only foods that could be carried on the buses were non-perishables.*

All that changed with the advent of the thermal insulated bag.

Not just a convenience, it also enabled many of us to save money. Periodically, we'd go to grocery stores to stock up on just about anything that would whet our appetites. Such a storage wonder also aided in the financial need department, considering our per diem! (Eventually that did go up, and by my last tours we were receiving $25 a day. Unfortunately, expenses had gone up, too!)

My tour bus seat was located directly across the aisle from the leader. Our singer, Bill Jones, had had that seat prior to his retirement in 1970, and now, from day one of the 1970 tour, I had "inherited" it—by Schoepper's dictum, not mine!

Riding back to our hotel from an evening concert, I mentioned to Schoepper that I wouldn't be riding the bus the following morning. He naturally asked why. I replied that I was going to the next town with Joe Rasmussen, our equipment truck driver, stage manager, and section cornet player, to pick up supplies for my "food and drink kit." No problem.

The next morning during our trip to the next town, Schoepper wanted to know what I had gotten. I proceeded to itemize everything for him, including a bag of pretzels. Such information elicited no interest from him whatsoever, at least for the time being.

Days went by. Our moods tended to follow that of Schoepper's, and his mood usually depended on what he thought of the performances. Some were good, some bad. Bad was not what you wanted to experience. He dared you to miss notes, and if you did, there'd be hell to pay. We learned the true definition of the term "work ethic!"

One morning I opened my bag full of goodies and selected pretzels. As I pulled a pretzel out of the bag and proceeded to take a bite, Schoepper, without looking, asked what I was eating. "A pretzel!" I'm thinking and chuckling to myself, "What does he think I'm eating?"

He asked for one and I complied. He enjoyed it, didn't bother to thank me, and that was it. We went on for the remainder of the week without incident.

The concerts were going well and all was right with the world. A week or so had gone by, and it was time to do some more shopping. I had done quite a bit of sharing with my newfound snacking partner and needed to replenish my supplies, telling him as much. He laughed a bit and then said, "We're out of pretzels. Get some."

"What?" I asked, startled.

His reply was abrupt.

"Don't forget the pretzels."

Okay, I thought. I knew him well enough to take it in stride, and that was that.

The morning following that evening's concert, we were traveling a rather long distance to the next town, departing at o-dark-thirty hour. At some point in the bus ride, I fell asleep.

It was a very restful, deep sleep . . . until I was awakened by somebody inquiring as to whether or not I had gotten pretzels.

Groggily, I replied that I had.

"I'll have one."

"Now?" I asked, rubbing my half-closed eyes.

"Yes!"

I gave him a rather disgusted look and handed him the bag.

He opened it, taking one stick out of the bag, took one bite, spat it out, and exclaimed, "These goddamned pretzels are stale!"

Without hesitation he threw the pretzel and the bag into the bus stairwell, moved his pillow over to the window, moved himself to the right side of his seat, and never said another word until we got to town.

The first and last words to any of us for that day, until the bus left for the concert site that evening, were memorable—and vintage Schoepper.

"No more pretzels!"

Of such things memories are made. ❖

The John F. Kennedy Center for the Performing Arts

presents

# The United States Marine Band

*Thursday Evening, November 25, 1971, at 8:30*

COLONEL ALBERT SCHOEPPER, *Conductor*

| | |
|---|---|
| W. PARIS CHAMBERS | March, "Chicago Tribune" |
| JOHANN SEBASTIAN BACH | Chorale and Fugue in G minor |
| HENRY HADLEY | Overture, "In Bohemia" |
| JOHN J. MORRISSEY | Brass Trio, "Concerto Grosso" |
| | FREDERIC ERDMAN, TIMOTHY ERDMAN, *Cornets* |
| | JAMES ERDMAN, *Trombone* |
| LEROY ANDERSON | Irish Suite |
| | The Irish Washerwoman |
| | The Minstrel Boy |
| | The Girl I Left Behind Me |
| BURT BACHARACH | Burt Bacharach Selections |
| arr. by Richard Raven* | |

INTERMISSION

| | |
|---|---|
| RICHARD WAGNER | "Elsa's Procession to the Cathedral," from "Lohengrin" |
| PIOTR ILICH TCHAIKOVSKY | Finale from Violin Concerto in D |
| arr. by Thomas Knox* | THE CLARINET SECTION |
| JOHN BARNES CHANCE | Variations on a Korean Folk Song |
| GEORGE M. COHAN | Medley, "George M.!" |
| arr. by William Jolly* | |
| AMBROISE THOMAS | Aria, "The Drinking Song," from "Hamlet" |
| arr. by Daniel Tabler* | MICHAEL RYAN, *Baritone* |
| GUISEPPE VERDI | Overture, "La Forza del destino" |

**Michael Ryan,** *Concert Moderator*

* U.S. Marine Band Arranger

*Program from the Marine Band's concert in November 1971 at the Kennedy Center for the Performing Arts, featuring the Three Erdman Brothers in Morrissey's Concerto Grosso.*

# Chapter 22

# Gone But Not Forgotten

Many times when roll call was taken and I wasn't on rehearsal that particular day, I'd find myself standing in the back of the band hall alongside people like Charlie Corrado, the longest serving accordionist the White House and Marine Band ever had; or Dave Johnson, the band's principal trumpet. They were the old-timers.

Then there were the younger guys like Jim Underwood, who spent just one four-year hitch, coming into the band one year before I did; and Tom Lee, a regular at the White House who played keyboard. Tom Lee earned some special distinction: during the mid-1970s, he persuaded Congress to change the law that prohibited military musicians from joining the American Federation of Musicians. It was a momentous achievement, one that spurred Tom to later become president of the AFofM.

Charlie Corrado was one of those we thought would be around forever. He left this world in 2004, but not before Darragh Johnson memorialized him in a March 29, 2004 story for the *Washington Post*.

## Memories that tickled the "First Pianist"

"That Charlie Corrado—he could play, and play, and play..." wrote Johnson. Charlie first enlisted in the Marine Corps, served on Okinawa, then tried out for the Marine Band as an accordionist, an instrument that was missing from the

215

band's instrumental roster at the time. According to Johnson, Charlie went on to entertain ten presidents, from Dwight Eisenhower to George W. Bush—41 years of White House performing in all—along with playing for 13 Marine Corps commandants, plus an assortment of dignitaries, from Prince Charles and Princess Diana to the president of Japan...to Duke Ellington and more.

"...He could do quiet, then spirited. And he could stay invisible—just what the Marine Band's White House protocol requires—except when President Bill Clinton suddenly was on the piano bench next to him, singing along," wrote Johnson.

"...And when Clinton needed music in the middle of the 1996 blizzard, when many roads weren't plowed and Corrado's unassuming cul-de-sac was a mess of snow, the National Guard sent a Humvee."

Darragh Johnson's *Washington Post* story was based on an interview with Charlie's wife, who did all the talking and told all the stories. At the time of that interview, Charlie sat alongside his wife but couldn't talk. By now he had ALS—amyotrophic lateral sclerosis, better known as Lou Gehrig's disease.

Those of us who played with Charlie knew he was a talented keyboard player, someone equally at home on the electric accordion known as the "Cordovox"; or the piano, which he taught himself to play during the 1970s, when he saw the accordion going out of style.

During that interview, the mention of Queen Elizabeth's visit to the White House drew laughter that comes with one of those remembered "moments." During a state dinner held in her honor, President Gerald R. Ford rose to dance with the Queen, and Charlie and the band immediately went into a medley of tunes suitable for dancing to. The medley included *The Lady Is a Tramp*. It wasn't a deliberate act of disrespect. The tune just happened to come up at the wrong time.

During an inauguration party for George W. Bush, his father, the former President, noticed Charlie playing the piano.

"Charlie! Are you still here?" exclaimed the former President, a backdoor compliment for all those many years of service.

After noticing his fingers couuldn't make the chord changes anymore, and carrying the accordion on his shoulder was a burden unlike any before, Corrado retired May 14, 2002. Like Lou Gehrig, he was music's version of the "Iron Man." And like Gehrig, he noticed a pain in his shoulder that just wouldn't go away.

Dutiful. Dedicated. A man who went about his work, never asking to be noticed. That's how we remember Charlie Corrado.

*At John Kennedy, Jr.'s birthday party, Charlie Corrado performs on accordion, Jr. with Ben Sanger on violin and Wiely Weaver, string bass. (Photo courtesy White House)*

## Dave Johnson warming up his trumpet like a Model T

Dave Johnson had a down-home wit. He used to amuse us younger and "greener" guys by simulating trying to warm up—more like "crank up"—his trumpet before rehearsal as if it were an old Model T Ford. Whenever I had car problems, he'd freely give me a lot of his sage, under-the-hood car wisdom, delivering it in an easy-going, "What? You didn't know that?" style that always had me believing I could successfully replace a starter motor or adjust valve lash—if I just followed his advice.

Such misplaced confidence would always land me in trouble.

"Tim, read your shop manual," he directed in that down-home, twangy voice one morning during a rehearsal break, dispensing "Advice for Dummies" on adjusting my valve lifters. So I did. I read the manual and followed the instructions.

I went car-less for over a month.

Another Johnson piece of advice had to do with changing my brakes.

"Brakes can be fun," he'd say. "You just have to know what you're doing." That was the grand qualifier, the mother of all weasel clauses—"You just have to know what you're doing." After attempting to remove the wheel lug nuts, which had seized and refused to move, I "wrenched" my back instead, landing in the hospital and traction for ten days.

Dave loved sailing. He had me convinced I should someday invest in a sailboat instead of "one of those stinkpot motorboats" that cruised up and down Chesapeake Bay. During summers, the bay was his second home. One summer afternoon, we hopped aboard his sailboat, where he instructed me on the fundamentals of sailing. We owned the Chesapeake that day, gliding across the shimmering wave crests in glorious, dangerous sunshine and by the end of the day, I felt as if I had experienced my first day of boat boot camp, Dave Johnson style.

Anyone else would have been disgusted with my seeming inability to grasp such rudimentary commands as "tack" and "ready about." Not Dave. He was just amused.

"Mr. Johnson, who liked the stability that the Marine Band offered a family man, started in the late 1950s, when the then-110-member group performed live weekly half-hour syndicated radio broadcasts and concerts at the Capitol, state funerals at Arlington National Cemetery, White House engagements and many other national shows," wrote the *Washington Post's* Yvonne Lamb in her article entitled "Trumpeter Reached the High Notes of Family, Career in Marine Band."

Dave and his daughter, violinist Susan Franke, became the first father-daughter duo in "The President's Own." Dave's grandson, Christopher, joined his mother as a member of the violin section,

"making the family the first to span three generations within the band. Susan's husband, Phil Franke, plays the euphonium."

Dave died of bladder cancer in June, 2007.

## James Underwood and his memorable Rain Dance

From 1969 to 1973, James Underwood did a four-year "hitch" with the Marine Band, then went on to become the first-chair cornetist and soloist with Leonard Smith's famed Detroit Concert Band. The last seventeen years of his life were dedicated to the Columbus Symphony as its distinguished principal trumpet.

Wherever he went, Jim was the focus of humor—his or someone else's. Everyone who knew Jim has his or her own story of the approximately 5'8" rotund funnyman who happened to be a gifted trumpeter. One of my favorites happened the day before he was supposed to play the difficult violin transcription on trumpet by Raphael Mendéz of "Czardas" with the Marine Band at the Watergate.

Jim was like some of us who would mimic a "rain dance" every so often, comically invoking the heavenly gods for some timely and serious precipitation. There were two possible reasons for soliciting help from the rain gods, and both had to do with raining out a gig.

There was always the summer heat. The popular Friday evening "sunset parades" were never played under less than hot and humid conditions in the wash rag known as the nation's capitol. After one of these gigs on the parade grounds of Eighth & I, our full dress scarlet woolen coats were always drenched in sweat. Playing a Friday evening parade in Washington's summer heat was no fun.

The other reason had to do with the fact that you were a soloist for both the Wednesday and Sunday evening concert. Depending on the nature of the solo, the nervous apprehension leading up to the evening of a concert at the Capitol or Lincoln Memorial could be enough for one to suddenly break into a spasmodic "rain dance."

On this particular Tuesday evening in June of 1972, Jim was having dinner with Mike Scarlatto, who some months before had come into the band's trumpet section.

Mike remembers that Jim simply did not want to perform the difficult solo the following night. I've heard Jim do it before, and I can't ever recall his having missed a note. Maybe he just didn't feel up to it. Whatever the reason, Jim told Mike that he was going to do the rain dance, with extra intensity and conviction, so that the rain gods would see to it that the concert be cancelled.

He kept his word. Going out the door to the restaurant, he broke into the rain dance, much to Scarlatto's laughing delight.

That evening, the rain began . . . and didn't stop until nearly a week later, in the "perfect storm" that became known as Hurricane Agnes. Although it had changed status from hurricane to tropical storm between the time it began in the Caribbean and when it finally ravaged the mid-Atlantic states, Agnes had had her say, dumping enough water on the district to force cancellation of one outdoor performance after another.

This, of course, included the concert in which Jim was scheduled to solo, as well as several Friday night sunset parades. Nearly a month went by without any of the Marine Band's traditional outdoor concerts and parades. There was no place to play. Everywhere was water, and every outdoor concert site in Washington, D.C. had been flooded.

The storm broke records for flooding. In neighboring Pennsylvania, the commonwealth incurred over $2 billion in flood damages, a tremendous sum in those days.

A few days after his little ritual, Jim admitted that he may have overdone his rain dance.

The storm put an exclamation point on Jim's rain dance by severely damaging the Watergate concert stage which had stood on that site since 1965, never to be rebuilt . . . and never again to serve as the stage for a Marine Band concert.

*Jim Underwood.*

Before Jim left the band about a year later, I had a chance to hear him perform Hummel's *Trumpet Concerto* with the band in a chamber setting. His rendering was a magnificent display of artistry. In my mind's ear I can still hear Jim as he rolls through all the passages of that excellent three-movement piece, a standard in the trumpet literature to this day.

In the late summer of 2006, Marti Underwood, his widow, sent me a CD recording of the Columbus Symphony performing Mahler's *Fifth Symphony* live, with Jim playing the principal trumpet part. Mahler's *Fifth* has many exposed, high-ranging trumpet parts, and Jim executed them all with exquisite power and precision. It was a performance that would have satisfied any world-class principal trumpeter. The miracle is that he performed with his face contorted, the horrific evidence of salivary gland cancer gone amuck. The one side of his face was so severely impacted that it took on the shape of a fishhook.

Prior to the Mahler concert, Jim had stopped playing the trumpet for nearly six months. So much air was leaking around his embouchure as a result of the cancer's debilitating effects, it prevented him from playing up to his usually high standards.

In February 2006, one of Jim's friends, a tubist in the Columbus Symphony, constructed a kind of "plate." Attaching it to Jim's trumpet, the plate was an engineering marvel in simplicity, fitting tightly against the side of Jim's mouth that was leaking air, and providing the necessary seal that would allow him to resume playing the trumpet.

The following April, Jim played the Mahler, brilliantly, miraculously, amazingly.

Five months later, he passed away.

He was a friend from my Marine Band career, and one who would leave an impression on me for the rest of my life. When I taught the concept of a trumpet sound to my own students, it was Jim's sound I was hearing in my mind's ear and wanted them to hear. Whenever I played the Hummel *Trumpet Concerto*, I tried to play it as Jim played it.

You'd think that one person having borne the stamp of another's musical imprint would stay in touch.    But I never called him. To my everlasting regret, I had never said another word to Jim Underwood after he left the band in 1973. ❖

# Chapter 23

# End of an Era

"*M*aybe Colonel Schoepper started to soften late in his career. One of our tuba players stumbled while leaving the stage for intermission on one tour concert. Unfortunately, he stepped off the riser and caught his toe on the safety rail. He fell headlong onto his tuba, the bell encountering the floor first. The instrument collapsed like an accordion with an enormous crash. Schoepper was standing in the wings and observed the whole thing. Was the unfortunate tuba player to be raked over the coals? There was an instant feeling of empathy throughout the band. Then, "Wha-ha-ha!" The Colonel burst into his unmistakable lusty laugh. As much as he tried, he couldn't be angry after seeing the flattened tuba.*"

—John Schaefer

*Freddie:*

April 28, 1972

Colonel Albert F. Schoepper retired. A full honors ceremony was held with the entire band on the parade deck in his honor. He was awarded the Legion of Merit Medal. At the conclusion of formalities, Colonel Schoepper handed over the Sousa Baton, the same baton that was presented to John Philip Sousa when he left the band and the Marine Corps in 1892 (it had now become a ceremonial relic), to Lieutenant Colonel Dale Harpham.

*The Schoepper Era had come to an end. The moment fills me with poignance. I liked Dale, but I knew I would miss that baton technique, the mark of Schoepper. The band would not be the same.*

*During Colonel Schoepper's reign (some called it the "Reign of Terror") the Marine Band was probably the best band in the world. Music critics as well as musicians from other service bands in Washington attested to that. I could not imagine any ensemble anywhere in the world being tighter than the Schoepper Marine Band.*

John Schaefer:

*"Years after Colonel Schoepper retired, he was invited back to attend the change of command ceremony on the parade deck for Colonel Bourgeois[10]. The band was sitting in the bleachers waiting for the ceremony to begin. A growl began among the band members—a truly audible one. What had happened? Had some incredibly beautiful young lady clad in a perky sundress just arrived? No, Colonel Schoepper was being escorted in. The older guys in the band had a truly visceral reaction to seeing him after all those years."*

Schoepper died on July 28, 1997, twenty-five years after his retirement, following a debilitating stroke. *Time* magazine reported that his death occurred on the same day as that of legendary pianist Sviatoslav Richter.

Shortly before his death, Freddie learned about the Colonel's condition and that his speech had been severely curtailed: he was limited to saying, "Why? Why? Why?" Deciding to pay the Colonel a visit in the hospital, Freddie prepared himself for the inevitable string of "Why's." As he walked into the room and approached the Colonel lying in bed on his back in a loosely tied, white hospital gown, Schoepper turned his head to Freddie and exclaimed, "Well!" his voice dipping up and down.

A few days later, on a subsequent visit to the nursing home in Arlington, Virginia where he had been transferred, Freddie and Mary Jo presented him with a cluster of green grapes and bouquet of flowers that she had collected from a lavender azalea bush; "The blossoms looked exquisite, like large orchids," said Mary Jo. His eyes lit up at the giving. "The look he gave when he touched the flower petals made it clear that he adored flowers," she said. "His eyes—they were very eloquent."

He tried eating one of the grapes but needed help putting one in his mouth. It was obvious he loved the grapes and flowers, but hated the help he needed in

---

10    Bourgeois was the successor to Colonel Jack Kline, who in turn succeeded Colonel Dale Harpham, who in turn succeeded Colonel Schoepper

eating the grapes. It was during this tender moment that Schoepper decided to come out from behind that authoritative façade, a curtain that had screened his humanity for the better part of his eighty years, displaying a rarely-seen gentler nature, smiling at her as if to say, "thank you." As the pair prepared to leave, he motioned to Tarrants with his hand, in a gesture and facial expression that said it all with a certain touch of finality. Though the words were barely discernible, Tarrants remembers hearing one quite distinctly. "Go," he commanded, waving with his hand as if to say, "Shoo, shoo! Don't come back." As they left, he continued to gaze at the flowers fondly, touching them.

Jim and I also drove from Lebanon to Arlington to visit Colonel Schoepper in the nursing home. Before leaving, we found out to our dismay what Freddie learned earlier: the stroke had left Schoepper speech-impaired, a fact difficult to imagine for anyone who had ever worked under his baton and suffered the verbal sting of a Schoepper quip.

Just what did "speech-impaired" mean?

Throughout the ride during what was a beautiful early-summer day, we reminisced about the Schoepper years that both of us had experienced, Freddie and Jim's experience together, then my own years later. At the same time we found ourselves bracing for the encounter about to occur. Ours was to be the final meeting with a figure once larger than life, now an eighty-three-year-old old shell of a man, the victim, like all of us are destined to be, of the aging process's ultimate decree.

The day nurse led us to his room, the door ajar. We rapped gently and walked in, a confining space, maybe seven feet across and ten feet deep, and smelling fetid. He was bedridden. Wearing big smiles, we greeted him, expressing our "hellos" in unison. His eyes widening, he smiled back faintly, using one hand in a feeble attempt to wave back and acknowledge his gratitude at seeing us. His face was sad and worn, but determined; his body a weightless shell, small fraction of the total authoritarian package we had come to fear and respect for so many years, an entity who, in our realm of experience and in another time, had no equal. We estimated he must have lost over seventy pounds, maybe more. But he recognized us immediately. Our instincts told us, thankfully, that his mind was still intact.

He spoke softly, the words unintelligible at first.

And then it happened, the final command.

No sooner had we arrived than he motioned to the bathroom. He had "to go." That meant the unthinkable: getting him out of his hospital bed and assisting him to the toilet, a kind of instantaneous nursing on the fly that neither of us was prepared to do.

While Jim went out into the corridor to summon a nurse, I bent down to help lift his frail body. His eyes engaged mine, his words now discernible, quietly spoken, over and over again.      "Why. Why. Why. Why."

Those were his sentences, his statements, his contribution to the conversation for that afternoon.

"Why. Why. Why. Why."

With shock, we realized the truth. Albert F. Schoepper, revered and despised, musician extraordinaire, once the leader of the world's premier military concert band, music director to four presidents, charmer to First Ladies, man with unparalleled adeptness in use of the language, musical despot who could strike down a career with a swath of words like an oak tree felled in one stroke of the blade, now here he was, reduced to a vocabulary of one three-letter word.

"Why. Why. Why. Why."

"Why. Why. Why. Why." ❖

COL. ALBERT F. SCHOEPPER, U.S.M.C. RET.
4013 N. WOODSTOCK STREET
ARLINGTON, VIRGINIA 22207

*Schoepper had a gentler side, as shown in this letter to Jim Erdman upon Schoepper's retirement from the Marine Band: "Dear Jim, I just want to express my personal thanks and appreciation to you for your part in the selection and presentation of the watch and plaque which I was so proud to receive. You always have done such a fine job in that role, and I was pleased that you were there when it came my time to be the recipient. I've written a letter, thanking the band, and I hope it finds its way to the bulletin board. With every good wish for you, Mrs. Erdman and the little one, Albert Schoepper."*

## Chapter 24

# Takeover

*John Schaefer:*

"*The fears of Schoepper haunted many of us for years to follow. The sight-reading prowess of the band was often described as being able to read all the spots off the page, literally.*

"*Two or three years after the Colonel's retirement, the band was performing a summer concert at the Jefferson Memorial. One of our clarinet players was challenged by his stand partner to do his duty and play every spot on the page. Well, it seems that an insect landed on their music six or seven ledger lines above the staff. An enormous squeak ensued, one they are still scraping off the walls of the Jefferson Memorial with palette knives. Those legends of ghosts in the basement of the memorial are probably due to the echoes of that squeak.*

"*Schoepper had conditioned us to put on a disguise whenever we made a mistake. People in other sections would quickly glance at the section from which an error was made, to see if it was possible to detect the offender. It was usually the one who was not glancing around to indicate "it's not me" or the one who couldn't hide his blush. Those short haircuts were dead giveaways. Much to our surprise, we saw a sea of bouncing shoulders and clarinetists struggling not to laugh through their horns. Times were changing. The Schoepper years were over.*"

**Freddie:**

*May 1972, one week after Schoepper retires: The new Director, Lieutenant Colonel Harpham, has the new seating arrangement posted on the bulletin board. I notice that he has me playing third chair, not assistant as I have been playing for the past ten years. He has placed the third chair man ahead of me to be Chuck's assistant! I visit Lieutenant Colonel Harpham's desk to find out what's going on. After a moment's hesitation, he says, "Frankly, Freddie, your sound sucks."*

*I stand there, speechless.*

*"However, when you get home, gather up all of your cornet solos and get them ready, because I want to feature you as our premier cornet soloist at all our concerts."*

*I am flattered at that, and we part on good terms.*

When Hurricane Agnes slammed into the country's eastern seaboard in June of 1972, no one knew it would also be ushering in the political firestorm of the century.

In a conversation with friends a short while after Agnes' wrath had passed, I made the passing comment that the *Washington Evening Star* had reported a break-in at the Watergate offices and apartments, just up the road from where our summer Watergate barge concerts had taken place. They were calling it "the Watergate Caper," the latter term soon to be replaced by the much more sinister word, "scandal."

**Mary Jo Terrants, who some-
day would meet Freddie and
eventually become his wife.**

*Freddie:*

*Late summer 1972: Mary Jo enters my life. The sun shines brighter. More flowers bloom. The earth moves as it never has before with positive power across the board, enriching and changing our lives forever.*

*September: Tour rehearsals begin with the full band. Harpham, unlike Schoepper, does not hold sectionals.*

*Jimmie and I are called upon by Harpham to perform as evening soloists on the West Coast tour this year every night, sixty-three straight nights. I am commanded to perform—guess what!—the Staigers "Carnival of Venice" once again, or should I say sixty-three more "agains." Jimmie is performing the Rimsky-Korsakov "Concerto for Trombone."*

*Seven weeks later, Walla-Walla, Washington: At tonight's concert, I will have performed the Staigers forty-nine times on this tour. We are all bored and weary as we disembark form the bus and make our way into the holding room where our coat trunks and instruments are. I don't really want to play tonight. I'm just so sleepy. No need to warm up. I drape myself over a piano and rest my head on it, face-down.*

*Just let me sleep!*

*We have some twenty minutes before taking the stage. I need to rest my eyes. As I'm napping, a young college student comes walking in to talk with one of us about the band and program. He walks over to Chuck Erwin and, after talking with him for a moment or two, says, "Where is the cornet soloist?"*

*"Over there," Chuck replies, pointing to the draped figure over the piano.*

*"Shouldn't he be practicing his solo?" the student asks.*

*"Oh, he's just getting himself psyched up," replies Chuck.*

*Before the tour started, I had performed the Staigers "Carnival of Venice" 138 times with the Marine Band. It seems as though people have no concept of the kind of schedule we are on out here, nor can they imagine performing the same solo sixty-three consecutive times, day after day after day.*

## The End of the War

In January 1973, the Paris Peace Accords formally ended U. S. involvement in the Vietnam War. Two years later, at 8:35 a.m. on April 30, 1975, the last ten U. S. Marines left the embassy in Saigon officially ending the U. S. presence in Vietnam.

In the early summer of 1973, Ruth Johnson, horn, became the first female member of the U.S. Marine Band.

231

*Summer: We now play on shore, right off the Potomac River, because the Watergate barge was damaged beyond repair during Hurricane Agnes last year and removed. What a shame! I miss that barge. It was such a unique setting.*

*Late summer: The Marine Band is booked to play for the California State Fair. Lieutenant Colonel Harpham charters a flight with United Airlines for himself, his assistant conductor, and Ruth Johnson. United will make the West Coast in six hours or less. The rest of us pigs get to fly in a C-130.*

**Fred and Jim play a game of cribbage to while away the eight hours spent on a military turboprop to El Toro Marine Base, California, 1973.**

*The trip takes eight hours. We sit on webbed bucket seats wearing ear protectors because of the engine noise (we all look like radio men with those things on). There is one—and only one—commode, and it is located right in the middle of the fuselage. On either side of the cockpit is a pipe to pee in. Good luck with the other number: if you have to defecate anytime while in the air, you will have to do so in full view of everybody, since it is an open commode perched about four feet above the floor! Upon landing, you must carry the bucket of excrement off the plane and dispose of it at the Motor Inn!*

*I am terribly disappointed in Dale for this, as we all are. And it certainly doesn't put Ruthie in good light, either. This is the "first class" treatment we're getting from our new director?*

*He has me performing the Staigers on this trip, and I sure don't want to play for him or this occasion after experiencing the indignities he just put us through.*

*On this concert and every concert thereafter, the new seating arrangement will have the cornets and trumpets near the back of the band in front of the percussion, bells facing the audience. This differs from the old seating arrangement, in which the cornets fronted the band and were flanked on*

*Schoepper's right side, practically right under his nose. I can't help but wonder if he had lost hearing in his right ear because he loved the brass so much.*

*Upon returning to Washington, we finish out the summer with concerts, the Friday "Evening Parades," patriotic openers, funerals, and White House commitments.*

In August 1973, Harpham guest-conducted the Interlochen National Music Camp Band in Michigan, and called upon Freddie and Jim to appear with him as his guest soloists. During the one and only rehearsal, the cornet section gave Freddie a standing ovation and labeled him "The Mechanical Monster." Freddie, of course, played the Staigers *Carnival of Venice* and Jim, the Rimsky-Korsakov *Concerto for Trombone*. After playing the last note, Freddie estimated that he had by that time performed the Staigers 205 times.

**Freddie as guest soloist at the Interlochen Center for the Arts, Interlochen, Michigan, August 1973, with Lieutenant Colonel Dale Harpham conducting.**

The famous pianist Van Cliburn also shared the stage as guest soloist with Freddie and Jim. While organizational change from the top down was apparent, some things never seemed to change—like tour, which would be opening again at Longwood Gardens in just a few weeks. For Freddie, it meant another go-round performing the Staigers, while Jim would again perform the Rimsky-Korsakov.

Both brothers would solo together yet again for sixty-three consecutive evenings from September through November. Meanwhile, the band had to collectively adapt to a new phenomenom occurring, and not just in the Marine Band but other service bands as well: for the first time, the admittance of women musicians into the band. This meant certain behavioral modifications. At the top of the list was the elimination of barracks language, which could sometimes penetrate the Sousa Band Hall like ham and eggs in the mess hall.

*Freddie:*

*April 1974: We are leaderless. Lieutenant Colonel Harpham is not showing up for rehearsals or concerts. What is going on? He is reporting to Quantico Marine Base daily to undergo hearings and seems to be in some kind of trouble. Who, then, is in charge?*

*Jack Kline takes over as Acting Director of the Marine Band. Chuck Erwin is asked to assume the position of Operations Officer and resigns as solo cornetist.*

## Damage Control

The story broke and left members in a mild state of shock. Harpham, it seemed, or so went the charges, had received financial compensation in addition to the "temporary duty" pay he was drawing while on military leave to guest-conduct band festivals. Very few people knew this, until someone within the band told an outsider—the band's own version of "Deep Throat" of Watergate Scandal lore.

The story found its way to the desk of Jack Anderson, noted syndicated columnist of "Washington Merry-Go-Round," and it soon appeared in newspapers around the country. Early in 1974, an active duty field-grade officer was placed on the staff of the Marine Band as deputy director to provide guidance on legal matters in order to ensure prevention of another mistake of this kind.

The director of Marine Corps public affairs became operational commander for the Marine Band except for White House commitments. The White House still has direct tasking authority over the band.

Lieutenant Colonel Harpham received an honorable discharge from the Marine Corps. The grandiose gentleman who had waited seventeen years to take over Schoepper's command managed to lose it all in less than three years, an omen to those events that eventually forced the resignation of a President a few months later.

To this day, the Marine Band's Deep Throat remains anonymous. ❖

## Chapter 25

# New Era

The days of Albert Schoepper were gone.

The fear factor, intimidation, pomposity, all gone.

So was the precision and that unique Schoepper sound that had defined the Marine Band from the 1950s through 1972. When Schoepper on that warm spring day in April passed the Sousa Baton to Dale Harpham, no one foresaw Harpham's demise. Having coveted Schoepper's job since the latter won it in 1955, Harpham was going to take the Marine Band to even greater heights than Schoepper. Instead, he experienced the kind of low that no Marine Band predecessor at that level had known—being forced to abdicate his position after the infamous Jack Anderson column and the Corps' subsequent investigation.

The leader now was Jack Kline, an amiable sort, a "one-of-the-boys" wannabe. Jack was a combat veteran of World War II. He went into the band later as a clarinet player, but made his reputation on the strength of his arrangements of *Witches' Sabbath* from Hector Berlioz's *Symphony Fantastique* and other classical orchestral transcriptions. Jack was a "good ol' country boy" and for those who hated Schoepper, a welcome breath of fresh country air.

FATHER AND SONS — Frederick J. Erdman, (second from left) 709 N. Third Ave., shakes hands with Lt. Col. Jack T. Kline, director of the United States Marine Band, last night at an appearance by the band at Annville-Cleona High School. Erdman's three sons (left to right), James Erdman, Fredric Erdman, and Timothy Erdman, all members of the Marine Band, surround him. The elder Erdman was honored last evening at the concert when he was invited to come forward and direct the band in which his three sons were playing. Erdman, who has taught private cornet and trumpet lessons in Lebanon for a number of years, has been largely responsible for the musical excellence of his sons. (Daily News Photo)

# Brother Trio A First
# In Marine Band Concert

By CURT SUTHERLY
County Correspondent

ANNVILLE — The United States Marine Band last night gave a rousing performance before a filled auditorium in the Annville-Cleona High School, and as an added feature, three Lebanon brothers, Fred, James, and Tim Erdman, who are all members of the band, performed as a trio.

The Erdman performance been with the band since 1956, is retiring in the near future. James will return to the Lebanon area to take up residence in Mount Gretna.

He plans to work as a registered piano tuner, performer and instructor of the trombone.

Jim's older brother, Fred, with the band since 1955, and a cornet soloist, will remain in the Marine Corps.

Follow In Footsteps harp soloist and one of the f individuals adept with such instrument in any conce band.

Pinkerton's rendition 'Green Sleeves" was favorite.

Baritone soloist Micha Ryan was also well receive He sang three numbers befo the assembly. Ryan's mo moving number was powerful "Shenendoah."

*A 1975 Lebanon Daily Newspaper clipping of the three Erdmans, Dad, and Lieutenant Colonel Jack Kline.*

> *Freddie:*

*June 1974: The concerts at the Capitol are now played in front of the West Capitol plaza. Yours truly is still playing assistant to the solo cornet player. Frustration is starting to set in with me. Poor leadership and lack of the kind of precision I knew so well under Colonel Schoepper spell dark days ahead for the Marine Band. By June of next year, I will have had twenty years of service, qualifying me for a lifetime of retirement income. Perhaps it's time to move on.*

## A New Direction

In September of 1974, Acting Director Major Jack Kline replaced Harpham on this year's tour. After playing thirteen consecutive tours, Freddie happily elected to stay at home. Jim, on the other hand, would make his nineteenth consecutive tour, but would not be a featured soloist for the first time in his career.

Freddie used the "home guard" time to study orchestral trumpet with one of the country's top orchestral players. Lloyd Geisler was an excellent teacher. He used to say, "When you practice, you're putting money into the bank. When you perform, you're taking money out of the bank." Among other things, he taught Freddie which pitched trumpet to use on the important trumpet passages of the orchestral repertoire. These are tricks of the trade, and Geisler knew them well, crediting them with helping him keep his job in the orchestral field. He took Freddie through ten volumes of orchestral trumpet excerpts. It was a fun and interesting time, and Freddie eagerly looked forward to his lesson with Geisler every Saturday morning.

Different orchestra parts for trumpet typically are written for differently pitched trumpets. Many trumpet parts written by J. S. Bach, for example, call for the D clarino, or high-register, trumpet. If a part might be designated, say, "In C," the trumpet player has several options. He can play the part on his B-flat trumpet and transpose up one step throughout the passage. He can simplify things for himself by electing to play the part on his C trumpet (the C-pitched trumpet is frequently used in places where the B-flat-pitched trumpet would be more difficult to play and/or project), which is pitched one step higher than his B-flat. Or, if the part still doesn't "lay" well on the C trumpet, he can select another pitched trumpet, such as a D trumpet, in which case he would have to play all the notes DOWN one step. Orchestral pros like Geisler instinctively knew which trumpets best suited the passage.

239

*Freddie:*

My studies of orchestral trumpet continue with Lloyd Geisler. He is getting me ready to audition for the New York Philharmonic. One of the pieces on the required list is "Samuel Goldenberg and Schmuyle," from Mussorgsky's "Pictures At An Exhibition." He wants to hear me play it. So, I pick up my D trumpet and play it. After playing through it, Geisler says, "They ought to hire you on just that alone."

November 1974: In the John Philip Sousa band hall, a short ceremony saw Jack Kline promoted to director of the United States Marine Band on November 1 and to Lieutenant Colonel on November 14.

March 1975, Avery Fisher Hall, New York City: There are 150 trumpet players here to audition for the second trumpet opening. After I've warmed up, I'm waiting for my call and hanging around backstage. I happen to be standing next to an old string bass player who plays with the orchestra. I say "Hi" to him and he says, "You don't want this job." I ask, "Why?" He says, "Too much bullshit."

I am finally called and escorted by the first horn player, James Chambers, into the auditioning room. As I seat myself, I see the trumpet part to Bela Bartok's Concerto for Orchestra. I get to play eight bars of it. "Thank you very much," says the auditioner behind the screen. I never got to play the Mussorgsky. That was it. Months of preparation for this audition, which consists of all of eight entire bars of music. What a crazy world! ❖

*Shortly after Jack Kline became leader of the Marine Band, Jim Erdman took this photo of the band's three living alumni leaders of the Marine Band: William Santelmann, Albert Schoepper and Dale Harpham. The three surround the band's legendary bass drummer, Vinnie Mauro. From left to right: Santelmann, Schoepper, Mauro, Harpham and Kline.*

# Chapter 26

# Bernstein Weeps

For any newbie in the Marine Band, that first experience of sitting on the bus as it drove us up to the doors of 1600 Pennsylvania Avenue was a sobering one. Here was this bunch of red-coated musicians about to enter the White House, the world's single-most-recognized home and repository of power. It could be both frightful and exhilarating.

## The Effect of Celebrity

Celebrity performers seemed to think that way, too. Regardless of their musical genre, they fully appreciated the reality of being in heady company. Those I had the pleasure of conversing with between rehearsal breaks, like Tammy Wynette and Roger Williams, expressed this much: for them, performing at the White House was a capstone to their careers.

Hearing such expressions of awe from the entertainment world's elite seemed to level the playing field. Because they considered us the White House's performing "regulars," they seemed inclined to have a special regard for us as well. "You work at the White House? Man!" We in turn were "wowed" at the thought of performing with the "big names," a privilege none of us took lightly.

There was also a steady stream of guest dignitaries, many of them celebrities in their own right. I can remember seeing a few of Nixon's Watergate cronies coming through the front entrance for a state dinner, before reading in the paper sometime later that these were the same people convicted of felonious crimes. One day they could be headed for the White House; the next day, jail.

Knowing that celebrities and politicians of high stature and hallowed dignity were strutting all around us, the idea of performing in their midst could be an unnerving experience.

## A Memorable Fanfare

One Monday morning on what was to be our "day off" for that week, I was called in to rehearse with three other trumpet players. The piece was a fanfare for President and Mrs. Ford, as they were to descend the Grand Staircase leading to the Entrance Hall, during a White House reception that was to be held later that evening.

Upon our arrival at Sousa Band Hall that morning, we were handed a newly composed, 12-measure fanfare with the assignment to do a few dry runs, then go home and memorize our parts. Memorizing a melody part was easier for me than doing the same for an inner part. Since I was playing the third part, I had to continually sing it to myself throughout the day until it became automatic.

Later that afternoon, we met again at the band hall, this time to rehearse our parts together from memory while playing our herald trumpets, which were pulled out of the cases and dusted off every so often for such occasions. Then we packed up the Besson heralds and headed for the White House.

Once there, we were directed to what was referred to as the "cloak room" in the basement where we stashed our White House cloaks and unpacked our instruments. With heralds in hand and new fanfare parts dancing in our heads, we walked upstairs and waited for our cue to march into the Entrance Hall and near the bottom of the Grand Staircase.

The cue came early. We marched in smartly and stood at attention. I was on the end of the four-man group. Just seconds before we were directed to perform, Vice President Nelson Rockefeller decided to walk over with a drink in his hand and stand a few steps directly in front of me. I had read stories and seen pictures of "Rocky" in the tabloids ever since I can remember learning to read, when our dad would bring home the New York *Mirror* everyday from work. At that same moment, Secretary of State Henry Kissinger walked over to say something to Vice President Rockefeller, and stood on my right. And there the two stayed— Rockefeller just in front of me on my left, Kissinger on my right.

These weren't just players, they were Goliaths of government, policymakers who could tilt the balances of power in any direction.

My brain went soft as putty.

"Ladies and Gentlemen, the President of the United States and Mrs. Ford."

We raised our heralds to perform the fanfare. The ensemble's sound was striking, brassy, and played with precise rhythm and tempo. But the notes I worked so hard to memorize throughout the day were gone, nowhere to be found in my distracted mind.

I had gone clueless.

Our performance succeeded in adding regality and majesty to the occasion, by a fanfare that had a certain surreal edge to it—thanks to my on-the-fly invention of a strangely harmonizing third part that was more cacophony than harmony.

*First Lady Betty Ford dancing with Tony Orlando. Tim Erdman is seated directly behind, performing with other members of the Marine Band White House Combo. (Photo courtesy Gerard R. Ford Museum)*

## Encounter with a Giant

Not everybody in the Marine Band came unhinged when in the presence of greatness. One of our contemporaries was Jerry Rogers, a fine clarinetist whom I came to regard as friend and colleague. Another was Ray Dryburgh. Ray and I knew each other briefly when I was going to Temple University in Philadelphia and he was freelancing as a trumpet player around Philly; a few years later, he followed me into the band. Jerry, Ray, and I did a lot of concerts, Sunset Parades, and funerals together.

Jerry and Ray also performed regularly with the Marine Band string orchestra that plays so frequently at the White House. Ray remembered an incident that occurred at the White House. I was still in the band, during the Jimmy Carter administration, a time when Leonard Bernstein was a frequent guest at the White House.

"During one visit," Ray recalls, "Jerry Rogers was playing the second movement of the Mozart Clarinet Concerto, when into the foyer walks Bernstein. He stops, listens for a moment, and proceeds to stand right in front of Jerry, no more than six inches away from Jerry's face. He's watching Jerry intently as he is playing . . .

"Jerry," continues Ray, "obviously keeps his cool and continues to play, despite knowing he is only inches away from a Giant of Musicdom.

". . . and tears begin to roll down Bernstein's face.

"At the conclusion, Bernstein gives him a big hug, kisses him on the cheek, and disappears into the dining room.

That was the last time Jerry played with the White House orchestra.

## To Sit or Not to Sit

Ray also remembers the time that Helmut Kohl was a dinner guest of President Reagan's. "He was an amateur cellist and well-versed in music," says Ray of the German Chancellor.

"Walking into the White House, Kohl stopped just inside the foyer entrance while the orchestra was playing Bach's *Gavotte Orchestral Suite, Number Three*. The trumpets were seated behind the orchestra and just in front of the front entrance of the foyer, where Kohl had just walked in. Kohl was blocking the entrance so that Vice President Bush and Mrs. Bush couldn't get in.

"Kohl looked down at me and asked, "What else are you going to be playing?

Ray really felt caught on the spot and didn't know if he should stand up in deference to the chancellor, or remain seated. He was afraid that if he stood up, the Secret Service might shoot him! So he remained seated and began leafing through the folder to show Kohl what they were going to be playing. John Bourgeois, the band's conductor at that time and who was conducting the orchestra, began staring at Ray. Getting increasingly angry, Bourgeois thought that Kohl should have come up to him and ask him what he was playing.

Ray happened to look over to his left and saw that Nancy Reagan seemed perturbed as well. But her husband, President Reagan, was "laughing his head off." ❖

# Chapter 27

# Escorts

In April 1975, the Marines evacuate American citizens and other foreign nationals from Cambodia and South Vietnam. Early in the morning of April 30, 1975, ten Marines stationed at the U.S. embassy become the last Americans to leave Saigon, ending the U. S. presence in that country. The war is over.

*Freddie:*

*As in last year, Jimmie and I are not called upon to solo on the spring concerts. I am curious about this but not complaining. I've had enough of soloing anyway, at least for a while. Besides, my aspirations have now changed to the orchestral world. I hope to get a job with a symphony orchestra. My spirit for the Marine Band has fallen, but not my pride. I continue enjoyable lessons with Geisler, getting increasingly inspired with the pitched trumpets and the music that calls for them. Mary Jo, my beautiful lady, is also an inspiration to me.*

*Though not a professional musician, she is enough of one to understand and appreciate my craft. Through her interest in music (she sings with a good soprano voice), I find myself wanting to learn more about music so that I can answer her questions more clearly. She likes concert band music, especially the brass. She also likes classical music and some pop music of the 1940s, 1950s, and 1960s. With an enticing voice and lovely personality, Mary Jo, in her late teens, worked as a telephone operator for Ohio Bell in Columbus, Ohio, and was used as a model for trainees. She studied voice, piano and music theory at Bowie State College in Maryland, and also sang second soprano in the college choir.*

That fall, Freddie would once again stay home on tour, and I joined him. Although Jim did make the tour, he would not be soloing again, just like last year. Kline instead chose to feature a harp soloist, James Pinkerton, and vocalist Mike Ryan. There were to be no brass soloists. In fact, none of the three of us had been featured as soloists since Kline took over in the spring of last year.

Not long after the winter thaw, those famous cherry tree blossoms of the nation's capital exploded in their magnificent fuchsia, a spring tableau that has inspired writers and poets throughout the ages—along with those whose responsibility was to plan the annual spring ritual known as the First Lady's Luncheon.

## New Mission

During roll call one morning, Drum Major Dennis Carroll called out about twelve names of band members, including mine, to meet with him after roll call. Usually when we were called in for something that hadn't been fully explained ahead of time, our first impulse was to think, "Well, what did I do wrong now?"

As we congregated in his office, Carroll began with a slight grin.

"Congratulations," he said. "You guys have been selected to be escorts." Puzzled looks passed among those of us unfamiliar with this ritual, which evidently was most of us.

We could see a common thought forming in our minds: Why not? If the band needed escorts, then we were the best-looking "bandies" for the job. Now for the *real* question . . .

Escorts? For who? For what?

Carroll explained.

Some years before, one of the coordinators of the annual First Lady's Luncheon at one of the plush downtown hotels got the bright idea to use younger players from the band to "escort," or usher, guests at the luncheon—among them Congressional Club members, the wives of senators and congressmen. It was one of those downtown affairs that always made the society columns. The First Lady always attended and was always escorted by the Director of the Marine Band. We had been chosen as this year's crop of "escorts."

As Carroll ended his explanation, someone quipped, "Does that make us gigolos?"

"Yes," I piped in. "We now have a new mission: we are United States Marine Band Gigolos."

Ha-ha.

## Quiet Dignity

In actuality, we would be ushering about forty Congressional spouses, each along a red-carpeted promenade. Our job was to walk them with quiet dignity to either the head table or to one of the circular, number-designated dining tables throughout the large banquet room.

Here was a mission loaded with possibilities for pratfalls and other *faux pas*. I could see myself gliding down the runway with a glamorous Congressional wife on my arm, in shimmering diamonds and dressed to the nines, only to trip over my size-12 feet and go down like Chevy Chase, pulling her down with me in front of hundreds of women whose husbands represent the country from every state in the union. That one possibility alone made all of us take our "mission" a little more seriously. Perhaps too seriously.

I had some interesting "draws," my very first being the wife of Congressman John C. Kunkel. This was a real coincidence and, I thought, just had to be a blessing. For many years the eminent congressman had represented my very own congressional district, which included my hometown of Lebanon, Pennsylvania. Truth be told, that's all I knew about him. I had never met Congressman Kunkel, or knew his politics. In short, I knew nothing about him.

Heck, I never even voted for the man.

But, of course, as a somewhat-nervous rookie "gigolo" and greeting Mrs. Kunkel as my very first assignment, I felt in need of some form of polite and socially correct small talk. So I said what anyone in my position of very limited intelligence would say:

"Mrs. Kunkel, it's such an honor to meet you."

"Why, thank you, young man."

Offering my arm and guiding her to the promenade, I continued.

"I just have to tell you that your husband, Congressman Kunkel, represents the congressional district I come from, which is in Lebanon, Pennsylvania."

"Oh," she said. "That's nice." She was a dear woman, very polite, her hair beautifully coifed, but I detected some uncertainty in her voice. That should have deterred me from saying the next line, but it didn't, and I did.

"I voted for your husband in the election last year."

(Liar.)

"Oh really," she said, without missing a beat, "that's strange."

"My husband has been dead for the past two years."

It was the longest walk of my life. I can remember thinking, "So this is what it's like walking the gangplank." Talk about feeling like a displaced person. This was a case of trying too hard. From that moment on, I vowed to limit any conversation on my part to little more than that of a chimpanzee's vocabulary.

## Can't Win

Walking back from Congressional Wife Number One and in recovery mode from my raw-egg gaffe, I was directed to Escort Assignment Number Two, then Number Three. Each went without incident, and everything was flowing smoothly by now. Then came Assignment Number Four: a tall, lithe, and hand-somely attractive woman. Drawing nearer, I offered my arm. She took it, then began to sob. I realized she had been trying to hold back tears and now just had to let go.

"Are you all right, ma'm?" I asked, shocked, moved, thinking of what to offer in the way of consolation, then reconsidering after remembering my vow of silence.

"No, I don't think so," she said between tears, raising a tissue to her nose.

"I'm sorry," I said.

"No, it's all right," she said, blowing her nose. "I'm sorry. I'm sorry I am this way. I'll be okay. You see, this morning I was served a summons for divorce from my husband. It just hit me, that's all."

She was Phyllis Holden Dole, first and soon-to-be-divorced wife of Robert J. Dole, war hero and esteemed Senator from Kansas, and future presidential candidate.

Another gangplank. This job wasn't all it was cracked up to be.

## Small Rewards

But there were perks. One was in shuffling off with some of the leftover booty: centerpieces and other special forms of tabletop gift-type memorabilia. At the conclusion of the First Lady's Luncheon, a lot of gift bags were left behind from no-show wives, so we were directed by our escort coordinator to take as many as we could carry for our own personal use. I took four bags. Inside each bag were beautifully monogrammed towelettes, special candies, White House matchbooks, exotic soaps and creams, and other tastefully done items. They made for some exquisite gift-giving the following Christmas.

## Special Assignment

Despite Mrs. Kunkel's verbal dissection of my psyche, my gigolo-ing was deemed a success, and I was "called back" again for the following year's luncheon . . . and the next. At each one, the Mmes. Kunkel and Dole episodes lingered fresh in my mind. By this time, I had learned to follow the exhortations from my own first wife, which was to greet each Congressional wife with a "How are you, ma'm" and stay mute—and out of trouble—the rest of the way.

Entering the hotel lobby, we gathered around for our briefing from the luncheon coordinator. "Gentlemen," she began, as she had the year before, and the year before that, "it's good to have you here again.

"Very little has changed. Most of you have done this before, so you know what to do. Each of you will have an escort assignment. You will greet the wife with a smile and keep the small talk to a minimum." (At the mention of "small talk" my heart skipped a beat, and I felt my face flush.)

"Then you'll offer your arm, and when her name is mentioned, casually lead the lady along the promenade and up to the head table. Give her a nice goodbye smile, and come back using a dignified but stepped-out pace for your next person to escort."

I felt a tap on my shoulder.

"Sergeant?" I heard a strange voice say from behind. Uh-oh, I immediately thought. They're going to ban me from this function after all.

Well, who could blame them?

"Yes, sir?" I replied to the gray-suited nondescript man. He was a member of the Secret Service, I was told later.

"We'd like you to carry out a special assignment for us."

Here it comes: the proverbial getting kicked upstairs, the demotion, the shameful punishment for all those guilty of sticking one's foot in one's mouth.

"We'd like you to guard the main entrance doorway."

I looked at him in bewilderment. "Right now?"

"Right now," he said, "until we're ready to open the doors and the luncheon is ready to proceed. You see, Sergeant, we've noticed that in past years, some of the wives have been going through the main doors into the hall early, well before they're supposed to, for the sole purpose of pilfering souvenirs and some of the tableware."

I nodded my head. "I see."

Apparently, some wives were brazen enough to enter the main hall, walk away with a centerpiece here, a gift there, then sneak out through some rear entranceway to stash the goods in their cars. Who would do such a thing? I thought.

"We'd like you to guard that door, and under *no circumstances* are you to admit anyone access through those doors."

"Yes, sir," I replied.

"When you're finished, we'll relieve you, and you can join your fellow escorts and receive your assignments. Okay? Understand?"

"Yes, sir."

Thinking this was a chance for my own private redemption from the Mrs. Kunkel affair, I went promptly to the double-door entranceway and stood at parade rest. Legs and feet slightly apart, hands clasped behind my back, I felt like the Colossus of Rhodes.

Minutes passed, then a middle-aged woman approached. "Excuse me," she said, expecting me to step aside.

"I'm sorry, ma'am," I said. "I can't permit you to enter at this time."

The woman smiled politely, raised her eyes, and sighed as if to say "Oh well" and heeled around.

Three more women approached with the same intent and were turned away in the same polite but firm manner. Potential felons? If so, I was doing them a favor, keeping them out of trouble and away from the long arm of the Secret Service. I began to wonder how being such a "guard" and "escort" would look on my resume someday. There had to be some socially redeeming value for these sorts of things.

Next was an attractive young blonde. She looked familiar, but that didn't matter. Orders were orders.

"I'm sorry ma'am," I said in my usual tone. "You're not allowed to enter the banquet hall at this time."

"I'd appreciate if you'd get out of my way," said the woman. (I remember the impulse thought: look out, Tim, this one could be trouble.)

"Ma'am," I countered, "I have my orders. I can't let you go through these doors."

"Move aside," she insisted in a low voice.

"No ma'am," I said.

She turned around and walked off in a huff. Ten seconds later, I was rushed and surrounded by three or four Secret Servicemen. Had they mistaken me for an assassin?

"It's okay, she can go through," one said.

"Right," I said, relieved, realizing that orders are orders for some but not for all. Especially when I was told that "she" happened to be Susan Ford, daughter of President Gerald Ford.

That would be my very last time as a Marine Band escort, an experience that was never listed on any of the many resumes I submitted throughout the ensuing years of my life. ❖

## Chapter 28

# "Would You Like to Meet the Queen?"

*Freddie:*

*November, 1975: About 10:45 a.m., after coming in from a very cold outside duty gig and feeling a bit depressed, I received word from the office that the Colonel wanted a meeting with me. My relationship with the band these days had become a mixed bag of emotions. The Schoepper era ended three years ago, his successor had been booted out, and my job had profoundly changed, accompanied by a sense of loss and the resulting lack of enthusiasm for playing in what I had once regarded as one of the finest symphonic bands the world had ever known.*

*Naturally wondering what it was all about, I walked through the door and into Lieutenant Colonel Jack Kline's office.*

*"Yes, Colonel, you wanted to see me?"*

*"Freddie," he began, "I just received a call from the director of the Royal Marine Band in England. He says that he, the band, and the British Government would like to help us celebrate our Bicentennial by having the Director of the United States Marine Band and one of his soloists appear as guest conductor and guest soloist at a concert they're giving in February at Royal Albert Hall in London. So, I thought it would be appropriate for me to bring along our longstanding, stellar cornet soloist."*

*"What would I be playing?" I asked.*

*"Well, how about 'La Mandolinata?'"*

*"Okay," I said, my voice trailing upwards.*

*"And they would like you to play the Staigers 'Carnival of Venice' as an encore, since that's so popular over there."*

*"When do we go?"*

*"Well," said Kline, "the concert is on February 3, so we'll be leaving a couple of days before that. I'll schedule in a day when we can rehearse those solos with the band."*

*"All right, Colonel."*

*On my way out the door, I felt pleasantly surprised. Kline made it his business to select me to be his guest soloist for this trip. It's been years since I felt this relevant. Time to start practicing again.*

## Jimmie Retires

On January 30, 1976, after serving twenty years as premier trombone soloist with "The President's Own," Jim Erdman retired. A retirement ceremony was held in his honor in the Sousa Band Hall. After accepting a score of accolades, Jim spoke to the band, then conducted it in a march of his choosing, *Alte Kameraden (Old Comrades)*. A reception followed in the band hall. As it drew to a close, Jimmie and Freddie shared a few parting words. And then, just like that, he was gone—the beginning of the end of an era, and what seemed a sad day for Freddie, who saw his younger brother as a bulwark of the trombone section, a major player who in every sense had upheld the aggressive, symphonic, operatic style that was a hallmark of the Marine Band's dominant brass section.

When Jimmie retired, the Erdman Trio would be no more.

Without realizing it at the time, my departing brother would no longer be on hand for advice and otherwise. Jimmie has said on occasion that, had he hung around, my career with the band might have been more successful, one that might even have continued into my own retirement.

During the last tour we made together as The Erdman Trio playing Morrissey's *Concerto Grosso*, I said something to him that offended him deeply. Tour pressure had gotten to me, and the remark was made, which I was to regret almost as soon as I had said it. Saying it and later wishing I hadn't is one of those pitfalls we all stumble into throughout life's travails. We went for weeks without speaking to one another. Finally, after getting up the courage to apologize, I walked up to his room one night after a concert and knocked on his door. He asked me to come in, and I told him I was sorry for having said what I did.

His act of forgiveness was an unforgettable brotherly moment. It taught me to think before I speak. But more importantly, it taught me how to forgive a brother.

*Marine Corps publicity photograph of its youngest master gunnery sergeant, James A. Erdman II.*

## Comeback Trail

It had been two years since Freddie had soloed with the Marine Band: the incentive to practice just wasn't there. It was getting increasingly difficult to remember those days in the fourth grade, this one-time pre-teenage musical phenom, wood-shedding for four to six hours each day, drilling constantly on vast amounts of technique, perfecting everything the cornet had to offer, and then some. But now, with Kline's decision to present his best soloist to an audience inside one of England's most prestigious concert halls, the sense of rejuvenation was palpable. Like an aging athlete on the comeback trail, Freddie returned to his old practice regimen, putting in three- and four-hour days on the horn, determined to be in the best playing shape of his life by the last week of December.

During one of his trumpet lessons, Lloyd Geisler noted his only concern, and that was a significant time away from "the horn." The schedule would be all-encompassing, one that might consume most of Freddie's time from the moment he would step off the plane at RAF Brize Norton Airport, north of London. There would be lots of introductions, conversation, back-slapping, and glad-handing. The Brits were a generous but hardy lot. They liked to make their guest feel at home, and their hospitality always seemed to come with a drink in hand. Geisler just might have a point, Freddie thought.

On Saturday, January 31, 1976, 9:30 a.m., a military staff car drove Kline and Freddie from the barracks to National Airport just outside Washington, D.C. The two boarded British Airlines, and Freddie's first transatlantic flight was about to begin. At 11:00 p.m. London time, the plane touched down amid darkness at RAF Brize Norton.

### Freddie:

*I remember disembarking and being met at the plane by a British Royal Marine captain, who greeted and assisted Jack with his luggage, but completely ignored me. I had a cornet, a uniform, and a suitcase to lug. It was cold as I followed the colonel and the captain during a seemingly endless walk. The captain led us to his motel room, located on the airport premises and about 200 or more yards from the plane. In his room, he hosted us each with a scotch while briefing us on the forthcoming schedule of events.*

*Sunday morning, February 1, Early Morning Practice:*

*After downing two scotches-on-the-rocks, I finally go to my room. It is close to 1:00 a.m. and I haven't had a chance to play all day, so I've got to get that horn out and practice for an hour-and-a-half on the "whisper" mute, which mutes the sound of a trumpet much more than an ordinary mute. During my practice, the captain calls down the hall to me, saying in a typical British accent, "Do you play reveille at the barracks?"*

*"No," I simply reply, and go about my business. It has been obvious to me right from the start that he has no concept, nor does he care who I am, good, bad or indifferent though I may be. In his eyes, I am just a sergeant, period.*

*At 3:00 a.m., it's time to get some sleep. We depart by motorcar at 6:00 a.m. for Deal, England, a four-hour-long trip. I set the alarm clock for 5:00 a.m. to give myself enough time to shave, groom, and get dressed.*

*The 5:00 a.m. alarm sounds and I force my way out of bed. I get two hours of sleep. Nearly an hour later, I'm out the door to meet the colonel and the British Royal Marines captain.*

*At 6:00 a.m., we board the motorcar and promptly leave the airport premises. Kline says "Good morning" to me. The captain doesn't say anything. So much for British hospitality.*

*Inside the car, a young military woman is tearing up the streets, some of which are very narrow. We motor through several small villages, and I realize that she has to be clipping along at sixty miles an hour!*

The sun was out, signaling a clear and beautiful day in the United Kingdom. By ten o'clock everyone had arrived on schedule at Deal AFB, which apparently had been a Royal Air Force base during World War II and now the headquarters of the Royal Marines Band.

The colonel and his soloist were escorted to the Commandant/General's quarters to meet him and socialize with him and his guests, including Colonel Neville, Director of the Royal Marines Band.

*Freddie:*

*We are immediately offered a scotch. As we talk with people, another drink is offered and in order to at least appear socially agreeable, I accept. An hour passes by. I am introduced to Warrant Officer Ron McCay, who will be my escort throughout my stay here in the U.K. Ron takes me to the staff mess, where we lunch with a playing member of Her Majesty's Royal Marines Band. Ron seems like a really nice guy. Ah, there's that British hospitality.*

*1:00 p.m. He takes me around the base to meet more people. We make two stops, where I am offered beer. These folks are so friendly. At 6:00 p.m., we "chow down" at the staff mess hall. Ron now says that we have to pay a visit to the staff club to "meet the boys" as he puts it—the members of the Royal Marines Band.*

## "Meeting the Boys"

*About an hour later, Ron and I enter the staff club. There are a lot of "boys" sitting at the bar, and all heads turn toward me as I walk in with Ron. I know there are comments being made about me, but I can't make out the words. I'm terribly uncomfortable being a standout in a situation such as this, but I manage to hide it pretty well and hold my ground while exchanging comments with them. They really are nice chaps, and they receive me most cordially.*

*A drink is offered. I graciously accept and once again indulge. After talking with them for about a half hour, I am introduced to the bartender, Scott—another very friendly chap. He offers me a drink, so I ask him for a lager, just to be polite. I really don't want any more alcohol, but I don't want to hurt his feelings, either. He seems to take a liking to me.*

*The "boys" then invite me to throw darts with them. One explains the rules. His explanation doesn't help. I don't have the foggiest idea of the rules for darts, but I play anyway. I'm doing pretty badly, and every time I turn around, someone has either a beer, a lager, an ale, or scotch in his hand for me.*

259

*Three ales, beer, lager, and one scotch later, I see that it's almost one o'clock in the morning. "Fellows, I'm going to have to call it a night so I can make the rehearsal at 9 o'clock."*

*"Oh, c'mon," someone says. "We have to see what kind of musician you are." They don't know that I have an hour-and-a-half of practicing ahead of me yet. "All right. I'll show them," I'm thinking. "No one is going to call a member of the United States Marine Band a wuss!" As I concede to stay a while longer, I am handed yet another drink.*

*2:00 a.m. I politely say, "Thanks much, guys" and walk out. Finally, I'm back in my barracks room, which is quite small and somewhat cramped, about seven-foot by ten-foot with a locker, a small sink, no bathroom, and a small cot. (A "water closet" is located down the hall, along with slippery toilet paper.) It's cold in here. There is no thermostat in the room, so I can't turn up the heat. Having practiced for one-and-a-half hours, it's now 3:30 in the morning. Time to take a couple of Vitamin B complex tablets to rebalance my system, and get to bed. Damn! It's cold in here!*

*Monday, February 2, 6:00 a.m., Scotch and Rehearsal:*

*Got to get up. Last night, Scott the bartender invited Ron and me to breakfast at his flat. (He resembles very much Randolph Scott, the movie actor.) Upon entering his flat at about 7:30 a.m., Scott offers us "a bit of scotch." No rocks. Ron accepts, but I refuse as graciously as I can.*

*"Oh, just a bit, Freddie."*

*"No thanks, Scott."*

*Ron tells Scott that I have a rehearsal to play at nine o'clock.*

*"Oh," says Scott. A few moments before he serves breakfast, he again offers me "just a bit of scotch." He just thinks I have to have it! Tiring of refusing his offer, I finally give in and think, "What the hell! Go ahead and take the bit of scotch with him." He is so generous and cordial. He cooks a good breakfast, too: ham and eggs with fried potatoes, toast and coffee.*

*8:30 a.m. As Ron drives us to the rehearsal site, I'm getting those all-too-familiar butterflies of anxiety, but I feel physically ready to perform after such a good, hearty breakfast, thanks to Scott. I am thinking back to last night, when I was doing quite badly at darts. As I was playing, one of the band members said, "He can play dots but he can't play darts." (They refer to musical notes as "dots" over here.)*

*8:40 a.m. We arrive at the rehearsal site, which is an old stone building dating back to the 17th century. The hall inside where we will be rehearsing is quite huge, with a seating capacity of about a thousand, I estimate. We go backstage, which, considering the spaciousness of the hall itself, is rather cramped for space. I get my horn out, then begin looking for a spot somewhere in here where I can warm up without blowing in someone's ear. There are a number of people back here. As I pick out a small space at a wall, Ron says to me, "Are you going to do some lip flexibilities?" I nod a "yes" to him. I cannot be disturbed now. I have to loosen up. "Lip flexibilities" are slurring exercises between intervals of varying lengths, designed to help the brass player loosen the lip muscles and tissues and prepare the embouchure for more strenuous, flexible playing.*

*Considering all the drinking I've done up to this point, "looseness" should be the least of my worries! But I feel no adverse effects; the butterflies are too busy. I must bring them under control.*

## Let's Show 'Em How It's Done

The rehearsal began at 9:00 a.m. sharp. Colonel Kline took the band through a couple of selections he chose from the Marine Band library. Just before ten o'clock, he called for Freddie. "All right," thought Freddie. "Let's show 'em how it's done." Walking out toward the band, Kline introduced him to the band, which responded with warm applause.

"Okay," says the Colonel. "Get up the 'Carnival of Venice.'"

When he saw that everybody had his part up on the stand, the Colonel turned to his soloist and said, "Ready, Freddie?"

"Yeah," he replied softly.

*Freddie:*

*As the Colonel gives the band the downbeats to the three major chords, I'm thinking, "We're in good shape, so just blow!" On the third chord, it is time for me to blow as I attack the first note, leading into the opening slurring cadenza. Feels good. Everything is working. Playing through all three variations, I am pleased with my execution and quite pleasantly surprised that I could play up to my standards after all that booze yesterday. Following the last chord, the band gives me rousing applause and the cornet section gives me a standing ovation. The Colonel then says to me, "Could we do this once more?"*

*"Sure," I answer. We play the Staigers again from the top to the end.*

*We then rehearse "La Mandolinata" twice. That ends the band rehearsal for this morning.*

*At this point, Colonel Neville presents a gift to the Colonel and one to me, an ice bucket on which is inscribed the coat of arms and "EIIR" (difficult for me to describe). The cornet and trumpet players then form a line, come up to me to shake my hand and congratulate me. On the way to lunch, Ron tells me that, after the first time through the "Carnival of Venice,"*

261

*all the cornet players lowered their instruments, held them underneath their chairs and waved them back and forth. "Why did they do that?" I ask. By doing that, he explains, they are saying they can't match your playing. He added that they expressed disbelief when they saw and heard me play through the entire "Carnival of Venice" twice and "La Mandolinata" twice, all within 15 minutes.*

*After lunch, Ron takes me to Canterbury Cathedral where, among other things, I see two sarcophagi. He also takes me to the shoreline of the English Channel, where Julius Caesar had landed his troops nearly two thousand years ago. A metal plaque sticks out of the sand, stating the date of the landing. I can also see Calais, France, from here.*

*6:00 p.m. Ron and I have dinner at his flat. He prepares steak, potatoes, and salad. Two hours later, he takes me to a stage play on base. By 11:00 p.m. we return to his room, where we fraternize for another hour or so. By 1:00 a.m. I am back in my barracks quarters and proceed to get the horn out once again for a light forty-five-minute practice. By 2:00 a.m., I plunk myself down on my bed and fall asleep.*

......................

## The Big Day

The alarm clock sounded at 5:00 a.m. Groggy and at first disoriented, he reached for the alarm and shut it off, then remembered, This was it! *The Big Day*, the day of the performance. He got up, shaved, groomed himself, and got dressed. Meeting Ron and the Colonel Kline about an hour later, the trio left Deal promptly in a motorcar for London, stopping off for breakfast along the way, as did the two buses carrying the band. Midway through the five-hour trip, Ron told the Colonel and Freddie that, after the concert, all the stars of the show would go up to Lord Mountbatten's box to meet the legendary World War II hero.

Kline then asked Ron if the Queen would be in attendance for the concert. "Naw," he replied, as if to say, "We don't expect to see her there."

By 11:00 a.m., everyone arrived in London then proceeded to one of the pubs downtown for lunch. And drinks, of course.

......................

*Freddie:*

*By 1:00 p.m., we had arrived at Royal Albert Hall for a dress rehearsal. There was plenty of time to warm up. The Colonel called for me to rehearse my solos once again. As I played through them, it felt as if the carpeted hall was "dead" in sound, with no reverberation whatsoever. My sound, I feared, was getting completely sucked up! It was like playing inside a box full of cotton! By this time I had grown to hate the acoustics of Royal Albert Hall. String players might have found this place an ideal performance venue, but certainly not brass players!*

*After rehearsing the solos, I make my way back to the backstage area and pass by the BBC's Richard Baker, the concert emcee. A news commentator, he is probably the UK's answer to our Walter Cronkite. "Fantastic!" he says to me as I pass by him. Acknowledging him with gratitude, I couldn't help feeling the remark was exaggerated. I didn't sound as good to myself as I did back at Deal.*

......................

By five o'clock the rehearsal was over. Ron took Freddie to a Chinese restaurant for a quick bite; they had to get back to the hall by seven o'clock, at which time Kline and Freddie were to meet with Richard Baker backstage. Baker needed general information about the U.S. Marine Band, Colonel Kline, and guest soloist Fredric Erdman. The interview went as planned, and the countdown began.

......................

**Freddie:**

*It's now 7:15 p.m. The concert starts at 7:30 p.m. I need to be with my cornet. My next challenge is to find a place backstage where my chops can have contact with both instrument and mouthpiece. There are a lot of people back here wanting to talk to Colonel Neville—almost every time I turn around, I seem to be bumping into somebody. This is impossible! I won't be able to blow a note without warming up in somebody's ear!*

*I spot a door across the way, walk over and open it, and see a tiny powder room inside, about five feet by three feet. Surreptitiously, I step inside and close the door. Hopefully, I can be by myself and warm up for fifteen or twenty minutes without anybody wanting to use it.*

*7:25 p.m. and five minutes before concert time. The adrenals are really pumped up, and the butterflies make an unwanted appearance.*

......................

## The Concert

At 7:30 p.m., the very eloquent Richard Baker greeted the audience with a few remarks, noting that the Band of the Commando Forces is in the United States on a Bicentennial Tour.

"And of course," he added, "the Bicentennial gives you the clue to this evening's program. This is a celebration in music of the Declaration of Independence. Actually, we are celebrating not so much the fact that they booted us out 200 years ago as that we are still speaking!"

The audience laughed.

"And," continued Baker, "I would like all you Brits present to give a special welcome to all the American friends who've come to join us this evening, not least the *chargé d'affaires* of the United States Embassy."

(Applause.)

"Now, of course, there is a very good deal of American music in the program tonight, and to start us off is a march, an American march, 'National Emblem.' And to conduct this and the first part of our concert, here is Captain J. R. Mason, Director of Music of the Band of the Commander in Chief, Naval Home Command."

(Applause.)

..............................

*Freddie:*

*As I expected, their style of playing this march differs from the way we play it. Next is a piece written by Don Gillis, followed by Leroy Anderson's "The Typewriter."*

*I'm getting that scary feeling again. We're getting so close to when I'll have to walk out on stage. Baker now introduces Colonel Kline. Meanwhile, I'm backstage, not knowing when I'll be next, since I don't have a printed program.*

*The Colonel conducts two selections. "I could be on after this one," I'm thinking. After the second selection concludes with more applause, there is silence.*

........................

Richard Baker's voice could be heard through the loudspeaker system once again.

"Colonel Kline was telling me earlier," he told the audience, "that many of the members of the U.S. Marine Band go to universities first to get their music degrees, and then they join the U.S. Marine Band. We do it the other way around. We teach them the music at Deal, and then they go on to be leaders of the profession. We have in fact no less than thirty junior musicians under training here tonight who are making their first concert appearance. So, that's pretty good!"

(Applause.)

"But, of course," Baker continued, "the best musicians in the U.S. Marine Band don't bother with university. Among them is Master Gunnery Sergeant Fredric Erdman, who is probably . . . (short pause) the best cornet player . . . (short pause) in the world. And he's going to play for us a fantastic solo written by another cornet player, Hermann Bellstedt, *La Mandolinata*. Sergeant Fredric Erdman."

............................

*Freddie:*

*My inner voice says, "Okay, let's get professional. Just get the first few notes out in the opening cadenza and we'll be all right." I walk through the band from backstage and make my way to the front of the stage. Bowing in acknowledgment of the audience, I see in front that the hall is filled to capacity (it seats five thousand). It's dark out there. I look over to Colonel Kline; he looks over to me. I give him the go-ahead nod. The Colonel starts the four-bar introduction to the opening cadenza of eighth-note triplets. After positioning my embouchure, I make my entrance and attack all triplets successfully. I'm getting more confident already. We've adjusted to the hall; now, we're just performing. The multiple tonguing is crisp and sharp; the notes are coming out the way I want them to. As the last chord is played, the audience applauds, cheers, and gives me a standing ovation as I bow twice and then make my way backstage (a long walk, it seems). I won't be coming out for a second bow. The path to the front of the stage is too long. They are still applauding. "Whew! Glad that's over!" I always hate the thought of having to do it, but if everything goes right, then I'm glad I did it.*

............................

As the second half of the concert got underway, Kline conducted two more selections. These were followed by George Gershwin's *Rhapsody in Blue* played by the guest piano soloist. Every now and then, Freddie would blow a few notes backstage at discretionary times—for example, during the Rhapsody's louder moments, when no one could hear him playing, just to keep his "chops" warmed up for the upcoming Staigers.

After the Rhapsody was played, along with two other pieces conducted by the Colonel, Richard Baker came back onstage, saying, "How would you like to hear Fredric Erdman again?" The answer came back in enthusiastic applause.

"The *Carnival of Venice!*" announces Baker.

..............................

*Freddie:*

*Here we go again.*

*I play through the Staigers and the execution is clean. As I play my final note on this interesting and challenging sojourn, I hear thunderous applause. As I return to the backstage area, the band and Colonel Kline perform another piece. Meanwhile, I'm back here thanking the Force, the Divine Source—God, if you will—for helping me sustain the schedule I have been on these past three days, and for giving me a performance matching my standards. I put my horn (my "teammate" Bach Stradivarius cornet) back in the case, feeling that I upheld the honor of the Marine Band and my country. This, in spite of having amassed a total of seven hours of sleep in three days (and four quarts of booze?) from the time we landed at RAF Brize Norton Airport to concert time tonight. Now, I can finally relax and enjoy the company of the British even more.*

*As the last number concludes, I must go back out, without my cornet this time, to take center stage with the other stars of the show: Colonel Neville, Colonel Kline, Capt. Mason, the guest pianist, and Richard Baker. We stand at attention as the band plays "The Star-Spangled Banner," followed by "God Save the Queen." Very stirring. After the last note is played, the concert is over.*

..............................

## Not Finished Yet . . .

Returning to the backstage area, Freddie picked up his encased cornet and made his way out to the hallway, behind the backstage area. There, he was met by several people wanting his autograph. One woman quipped, "Bloody good!" and offered him a program for autographing. After signing his last autograph, Freddie took off for the staircase leading up to Mountbatten's box. Making his way up the ornate, golden staircase, Freddie looked up and saw two ladies on the top landing looking down at him with smiles. As he reached the top landing, one of them gently took hold of his elbow.

"Would you like to meet the Queen?" she inquired.

......................................

*Freddie:*

*"Oh, absolutely!" I reply. This was totally unexpected!*

*She leads me by the arm into a room off to the right of the landing. We walk across to the far wall. And there she stands—Queen Elizabeth II—facing me with a nice smile. As I stand in front of her, her Lady-in-Waiting, who still has me by the arm, introduces me.*

*"Well, it's an honor to meet you, Your Majesty."*

*I wasn't prepared for this.*

*"You were fantastic," says the Queen.*

*"Thank you."*

*I notice she's wearing a brown tweed suit and looking somewhat matronly.*

*"I don't know how you do it," says Her Majesty.*

*"Well, I had a good audience to play for."*

*She smiles. "Well, good luck for the rest of your wonderful career."*

*I thank her.*

*And that was it.*

## Lord Mountbatten

*The Ladies-in-Waiting and a bodyguard lead her out of the room. The Queen's visit to me was so hasty and secretive that I don't think anybody realized she was in the room. I think she didn't want to be seen, so sometime during or after the concert, she arranged with her Ladies-in-Waiting to sneak her into the room and stay just long enough to meet me. As I look around the room, I notice that everybody's attention is on Lord Mountbatten. I know that all of the other stars have already met Mountbatten, so I amble on towards him. He is standing in the middle of the room and chatting. Ron or somebody introduces me to him.*

*"It's my honor, Your Lordship," I say as he shakes my hand.*

*"Tell me, how come you're still a Master Gunnery Sergeant?"*

*"Well, I've been meaning to talk to you about that, Your Lordship."*

*Laughter erupts from him and everybody around him.*

*"How do you move your lips so fast," says His Lordship, pointing to his lips.*

*Now I really have to think of something to say.*

*"Well, ah, you see, sir, it's all done with the tongue." I point to my tongue.*

*"The tongue!" He chuckles, and so do the others. "Well, it was nice meeting you," says His Lordship.*

*"It was my pleasure," I respond.*

*He makes his way out as the reception breaks up.*

**Inside the reception room of Lord Louis Mountbatten in Royal Albert Hall. Left to right: British Secretary of the Navy, Captain Shilito, Freddie, Lord Mountbatten, Colonel Jack Kline, Colonel Neville, the BBC's Richard Baker, and P.J.F. Whiteley, Commandant General of The Royal Marines.**

## Time for a Drink

*I walk out of the room and descend the staircase. At the bottom, I meet Ron, who has my cornet case in his hand. He introduces me to two friends of his, a married couple. The wife gives me a big hug, and we all go out to dinner. We are driven by motorcar to an Indian restaurant in downtown London. After being seated, I'm thinking, "Now I want a drink!"*

*I have to unwind. Following my order of Indian cuisine, the drink is served and I imbibe with sheer pleasure. I need this! The meal is delicious. I'm having a wonderful time in the company of newfound friends. The husband looks and sounds like W.C. Fields—very funny. His wife is gracious and charming. We all enjoy a delicious meal and wonderful company. W.C. Fields picks up the tab and we're now off to their flat for the night.*

*February 4, 7:15 a.m. The Day After: I awake to find that Ron is gone. Everybody has left for work, and I'm still in bed!*

*Ah, good. I can sleep in!*

*9:30 a.m. I wake up, and the wife offers to drive me around downtown London. We sightsee at Big Ben, London Bridge, Parliament, Piccadilly Square, the Wedding Cake, etc., and she, at my request, stops at that famous department store, Harrod's. There, I purchase two beautifully knit sweaters for Mary Jo. She then takes me to a Howard Johnson Motor Inn on the Thames, where a room has been booked for me. As we part, I of course thank her for the great time we had last night and for getting me to the hotel here. The next morning, I make a transatlantic phone call to MJ. I forget that she is still at work, because she is six hours behind me. But she is excited to hear from me anyway.*

*Friday morning, February 6: The Colonel and I are taken back to RAF Brize Norton Airport for our return flight to Washington, D.C. via British Airways.*

## Grandma's Pride

*Some time after my performance in London, I had occasion to go up home to visit my parents in Pennsylvania. I also decided to visit Grandma, who was in a nursing home and well into her nineties. As I entered her room, I noticed that she was seated and in friendly conversation with one of the nurses. Making my way across the room toward her, she turned and gave me a look of surprise, accompanied by a big smile.*

*As I stood in front of her and the nurse, Grandma, with great enthusiasm and pride, said, "Dorothy, this is my oldest grandson, Freddie." Without missing a beat, she added, "This is the one who played for Queen Mary."* ❖

# Chapter 29

# Freddie Who?

Freddie received letters that praised his playing, some from Royal Marine bandsmen, as well as a very complimentary letter from Secretary of the Navy J. William Middendorf II.

In October, 1976, Freddie's performance was chronicled in the *ITG (International Trumpet Guild) Newsletter*: "ITG member Fred Erdman, premier cornet soloist with the U. S. Marine Band was honored with a request from the Royal Marine Band of London, England, to be their soloist at a concert to be attended by the Queen of England. After receiving the necessary clearance from the U.S. Marine Corps, Fred made the trip and played his usual flawless performance, after which there was a reception and Fred met and talked with Her Highness, the Queen, who was very enthusiastic about his playing. It was quite an honor and an occurance that does not take place very often, where a soloist from another country is invited to appear with a military band. Fred, a native of Pennsylvania, has been soloist with the Marine Band for some years. He studied with his father and, after joining the Marine Band, continued his studies with Lloyd Geisler."

By Spring 1977, the band resumed its spring and summer concert series, now at the West Capitol plaza every Wednesday evening, a venue that Freddie felt was not as good acoustically as the East Capitol plaza. He missed playing there.

The Colonel had not asked him to solo.

## Expanding Horizons

At Lloyd Geisler's house, Freddie resumed his lessons. Geisler was fun to play for, and it was interesting to learn all about transpositions involving the differently pitched trumpets. Freddie owned a B-flat Bach trumpet, C trumpet, a combination D/E-flat Schilke trumpet, and a French model Couesnon (pronounced "Cway-non") piccolo trumpet. His lessons gave Freddie an opportunity to play all of them. In terms of technique and endurance requirements, he was finding the orchestral literature much, much easier to play than the standard concert band repertoire.

On April 16, 1976, Kline accompanied Freddie to the post's commanding officer's office, where Freddie was awarded a special commendation, given by Colonel W. H. Rice, in recognition of his performance in London. He was not going to go on the fall tour again, which gave him time to take some coursework. He decided to take a semester of conducting with Lloyd Geisler at the Army post of Ft. Myer, Virginia, just on the other side of Arlington National Cemetery.

> Freddie:

*We have only three students in the class. The assignments include Mozart's "Jupiter Symphony," Strauss' "Till Eulenspiegel," a Mozart piano concerto, and the last movement to Ravel's ballet, "Daphnis et Chloé."*

*I'm enjoying this class, except for the fact that Mr. Geisler keeps jumping on me for one thing or another, more than he is the other two. On our final assignment, Daphnis et Chloé, I study and practice with the score while the record is playing. Every day and late into the night, I'm looking for the smallest mistake he might stop me for. He's got me so damn furious! He has never complimented me like he has the other two. "All right," I say to myself, "I'll show that little red-headed bastard!"*

*I'm determined to be mistake-proof when next week's class comes around.*

*Next week comes. We are now at our final class for this semester, and it is my turn to conduct.*

*Geisler turns on the record, starting at the last movement of Daphnis et Chloé. As I conduct my way through the movement, Geisler does not stop me. After the final chord is released, Geisler says to me, "You must really like that piece to be able to conduct it so well."*

*I certainly did not expect such a compliment. I forgive Mr. Geisler for his seemingly undue criticism of these past four weeks. I think he really got the best out of me. What a coach! Two weeks later, I receive in the mail his grade for my conducting: "A."*

## Pulling Strings for a Brass Conference

Throughout the winter of 1976 and spring of 1977, Freddie resumed his orchestral trumpet excerpts with Geisler. The two had progressed as far as Volume 8 (of ten volumes) of the "Orchestral Excerpts" series, edited by Roger Voisin, for many years the Boston Symphony Orchestra's principal trumpet, and one of the first to have ever held a full-time contract in the American orchestra field. In August 1977, after returning from leave, Freddie was told to report to Kline's office, that there had been a problem with the solo cornet part on last Sunday evening's concert at the Jefferson Memorial. Kline then told him he wanted Freddie to take over the solo cornet chair—shades of the 1962 tour, when Freddie was called upon once before, by Schoepper, to "rescue" the cornet section.

In early December, Luke Spiros, who for the past several years had succeeded Arthur Lehman as the band's principal euphonium player, had an interesting proposition for Freddie. "The Greek" happened to know trumpeter Charles Colin, a famous pedagogue and music publisher in New York who also happened to be Luke's godfather. Paying Colin a visit, Spiros played a recording of Freddie's performance of the Staigers *Carnival of Venice*.

"Who's that!?" Colin exclaimed.

"Freddie Erdman," said Spiros.

"Freddie who?"

"Freddie Erdman," repeated Spiros. "Premier cornet soloist with the Marine Band."

"That is the most amazing rendition of the *Carnival of Venice* I have ever heard," Colin said in awe. "Can I get Freddie up here to play for the Brass Conference?"

In New York City, the New York Brass Conference for Scholarships has been a yearly gathering of the finest brass players of the world in both the classical and jazz idioms, attended by the full spectrum of players and brass-playing aficionados.

"I don't know," replied Luke. "The Marine Corps has an issue about Marine Band soloists playing outside engagements." (Such oversight resulted from the

Harpham debacle and the subsequent takeover and close monitoring of the band by the Marine Corps.) "But I'll see what I can do. We might have to get the Marine Band up here to play a concert. That way, we could slip in a featured solo spot for Freddie."

Colin frowned, then smiled. "I'd like to hear him play my favorite cornet solo, *La Mandolinata*." Not too long before this conversation took place, The Greek had been teaching computer technology to the band's copyist, who happened to personally know Secretary of the Navy J. William Middendorf II. Middendorf occasionally visited the John Philip Sousa Hall to have the Marine Band record some marches that Middendorf himself wrote. On one of these occasions, the copyist introduced Luke to him, and The Greek ended up playing for Middendorf at several embassies, in order to record some more of his marches.

In early December, Charles Colin wrote the Commandant a letter requesting his permission for the Marine Band and its soloists, Luke and Freddie, to perform for the New York Brass Conference the following January.

The request was denied. Any appeal would seemingly be futile, since appealing a decision by the Commandant of the Marine Corps is like fighting 100 City Halls all at the same time. But The Greek's connection with Middendorf managed to return dividends. A couple of weeks after the letter of permission had been turned down, fate intervened. Walking into a Howard Johnson's restaurant, Luke by chance saw Middendorf and walked over to him. The two struck up a conversation immediately, and following a few pleasantries, Luke sensed the timing was right.

"By the way, you know Charlie Colin up in New York, don't you?"

"Yes," replied Middendorf.

"He and I are trying to get the Marine Band up there in February to play for the New York Brass Conference, so he can hear Freddie play Charlie's favorite cornet solo." Spiros went on to explain that Colin had written a letter of request to the Commandant and had been turned down.

"Are there any strings you could pull to get us up there?"

"I'll take care of it," said Middendorf.

The very next day, the phone rang in the Commandant's office. It was Middendorf.

"The Marine Band will be going to the New York Brass Conference in January."

And that was the end of that.

# Count on the Marines

*Mid-January 1978:  After Colonel Kline rehearses "La Mandolinata" with me, Luke comes up to me and says, "Freddie, you're not playing that as fast as you used to."*

*"Wait 'til we get to New York," I reply.*

*I had a strategy. By slowing up the variations just a bit, I felt I was giving the Colonel a better feel for where the main beats were with all of those sixteenth notes flying around. Besides, I want to save that energy for a faster speed when I would get to play it up in New York.*

*January 20, 1978:  A snowstorm is predicted for the East Coast. It is already snowing as the band takes off from the barracks by bus. The concert is scheduled for eight o'clock tonight. Estimated travel time is four hours. As we're buzzing along Interstate 95, it is snowing heavier, driving conditions are worsening and we now think this concert might be cancelled. So much snow is accumulating! We are now seventy-five miles away from New York City when we get word that New York is shut down. No buses, trucks, or cars are entering New York. But—we are!*

*7:00 p.m   We arrive at the Roosevelt Hotel in downtown New York, site of the conference and where the concert will be played. Luke and I, followed by the rest of the band, walk into the hotel dining room for a quick bite to eat. "Luke, you are a god!" exclaims Charlie Colin. He had been sitting in the dining room, waiting for our arrival.*

*7:30 p.m.  Following a quick sandwich and salad, Luke and I check into a room that Luke has booked for us.*

*7:40 p.m.  We have less than fifteen minutes to warm up in the room. At five minutes to eight o'clock, we leave the room to take the stage. As I get on stage, I notice that this "hall" looks more like a long conference room and not at all like a concert hall. This is where all solos and ensembles will perform.*

## Almost a Spiritual Experience

*8:00 p.m.  Colonel Kline walks out to the podium without an introduction, as there is no moderator for this concert. Everything is played without announcement, although programs are being provided to the audience. I am not only soloing, but playing the solo chair as well. After a march and two selections, I make my way out to the front of the band. This audience will be the most empathetic and most critical of my entire career, since it is made*

275

up of big-name New York brass players, as well as those making the trip from nearby major metropolitan areas such as Philadelphia and Boston.

The audience greets me with warm applause. As I assume my position, I see that the hall is about half-full and mostly dark. I get the sense of standing inside a long dark tunnel, because of the distance between where I'm standing and the far back of the room. I can only see the people in the first two rows, a somewhat ominous feeling.

I give the Colonel the "okay" nod, and he starts the band playing the opening four-bar intro leading into my entrance.

I attack the opening series of eight eighth-note triplets, and finish the cadenza. The execution is satisfactory to me all the way, and the entire cadenza is note-perfect. The acoustics are terrible—hardly any reverberation whatsoever. After finishing the cadenza on a high-C fermata (a note held for a length of time at the player's discretion), the band goes into the two-bar intro that leads into the theme of the piece. Coming into the melody line, I feel more confident. Everything is working throughout this solo—lips, tongue, fingers. Everything is there.

We come to the end of the theme section. The band plays a nineteen-bar interlude. I then play a very short cadenza. After a middle-C fermata, I lead into the first multiple-tongued variation. I set the tempo, playing it faster than I did at rehearsal. The Colonel has to hang in there with me, because I'm takin' off! As I play through the first variation, something bordering on the mystical seems to be taking hold. I am experiencing something I've never experienced before.

Is this a spiritual experience?

After playing the first variation, I hear applause from the audience.

This is followed by another nineteen-bar interlude leading into another cadenza that ends on a written high-C fermata, which in turn leads into the second and last variation.

That "someone" or spirit continues to guide me to everything required for perfect execution of this piece.

At the end, the audience applauds and gives me a standing ovation. Note for note, it was my best performance of "La Mandolinata."

## Meeting the "Brass" of Brass

During the second half of the concert, Luke Spiros performed Hermann Bellstedt's "Napoli."

Just as the first half ended, Luke grabbed Freddie's arm and took him off stage and over to where several of the big-name brass players were standing. Luke had known these guys for a number of years and introduced Freddie to them, one by one. Among them was Raymond Crisara, whom Freddie was especially thrilled to meet. A leading studio trumpet player, Crisara was Freddie's number-one idol when he was growing up. From time to time, he would hear Crisara play a cornet solo with Paul Lavalle's "Cities Service Band of America" during its concerts on the radio, which back in the early 1950s were broadcast live every Monday evening at nine o'clock. After Crisara and Freddie shook hands, "Boy! You have quite an act to follow!" said Crisara to Spiros.

*Freddie:*

*In the second half, Luke does a beautiful job on "Napoli," and the band winds up playing a transcription of Liszt's "Hungarian Rhapsody."*

*Luke, John Wright, my very capable assistant, his wife, and I go out to dinner. The rest of the band goes back to Washington in the morning. Luke and I are staying overnight at the hotel so that he can introduce me to more famous players of the brass world. The following morning in the reception room, I meet Gerard Schwarz, noted trumpet and cornet player of New York; and William Vacchiano, principal trumpet with the New York Philharmonic, both very gracious gentlemen. In the afternoon, I find myself playing a rotary valve E-flat cornet in a small brass ensemble led by Gerard Schwarz, who is playing the B-flat piston cornet.*

*(Rotary valves on a cornet are similar to those on a French horn.)*

*It is fun as we play Civil War-era pieces for the conference audience. In the middle of the day, Luke and I head for Grand Central Station and take the train back to Washington.* ❖

# Chapter 30

# "Doing It Right"

As if to match the fresh bloom of cherry blossoms evidencing the return of springtime in 1977, the Marine Band, in its resplendent scarlet tunics and blue-trouser uniforms, began its spring concert schedule in Department Auditorium in the U. S. Commerce Department building, then went outdoors for those summer evening concerts at the Capitol plaza and Jefferson Memorial. Despite his success and subsequent accolades from appreciative members of the Royal Marines, Colonel Kline did not call upon Freddie to solo.

Freddie had just turned forty-one years of age. His face was fuller, but his waistline was still a trim twenty-eight inches. He hadn't stopped his training and still ran a few miles every other day to stay fit, sometimes working out as well in the weight room at the Marine Barracks. Brother Jim had retired, and there was little doubt that Freddie missed his outspoken younger brother who shared the featured soloist spotlight with him for the past twenty years. Both had logged countless miles together on all those tours, frequently soloing together as brothers day after day, night after night, earning their reputations as world-class performing artists.

## Studying with a Master

Jimmie had left me behind as well. Though I had never come close to attaining their status as perennial tour soloists, I had also been studying trumpet with Geisler by this time, and became increasingly curious and excited about the world of orchestral trumpet playing. Occasionally, Freddie and I would get together, play duets, and compare notes on the one person we had in common: Lloyd Geisler. By late summer, my second child, Rebecca Suzanne, was born, so I declined to go on tour and instead continued my lessons with Geisler at Catholic University.

As the Marine Band's solo chair cornetist, however, Freddie was obliged to perform on this year's upcoming sixty-three-day-long tour. As he was about to find out, the 1977 tour of the southeast turned out to be the easiest tour he ever played. "His playing sparkled; he never missed a note. Your brother's phenomenal!" I was told by some of the tour veterans on their return to the barracks in November. When I saw him, he looked refreshed, relaxed. And I knew instinctively: he, this man, one of two brothers I had idolized for years before myself coming into the Marine Band, had scaled the summit of cornet playing, during the most rigorous performance schedule known to man. And he seemed the happiest for it.

Freddie had approached the pinnacle of his career, reaping the fruits of all that practice to master the cornet during his school-age years. I on the other hand was suffering through a nightmare. It began innocently enough inside Geisler's Catholic University teaching studio one autumn afternoon. Freddie was gone on tour, and I was the last Erdman left on the "home guard," sharing first chair honors for the few kiddie concerts we played, plus doing substantial work with the combo at the White House.

I did the same thing in 1976, the last year President Ford was to spend in office. One night in that particular year, I found myself standing for photos between President Ford and guest artists Tony Orlando, who was being honored along with tennis great Jimmy Connors during a celebratory night of dining and dancing. The following year, after Jimmy Carter was elected to office, one of the church members at the Moravian Church we attended in Upper Marlboro came up to me. "I saw you on the Mike Douglas show," she said. I was taken aback, having no idea what she was referring to. "You were standing between President Ford and Tony Orlando. Mrs. Ford was showing it as part of her scrapbook." Then I knew. In addition to everything my brothers had accomplished, I now had my own little claim to fame, a photograph that would someday hang in the Ford Library. And I was in it, an honor I have never stopped cherishing.

For the past couple of years, I was also going to Catholic University as a declared graduate student in music performance, the curriculum of which called for trumpet lessons inside Geisler's studio. God bless him, that little red-headed Irishman. He had instructed so many pros in the business, and I could see why he was so popular. When it came to orchestral literature for the trumpet, the man fell into the category of "has forgotten more than the rest of us know." There was so much "music" about him; he even instructed the university's voice majors in the art of song and lyricism. He had a wonderful sense of the melody line and how to shape it, and would sing along a passage in your ear as you were playing (a teaching technique I later adopted for my own students over the years).

We were studying the *Concerto for Trumpet* by Joseph Haydn, which is considered "standard fare" for the instrument. Everything was going smoothly until the end of the first movement, where the eighteenth-century composer employed the use of widely spaced intervals to "bring home" the end of the first movement. Entering the passage where notes jumped by ten steps here and twelve there, I began missing the top notes of some intervals. "Let me try that again," I'd say, for the second, third, and fourth time, each time playing with the same mixed result. Frustration was beginning to set in. Feeling that I was disappointing not only myself but also my teacher, I wanted to pack things up and leave on the spot.

Where my Marine Band career was concerned, it would have been better if I had.

## Frustration

"I don't understand," I complained to Geisler, putting down my trumpet, adding, in a remark he must have heard a thousand times before, "I've practiced these jumps at home and never miss! Why am I missing them here?"

"Tim," he observed, "I'm not sure why you're missing, but I notice a lot of movement around your embouchure when you go to make the interval."

"What do you mean, Mr. Geisler?"

"Here, watch me," he instructed, picking up his trumpet and, without as much as a single-note's worth of warm-up, proceeded to play the passage of intervals flawlessly. On top of that, there was absolutely no movement around his mouth where mouthpiece met lips.

His demonstration was effortless. I was astounded.

"How did you do that?"

"I'm not sure," he replied. "It's always the way I played, so I never had to figure it out. But I think that's your problem. Your embouchure sometimes becomes unstable, especially when you attempt to play such difficult passages like the interval section in Haydn."

The answer frustrated me. I knew Geisler's teaching forte was his knowledge of the literature and when to apply which trumpet to which part. But any knowledge of a proper playing embouchure had to come from somewhere else, because the man behind the horn never had to figure out what he was doing wrong and how to correct it. He had, after all, always been "doing it right."

That afternoon, immediately after packing up my trumpet and leaving Geisler's office, I headed over to the bookstore on the grounds of Catholic University and there, in the music section, were several copies of a modestly thick, blue-covered book titled *The Art of Brass Playing*. The author, Philip Farkas, was a former member of the Chicago Symphony Orchestra's French horn section, and was considered (I later discovered) to be the foremost pedagogue in brass playing. I bought the book on the spot and took it home, reading it from cover to cover over the next twenty-four hours. It was a comprehensive source of information that, unfortunately, contributed to ending any hopes of furthering my own career in the band my brothers considered the world's best.

## Making a Major Change

After absorbing everything Farkas had to say, I was convinced: If I was going to carry out any future playing responsibilities at the highest level with the band, especially lead playing, I needed to improve the mechanics of my playing, I needed to change the way I played the trumpet. Right there on the spot, I decided to adopt a picture-perfect pose that Farkas depicted, one of several photographic close-ups of embouchures of members of the Chicago Symphony Orchestra's brass section. That very night, I decided to try puckering down on my lips, as if I were going to whistle, then back off the corners of the mouth ever so slightly. It seems like an insignificant change, but as I was to discover over the ensuing days and months, the "slightly altered" configuration turned out to be a radical departure from the way I used to play.

As Freddie would point out later, I was calling upon the tiniest of muscles that up to now had never been used, at least to this extent. During the first two days of practicing, using what Farkas referred to as the "smile-pucker" embouchure (instead of the "smile," where the corners of the mouth go back as one plays higher, the kind of embouchure I had employed all my life), everything seemed to be going well.

## Trapped

And then it all began to unravel. It suddenly seemed as if I were learning to play a brass instrument for the first time. The trouble revealed itself during the morning warm-up just before rehearsal. I'd get up at my customary time in the morning to report in for roll call at 8:45, put the cornet and mouthpiece to lips to play—and nothing would come out. If you can imagine the anxiety, the feeling of helplessness, when everything you've invested into making something work, and it wouldn't, then you can imagine the panic I suddenly felt. By this time, the change was irreversible. I felt trapped, with nowhere to hide.

I was determined to stick by my decision to change, but the more determined I became, the worse things got. Each morning before rehearsal, I'd replay the same results from the day before, with no response, notes barely coming out, a totally foreign feeling, all hell threatening to break loose if I was ever exposed while having to play a solo passage. Each morning was "ground-hog day," embodying the definition of insanity that says it is "doing the same thing over and over again and expecting different results."

The day I changed my embouchure was exactly two years before my current hitch with the band was up. At the moment I made the change, I told myself, "Tim, you've got one year to make this work. Otherwise, it's out the next year."

It would prove to be my own worst self-fulfilling prophecy.

*Freddie:*

*March 1979, another visit to New York: Luke the Greek and I return to the Roosevelt Hotel in New York City for the annual New York Annual Brass Conference for Scholarships. Last January, Charlie Colin had me placed on the NYBC board of directors and had asked Luke and me to perform again for this year's conference. After rehearsing "Carnival of Venice" with the New York University band, we take the subway back to the hotel. The day of the performance, the band conductor panics during the last variation of the Staigers. He rushes like hell on wheels and finishes about eight bars before I do! In spite of that, the audience gives me a standing ovation. For an encore, I play Jules Levi's "Our Own Make Polka."*

*Raymond Crisara greets me afterward and quips, "You are a giant!"*

*Spring 1979: Our younger brother Tim quietly out-processes from the band. His departure leaves the band with me as the only Erdman, the first time that has been the case since 1955.*

My last year was an exercise in futility. It was almost as if the embouchure had a mind of its own. Some days it worked, and other days it didn't. "The President's Own" is no place for unpredictability. The pressure of going into work each day became unbearable.

Unlike my two older brothers, I was not to retire from the Marine Band. After nearly nine years of service in the United States Marine Corps with the Marine Band, I took an honorable discharge and moved our family back to Pennsylvania. We settled in Harrisburg, where our fourth daughter, Amanda, was born. The first three —Jennifer, Rebecca and Catherine—were all born at Andrews Air Force Base.

Four of my trumpets went up for sale. Fortunately, no one had expressed an interest in them. After taking off for several months from any kind of playing whatsoever, I resumed putting the mouthpiece to lips. The embouchure change by now had somehow solidified itself, and I went on to enjoy a couple of years performing principal trumpet with the Harrisburg Symphony. At the same time I put my journalism degree from Temple University to work as a technical writer for one of the area's major manufacturing firms. Subsequent years of free-lancing on my trumpet with numerous ensembles added to the whole experience, as well as the opportunity to have taught at various colleges over the years as an adjunct trumpet instructor. Although my approach to playing the trumpet was different from the day I entered the Marine Band, the change served me well.

In 1988, the Pennsylvania Air National Guard 553rd Band, now known as the Air Force Band of the Mid-Atlantic, welcomed me as a member of their fine cornet section. A world of difference in the culture of Air Force bands and that of the band I recently came from was at first unsettling. Adustments were made, however and along the way I made many friends in that small but illustrious unit. During our two-week summer camps, we played in countries throughout Europe and Scandinavia in addition to many cities and towns throughout the Atlantic states. Our little 37-member Guard band produced some top-notch area musicians who also worked as public school teachers and in many other walks of life.

As for those events during my last years in the Marine Band and any lingering regret, it is far outweighed by the moments of having played alongside world-class players—my brothers and others. The dream was fulfilled, a dream that started while attending that first Watergate concert back in the mid-1950s, listening to the likes of first Freddie, then Jimmie. With Mom and Dad by my side, I was fortunate to have experienced his authoritative baton as well as those of R. Leslie Saunders and Colonel D. Keith Feltham, all the while sensing the shadow of Shoepper. I will always be grateful that my turn indeed did come some fifteen years later. ❖

# Chapter 31

# Saying Goodbye

As Colonel Jack Kline approached his retirement, a debate sparked up at Marine Corps headquarters over choice for the Marine Band's next Director. Would it be Major Snellings, an outsider, or Lieutenant Colonel John Bourgeois, Marine Band assistant director? Less than a month later, the argument was settled. John Bourgeois won the appointment. Bourgeois told Freddie that he was (a) "my solo chair man," and (b) wanted Freddie to perform—you guessed it—the Staigers *Carnival of Venice* every night on tour this year.

*Lieutenant Colonel John Bourgeois, 1978. (Photo courtesy Department of Defense)*

## Teacher Retires

That fall of 1979, the band traveled as far north as Vermont and west to Minnesota. At forty-three years of age, Freddie found himself still playing 126 concerts, two concerts a day—no days off. More importantly, he was still playing up to his own high standards. He later reminisced, "Those past three years were, in terms of performance, the best years of my life."

On November 4, 1979, Iranian students and militants stormed the United States Embassy in Tehran, Iran, and took sixty-six hostages, including eight U. S. Marines who were serving as guards. The world was transfixed by the 444-day ordeal that, in many ways, changed the political face of the Middle East.

In November 1980, Ronald Reagan overwhelmingly defeated Jimmy Carter in the presidential election. As tradition dictated, "The President's Own" provided the pre-ceremony music at the Capitol for the swearing in of newly elected President Reagan on January 20, 1981. Moments after he took the oath of office, the hostages were released and the nation breathed a huge sigh of relief.

*Freddie sharing his cornet with First Lady Nancy Reagan and a special White House visitor.*

As Reagan was coming in, another standout was on his way out. Lloyd Geisler, our beloved teacher, retired as principal trumpet and assistant conductor of the National Symphony Orchestra. He had also given up teaching, so Freddie's enjoyable lessons with him would come to an end. It was time for Geisler to collect payback for all those pressure-packed years of playing principal trumpet, an occupation rated near the top of the charts for stressful employment.

Enjoying a reputation as one of the most precision-playing principal trumpeters in the world, Geisler had once provoked a headline in one of the major Washington metropolitan dailies. A music critic in attendance heard him "chip" an attack during a performance with the National Symphony—a first, and this after more than three decades on the job. The paper's review headline read the next day, "Geisler Misses a Note!"

Now, instead of playing the trumpet, he would devote his time to practicing golf. Instead of practicing any longer for those delicate entrances and soaring passages in the orchestra, a job that only a small fraction of trumpet players aspire to (and a tinier fraction attain), Geisler would soon be swinging the sticks in Florida. There was no question in Freddie's mind: he would definitely miss the little red-haired Irishman.

*Freddie:*

*September 1980, West Coast tour: John Bourgeois wants to give me a year off as tour soloist but still wants me to play the solo chair on tour. In terms of playing, this is a very easy tour. I just sit back and play the book with John Wright, my assistant. We still live the same daily grind-out schedule.*

*March 1981, Disagreement: Bourgeois and I are not getting along very well. I don't agree with what he's doing on the conducting podium as both director and conductor. I think he is favoring the reeds over the brass and seems to be trying to convert the band into a symphony orchestra. On too many occasions, he is subduing the solo cornet stand when and where I think the part should not be subdued. This is making me increasingly angry. We are losing the traditional playing style this band has long been noted for. But, if John wants a different style, that's the way it will be. I just don't like it. I'm utterly frustrated and infuriated!*

*Late March: During rehearsals, Major Bourgeois and I continue to have conflicts and they are getting worse. Suddenly, something is going on with my playing! It's either nerves, adrenal glands, or both, because I'm getting a quiver in my tone when playing in the lower register. I'm playing the solo chair, still strong but shaky on solo passages. I'm sure everybody is noticing this, but nobody is saying anything about it to me. Even though I'm getting by, this is getting to be too much pressure. Mary Jo says I'm looking just a little rough around the edges; maybe go to the doctor and have myself checked out.*

*April 1, 1981: A visit to the doctor reveals a blood pressure reading of 188 over 112 on the right arm. The left arm reads the same. On the basis of that, plus not looking or sounding good, it becomes obvious to me that I've got some health issues. Not to blame this on John Bourgeois, but I think that our conflicts have finally caught up with me.*

*April 2: Feeling that my playing is on the decline, I walk into Bourgeois' office and tender my resignation as the solo cornetist.*

*"Okay," John replies, "but there is no way you are going to retire, because I want you to stay on as our cornet soloist." After roll call, John has me standing alongside him in front of the band as he makes an announcement about my resignation. He is most gracious and complimentary about my job as the solo cornetist. After rehearsal, John takes me out to lunch along with Chuck Erwin and Tim Foley (assistant conductors). I am touched by John's gesture. From now until whenever, I will be playing assistant solo cornet to Terry Detwiler.*

## The Pressure's Off

In June 1981, after having consulted with a nutritionist during the past two months, Freddie saw his blood pressure fall back to "normal"—130 over 71. According to those who knew him, he was looking a lot better. "My thanks have always gone to Mary Jo, who alerted me to go to the doctor," he recalls.

One month later, Major Chuck Erwin asked Freddie to perform Leonard Smith's *Spanish Caprice* during the Wednesday evening concert at the west side of the Capitol plaza, and the Sunday evening concert at the Jefferson Memorial, the very solo Freddie heard Chuck rehearse with the band back in June of 1955. "That Wednesday evening was nice and balmy," Freddie remembers, "a fitting backdrop for a very satisfactory performance of that solo. At the Jefferson Memorial, I got halfway through the opening cadenza when it began to rain. At that point, we all packed up and went home."

He would not make the tour that September. In his twenty-six years with the Marine Band, Freddie had made twenty-two tours, ten of which he had performed as featured evening soloist, and seven of which he had served as the first chair solo cornetist.

Even though each June moved him closer and closer to retirement, Freddie still had more soloing ahead. In July 1982, Bourgeois called on him to perform the Walter Rogers cornet solo *War Song-Columbian Fantasy* three times: first at the Capitol plaza on Wednesday evening; then on Sunday evening at the Jefferson

Memorial; and one more time outside in the stadium of the University of Maryland for the July 4th celebration concert. "The Capitol performance meets my standard," said Freddie. "The second performance at the Jefferson Memorial was better, and the third performance was even better. I would never play that solo any better than I did that night out at the University of Maryland."

In December of that year, Freddie received a complimentary letter from Frank Scimonelli, noted post horn soloist with the U.S. Navy Band for many years in Washington. During the same time period, he was moved down to the second cornet part. The following spring, Tim Foley, assistant conductor to Chuck Erwin (and who would eventually become the band's next leader after Bourgeois), asked Freddie to perform Frank Simon's *Willow Echoes* at the Navy Memorial downtown. Later that summer, Foley asked him to solo at the Jefferson Memorial, playing Steinhauser's *The Surf Polka*. It would mark Master Gunnery Sergeant Fredric Erdman's last appearance as a soloist with the United States Marine Band.

*Freddie:*

*Fall 1983: Terrorist bombs murder over 200 Marines in Lebanon. We helicopter up to Dover, Delaware to play as the remains are being flown in.*

*New Year's Day 1984: We play the "Surprise Serenade" for the new Commandant, Gen. Paul Xavier Kelly.*

*The powers that be have now put me out to pasture—I'm playing the third cornet part, next to last chair. In a way, it's kind of fun: no solos, no solo chair work, no pressure.*

*Marines participate in operations in Grenada.*

*1985: My last "Surprise Serenade."*

After thirty years in the United States Marine Band, Freddie's career had come full circle.

*Freddie:*

*May 31, 1985, Farewell Roast: A luncheon is given in my honor by the cornet and trumpet section! Lots to drink, lots to eat, lots of fun. And of course, I get roasted.*

*In attendance are the three directors: John Bourgeois, Chuck Erwin, and Tim Foley. Also present are Drum Major Carroll, Frank Byrne (tuba), Michael Ryan (vocalist), Tom Knox (arranger), Lucas Spiros (euphonium), all still on active duty. Retired friends and colleagues are there: Arthur Lehman, John (Buddy) Burroughs, Bob Isele. And of course members of the cornet section: David Rorick, Roy Griffin, John Wright, Terrance Detwiler, Bruce Gettinger, J. Carlton Rowe, David Sapp, Barry Stoner, Darrell Grabau, David Sorenson, Edwin Gay, and Mark Brown. Following the main portion of the meal, the roasting begins. They then present me with an album book containing the signatures of all the guests. In addition, it also includes salutary and congratulatory letters from many musicians who have known me down through the years. I am both humbled and exalted.*

*June 14, 1985, Flag Day and almost home:*

*Although this day marks the date of my enlistment back in 1955, crediting me with thirty years of service, I am asked to extend the date of discharge to June 26 because of accounting problems at headquarters. So, twelve more days to go. Yours truly is preparing his speech for the retirement ceremony and making arrangements to have a Greek buffet catered for the conclusion of the ceremony.*

*Tuesday, June 25, 1985: At the end of rehearsal, I am urged to take the band through the march I'm going to conduct at the conclusion of tomorrow's ceremony. I have selected a simple Austrian march titled "Schönfeld." As I take my position on the Sousa podium (everybody in the ensemble looks like they are five feet below me!) I ask the band to get up the march. Wielding my Schoepper baton, the impact of uniformity of attack, intonation, and sound coming from the band hits me like a freight train. This impact I shall never forget.*

*Wednesday, June 26, 1985, 11:00 a.m.  Music on the Cordovox was provided for twenty minutes prior to the start of the ceremony. I am attired in the full dress uniform. The ensemble is also attired in full dress and is seated in place, awaiting the start of the ceremony.*

*Thirty Years of Meritorious Service*

*At precisely 11:30 a.m., the band's vocalist, Michael Ryan, announced the presentation of the colors. A ceremonial color guard stepped off immediately, marching down the aisle toward the band as it played the trio strain of Bagley's "National Emblem" march. Taking its position in front of the podium, the color guard was given the command, "Present Arms," to which the band played "To the Colors." The bugle call "Attention" was sounded next. Colonel Bourgeois and Freddie entered the hall and walked in military fashion straight towards the color guard to "honors" position, then stood at attention. The color guard executed a "Present Arms" salute. The audience came to attention, and the band played "The Star-Spangled Banner."*

"Attention to orders!" barked Michael Ryan, who then proceeded to read the citation accompanying an award known as the Meritorious Service Medal. As Ryan concluded his reading, Bourgeois pinned the prestigious medal onto the upper left side of Freddie's scarlet tunic, then returned to his position. After the letter of retirement was read, Bourgeois presented the retirement package consisting of gifts and letters, including one signed by President Reagan. The band played *The Marines Hymn,* and the color guard executed "Present Arms" and "Order Arms" movements with their rifles, then retired the colors and marched its way back through the exit door. The formal part of the ceremony was over.

Colonel Bourgeois moved to the lectern, told the audience to be seated, then gave his remarks. He was followed by Chuck Erwin, now Lieutenant Colonel Charles Erwin, who presented Freddie with a gold watch. Terrance Detwiler presented more gifts, including an old silver-plated 1890 model short cornet, made into a lamp and given by the cornet and trumpet section.

It was now Freddie's turn at the lectern.

*Freddie:*

*I begin my speech by expressing my thanks to Colonel Bourgeois, Lieutenant Colonel Erwin, Major Foley and staff for bestowing on me the honor of the Meritorious Service Medal and Award. I also extend my thanks to Colonel Schoepper, who is sitting to my left in the front row, for giving me the opportunity of performing both as a soloist and as a solo cornetist with this great band. And one more word of thanks—to Mary Jo, for supporting me in all my musical endeavors.*

*In my remarks, I express the many things I enjoyed about the Marine Band. "There are a few exceptions, of course. (Lots of chuckling from the band.) "The camaraderie, the sense of humor, and the high degree of intelligence by which I've been surrounded all these years. And, oh yes, the outstanding musical qualities of this band. The flawless intonation and tonal quality, dare I say, was, at times, cosmic—just for a moment."*

*At the end of my speech, I tell the audience that I have chosen a march in honor of my mother who is of Austrian descent: "It is titled "Schönfeld." I ascend the podium, look at the band for just a moment, and then give the downbeat. Man! There's that impact again! Big gorgeous sound and uniformity of attack. It's all there! God! What a feeling! It is an experience. At the conclusion of the march and applause from both band and audience, Michael*

*Ryan asks everyone to join in congratulating me by going through my receiving line and attend my reception to the rear of the Sousa Hall.*

*Mary Jo, my beloved, comes up to stand beside me. An hour or so later, the crowd at the hall has pretty much thinned out. I've talked to a lot of people in that hour. Mother, Daddy, Jim and Tim, Aunt Ruth, our cousin Ginny, and many friends and colleagues of mine were here today. It is a sweet and sour day. Sweet, because I am free from "bondage." Sour, because I will miss the band.*

*MJ and I go downtown to the Iron Gate Inn for dinner to complete the day.*

## The Final Numbers

*During my thirty-year career, I had played for seven presidents: Dwight D. Eisenhower, John F. Kennedy, Lyndon B. Johnson, Richard M. Nixon, Gerald Ford, Jimmy Carter and Ronald Reagan. As a soloist, I performed 537 times in ten of the twenty-two tours I made with the Marine Band.*

*As part of a trio on the road, I played 256 times in four of those twenty-two tours. In addition, my solo performances in Washington and guest soloist appearances since my first solo performance on the Watergate Barge, Washington, D.C., July 17, 1955, totaled nearly 1,500 performances in that capacity.*

*On the first chair solo cornet, I performed 838 times on the road and in Washington, D.C. inclusively. Those thirty years were a unique experience, and one few musicians ever could hope to have.* ❖

## Epilogue

# Life after the Marine Band

Back in 1970, R. Leslie Saunders, Jimmie's trombone teacher, died of emphysema. With his passing, no one would ever again see the likes of a Saunders baton-throwing rage, the same baton (one of many, actually!) that produced such a top-quality high school band. I visited him in the Good Samaritan Hospital in Lebanon by his bedside shortly before his death. Like Schoepper, I was shocked upon seeing Saunders in that state of deterioration, his body a shell of itself, so much of it laid to ruin by cigarettes and hard liquor.

Dad was good friends with both Saunders and Schoepper.

In later years while they were still alive, Schoepper and Dad manged to keep in touch by exchanging letters several times a year. Colonel Schoepper never forgot our family. He showed up for Dad's retirement banquet from the Bethlehem Steel, as well as the concert and subsequent "evening" held in Dad's honor when the local college established a scholarship in his name. The two conductors seemed linked in so many ways, including the final one. Schoepper's death in 1997 was followed by our own father's demise one year and five months later. On Christmas night, 1998, at 7:30 p.m.inside the intensive care unit of the same Good Samaritan Hospital, Dad died. As his heart monitor ticked down to zero, I was lucky enough to be by his side.

The passing of men like Saunders, Schoepper and Dad signaled an end to the era of old-school leaders, at least for us. They were part of what newsman Tom Brokaw labeled "The Greatest Generation." They and countless others from that period accepted nothing less than excellence from the men and women they led.

After Jimmie left the Marine Band in 1976, he built a home in the mountain resort and arts community of Mt. Gretna, Pennsylvania where he and his wife Kathy reside there to this day. In 2011, at the tender age of 72, he performed a trombone recital at Lebanon Valley College. It was a pristine performance, one befitting the kind of world class musician he still is. What's more, it was accompanied by the announcement that this would be his "final" one, a statement believed by few if any in the audience.

Upon his retirement from the Marine Band in 1985, Freddie was hired as solo cornetist with the Capitol Band of Washington, D.C. and as assistant solo cornet with the Virginia Grand Military Band in 1995. In 2013, his wife Mary Jo was laid to rest in Arlington, Virginia.

My wife Carolyn and I live in Lebanon, Pennsylvania. She plays the accordion and is featured in the concert band I conduct, known as the Lebanon Community Concert Band. LCCB also happens to be the last band Dad would ever conduct. The band was formed in 1992 by the Lebanon chapter of the American Federation of Musicians, and Dad was asked to lead as its first conductor. Nine years and two more leaders later, I became its third conductor. Whenever I lift up the baton to lead the band, my mind's eye sees the authoritative images of Dad and Albert Schoepper.

My very first rehearsal as the band's leader occurred on the evening of September 11, 2001. I can remember the band's musicians walking into rehearsal inside Lebanon's senior center in the aftermath of the tragic events at the World Trade Center that had occurred earlier that day. Some of those musicians had the kind of dazed look on their faces that I'll never forget. We began that rehearsal with a prayer, followed by the Star Spangled Banner, then proceeded with Richard Rogers' *Victory at Sea*.

A community band like ours can never begin to match the flawless musical execution of the Marine Band. The one commonality, however, is the love of music and the drive to perform, reminding me that all musicians, from amateur to professional, form a joyous community of music.

Back in the 1990s, Jim got together with Chuck Erwin and a few of the other old-timer retirees to organize a Marine Band reunion, the first of its kind that we knew of, at least for our generation of performers. There have been subsequent get-togethers since.

At that first reunion of "The President's Own" United States Marine Band, one person stood up to give the keynote speech. "In reviewing this chain of directors," Col. Albert F. Schoepper said, "you lean towards the one who hired you and did the most for you. And you will name as the lowest son-of-a-bitch the one who did the most to you. So be it. I was privileged to build and leave behind a great and trouble-free band. And as I walked out the barracks gate on April 30, 1972, it was with the detachment of Pontius Pilate and the certitude and prophetic foresight of Louis XV.

"Enough! It's time now for me to yank my chain, and to express my gratitude to the members and their ladies of the Reunion committee, for giving us this truly memorable night. It is a virtuoso performance for all the virtuosi who are here. My thanks to all!"

There was no mention of "guaranteed notes" in that speech. But we all knew what he was thinking.

To hear the Marine Band and The Erdman Brothers, visit www.guaranteed-notesthebook.com. ❖

*Left to right, Freddie Erdman, Gil Mitchell (U.S. Army Band, ret.), Tim and Jim Erdman. This picture was taken at a reunion of former students of Ernest Williams in Reading, PA.*

*Left to right, Brothers Jim, Freddie, Tim and Mike, May, 2013.*

# Appendix 1

# Letters Received Upon Performance at Royal Albert Hall, London

BAND OF H.M. ROYAL MARINES
ROYAL MARINES BARRACKS, EASTNEY, SOUTHSEA,
PORTSMOUTH, PO4 9PZ
Telephone: Portsmouth 22351, Ext. 6138
13 February 1976
Dear Fred,

I just thought I would write a short note to say what a great pleasure it was to have met you and to have listened to your supreme musicianship at the Royal Albert Hall on 3rd February.

Everyone was full of praise, not only of your ability, but the unassuming and highly professional approach you exhibited on Tuesday night.

You are well aware of the high respect I hold for the U.S.M.C. but that night both you and Colonel Kline proved yourselves Ambassadors Supreme.

My only regret is that you were unable to come to Portsmouth and see our historic city, perhaps, some other time.

Yours sincerely,

David

The Secretary of the Navy
Washington, D.C. 20350
24 February 1976
Master Gunnery Sergeant Frederick [sic] Erdman, USMC
Marine Corps Band [sic]
Marine Barracks
8th & I Streets, S.W.
Washington, D.C. 20390
Dear Mastery Gunnery Sergeant Erdman:

I have recently received a letter from Mr. Frank Judd, The Parliamentary Under-Secretary of State for Defence for the Royal Navy, who was quite impressed with your performance on Tuesday, 3 February 1976 at the Royal Albert Hall. I would like to extend my personal compliments along with Mr. Judd's thanks for a job well done.

Your outstanding professionalism has contributed significantly to Anglo-American relations and is in keeping with the highest ideals of the U.S. Marine Corps.

A copy of this letter will be placed in your service record.
Sincerely,
J. William Middendorf II


Lieutenant-General P. J. F. Whiteley, OBE
Commandant General Royal Marines
Ministry of Defence
Main Building
Whitehall
London S.W.I.
01-218-7675
Master Gunnery Sergeant
    Frederick [sic] Erdman USMC
Headquarters
United States Marine Corps
Washington DC 20380
5 February 1976

Dear Master Gunnery Sergeant Erdman,

I am writing to thank you for the outstanding performance that you gave us on Tuesday evening at Royal Albert Hall. I do not believe that Richard Baker was understating the case when he introduced you, and I am sure that the presence of yourself and Colonel Kline and the enthusiastic reception which the audience gave you, did much to cement the relations between our two corps.

With my gratitude and my best wishes,

Yours sincerely,

Peter Whiteley ❖

# Appendix 2

# Letters Received Upon Retirement

May 22, 1985
MGySgt. Fredric Erdman
Cornet Soloist Extraordinaire
United States Marine Band
Washington, D.C.
Dear Fred:

I deem it most appropriate to address you in the above manner. You have spent both countless and diligent hours earning the respect and admiration of this organization as one of its premier soloists. In the long history of the Marine Band, few have attained this prestigious position.

Traditionally, until recent years, all auditions were held by the Director or his Assistant(s). Word would filter out to the musicians about who did or didn't pass the audition—and a complete rundown of the technical abilities were, of course, included.

We were not surprised, therefore, after your audition when descriptive terms such as "fantastic tongue," "unbelievable finger dexterity," "amazing slurring ability," "extraordinary lip trills," etc., etc., reached us. One more "flash in the pan." Then when we saw this young, skinny, bushy-haired, sleepy-eyed kid check into the Band, we knew our worst expectations would be realized.

It was only after this "kid" stood in front of the Band and played that first solo did we realize a new chapter on the art of cornet performance was being inaugurated.

Your consistency as a soloist throughout a long and triumphant career will never be surpassed. It was a privilege to be your section leader and co-worker for the majority of those years and I wish you a long and successful retirement which you so richly deserve.

Sincerely,

Charles P. Erwin

LtColonel, USMC

Assistant Director, U.S. Marine Band

24 June 1985

Fred Erdman, MGySgt., USMC

Dean and Faculty, The Erdman Conservatory

Suitland, Maryland

Dear Fred,

Thank you so much for the privilege of attending your retirement ceremony. Although you may dispute this, in my heart of hearts I have always considered myself a "musician" and rather than dwelling on the contributions you have made to the world of musical performance through your artistry, I would like to stress to you how much your pedagogy has enriched my own life, of which music is a most essential part. You have a unique ability to analyze your own "moves" and communicate this analysis to a student. Many great performers simply cannot communicate this way because their technique is so automatic that they never take time to analyze what it is that they do. You are truly a most gifted teacher, and lessons with you, the feeling of being able to improve (even at my ripe old age), gives me a personal sense of accomplishment that enriches my life.

When I first heard you play at the New York Brass Conference, I could not believe my ears. I have never heard such an ovation from the crowd at that conference. The knowledge that you are part of a lineage that extends back to Arban, Levy, Arbuckle, Clark, Simon, Bellstedt, Walter Smith, fills me with deep gratitude that you have undertaken the sometimes unpleasant chore of assisting me in my amateur enterprises.

Most of all, your intelligence and sensitivity have made me value you as a friend. I am most moved by the story of your childhood and the disruption and then reconstitution of your family. I also have an admiration for your father as a teacher and as a man who lovingly raised his children under the most difficult circumstances. Always interested in the "process" of creativity, I see many unique things in your childhood which compelled you to attain the level of artistic greatness which you had when you were already an adolescent.

I hope one day to surprise you and actually play Characteristic Studies Number 1 and Number 2 with one breath and no mistakes. Perhaps by then we will both be collecting Social Security, but in the meantime I want to thank you very much for putting up with me.

Sincerely,

Ray

Raphael J. Osheroff, M.D.

Medical Director

Northern Virginia Dialysis Center, Inc.

Alexandria, Virginia ❖

BUCKINGHAM PALACE

26th June, 1985

Dear Mr Erdman.

The Queen has commanded me to thank you for your letter of 1st June.

Her Majesty sends you every good wish for a long and happy retirement.

Yours sincerely

Robert Fellowes

Mr. Fredric Erdman.

*From Buckingham Palace, with embossed letterhead in red, a note wishing Freddie a "long and happy retirement."*

# Acknowledgments from Freddie and Tim

**F**red: My heartfelt thanks to Mary Jo Tarrants who inspired and encouraged me to write these memoirs and contributed numerous meaningful passages. Thanks, too, to my brother Tim for so generously re-writing, pre-editing, writing the narrative while adding his own unique stories, and to my brother Jim for his valuable input and contributions. My gratitude also goes out to bandmates Leslie Hunt, Lucas Spiros, John Schaefer, Charles Erwin, Raymond Dryburgh, and Johannes Rasmussen for contributing their stories.

This memoir might not have been written without the influence of my good friend and colleague Michael Ressler, Marine Band historian, who provided research for the book and who actually planted the seed for its creation. Thanks to our editor, Cathy Murphy, for her incisive comments and affectionately rendered recommendations and to Carlton Joseph, another good friend and computer scientist for his very kind devotion in building the book's website.

Thanks to Nia Payton, the friendly front office manager at the Hunt Valley Hampton Inn in Hunt Valley, Maryland, for her warm hospitality and making the Erdman brothers feel at home as we reunited for a brainstorming session on *Guaranteed Notes*.

And special acknowledgment to Jarold A. Kieffer, past Executive Director of the National Cultural Center (later renamed the John F. Kennedy Center for the Performing Arts) who so kindly gave me his permission to use material from his book, *From National Cultural Center to Kennedy Center: At the Front End of the Beginning*.

**Tim:** The chair/uniform artwork that graces the cover of *Guaranteed Notes* is based on a painting by Boyd Conway for James Erdman. In addition to being a talented artist, Mr. Conway was also a percussionist with the Marine Band during the same period in which the Three Erdman Brothers served.

While a number of conductors and mentors have figured prominently in the shaping of my career in music, one immediately comes to mind—that of our father, Fred Erdman. His influence on me has lasted a lifetime. He put us on a course that eventually led each of us into one of the world's greatest bands. He also had a pretty good stroke of the pen himself, and his writing talent inspired me to pursue an eventual degree in journalism from Temple University. It is to him that I dedicate the narrative part of this book.

As a youngster following my older brothers' shining career in the Marine Band, Captain Albert Schoepper...then, Major Albert Schoepper...and finally, Colonel Albert Schoepper...stayed in front of me like a looming specter, one I expected to face someday, pending my own entrance into the Marine Band's cornet section. If I needed motivation to practice, it usually stemmed from the stories my two brothers brought home of Schoepper's insatiable quest for perfection.

A debt of gratitude is also extended to Dr. Howard Applegate, who painstakingly read through this book several times and gave valuable advice on how to improve it. My wife Carolyn deserves a word of thanks for her proofing and helping me bring this book to its proper completion. Thanks also to Cathy Murphy, our editor, for her professional guidance and enthusiasm: where we Erdman Brothers initially shrugged off what we thought of as just ordinary everyday occurrences, she saw a story to be told that others might actually enjoy.

I was fortunate enough to be a part of that story, in no small measure thanks to my brothers Fred and Jim, constant sources of inspiration for my own development over the years as a professional musician; and my brother Michael, whose deep appreciation for music runs second only to the loving concern he has always expressed for his three older brothers.

And finally, to our mom, I say "thank you." She no doubt embodied the adage, "behind every successful man is a woman." Without her and the strict but loving upbringing she provided all four of us, it's a good bet that these events would not have happened, and that this story would have never been told. ❖